St. Louis Community College

Library

5801 Wilson Avenue
St. Louis, Missouri 63110

Joe
DiMaggio

Joe DiMaggio

An Informal Biography

George De Gregorio

STEIN AND DAY/Publishers/New York

Published in the United States of America in 1981.
Copyright © 1981 by George De Gregorio
All rights reserved
Designed by L.A.Ditizio
Printed in the United States of America
Stein and Day/ *Publishers*
Scarborough House
Briarcliff Manor, N.Y. 10510

Library of Congress Cataloging in Publication Data

De Gregorio, George.
    Joe DiMaggio, an informal biography.

    Includes index.
    1. DiMaggio, Joe, 1914–   2.   Baseball players—United States—
Biography.   I.   Title.
GV865.D5D4   796.357′092′4[B]   80-6159
ISBN 0-8128-2777-5   AACR2

Chapter One is composed of a two-part series the author wrote for *The New York Times*. It is © 1978 by The New York Times Company. Reprinted by permission.

To Barbara—

a champion in her

own right

In Doylestown, in those days, all that mattered was sports, and even today across America things are not much different. Assessing those distant days as honestly as I can, I must confess that our team was never really first rate. No boy I ever played with or against could even make a first-class team today, and if our team were to play a modern high school, the score would be something like 97–22, with us losing. And yet, in our little world we were champions, and from that simple fact radiated an inner confidence that has never left me. I could never become a bum, because I was a champion. Realizing this, I was able to lift myself onto a level of existence I could not have otherwise attained.

—James Michener, *Sports in America*

Contents

Acknowledgments

For their advice and help in the preparation of this book I would like to thank Dave Anderson, Benton M. Arnovitz, Jim Benagh, Howard Celnik, Bernice Courtney (for permission to reprint the lyrics to "Joltin' Joe DiMaggio"), the late Arthur Daley (who encouraged the project from the start), James Furlong, Richard Goldstein, Lowell Lifschultz, Le Anne Schreiber, Ernie Sisto, and Larry Smith. Also, the information departments of the Baseball Commissioner's office and the American League, New York Times Photo Library, Associated Press Photo Library and United Press International Photo Library.

Illustrations

Foreword

The idea for this book came to mind several years ago when the vice-president of a large insurance company in New York, a boyhood friend and my roommate at college, said to me one night during a visit to my home, "You ought to write a book about Joe DiMaggio, describing what a great player he was. I think there have been a lot of facets to his playing ability that have never been put down. He was really a great all-around player."

My friend was not the only person who held DiMaggio in such esteem and much has been written about his abilities as a player. My friend's remarks can be forgiven because when we were youngsters growing up in New Haven, Connecticut, he affected the DiMaggio stance at bat so often that the other boys in the neighborhood invariably chanted, "Here comes the great DiMag," whenever he took his turn at the plate. My friend did not go on to become a major league baseball player, though he dreamed, like the rest of us, of becoming another DiMaggio. He did manage, however, to win a niche in *Who's Who in America* as a vice president of the United States Life Insurance Company.

I did not exactly promise him that I would write this book, but I did keep his suggestion in mind. I hope he isn't disappointed.

—G. De G.

Joe
DiMaggio

1

A
Hitting Streak
Not Soon
Forgotten

$\mathcal{F}$ ROM MID-MAY to mid-July in 1941, Joe DiMaggio forestalled any onset of the American baseball fan's mid-season torpor, replacing day-to-day monotony with a state of day-to-day euphoria.

DiMaggio's streak—hitting safely in 56 straight games, a record that has never been matched—came at a time when Europe was already at war. Americans, filled with foreboding, stumbled faint-heartedly through Civil Defense drills. Roosevelt's fireside chats brought dire warnings of a blueprint by Hitler. The country wanted diversion from thoughts of war, and sought it in baseball games, Andy Hardy films, zoot suits, the "Hit Parade," and the bobby-soxers' craze over a scrawny young crooner from Hoboken, New Jersey, named Frank Sinatra.

DiMaggio had been notified by the Selective Service Board that his draft number was 5,423 and that he would be registered in Class 3, assuring him of at least one more season in baseball. But there was anxiety in the New York Yankee front office as well. In mid-May the club was in fourth place; DiMaggio was batting .306, far below his career average, and the team lacked sparkle and élan in the field. The Yankees had lost four games in a row and seven of their last nine. They were five and a half games behind the league-leading Cleveland Indians. Edward G. Barrow, the Yankee president, feared a repetition of the team's poor start and loss of the title in 1940, when DiMaggio missed the first 30 games with a knee injury. Barrow issued broadsides to the effect that wholesale changes and the trading of star players, including DiMaggio, were not remote possibilities if the Yankees did not right their course.

As the heir to Babe Ruth and Lou Gehrig, DiMaggio was singled out as the figure most responsible for the apparent decline. He had won the league batting crown in 1939 with .381 and in 1940 with .352. He had been named the American League's most valuable player in 1939, his fourth straight year on a world championship team. No one else in baseball could boast such a ledger. DiMaggio had placed his stamp on this team as its leader, but now, though he was only 26 years old, the fans were beginning to wonder whether his reign as the monarch of the New York dynasty was nearing an end. If so, then surely the dynasty itself was in trouble.

Then, on May 15 at Yankee Stadium, DiMaggio began his streak with a seemingly inconsequential single off Edgar Smith, a left-handed pitcher for the Chicago White Sox, who routed the Yankees that day, 13–1. The team's tailspin was magnified in the columns of New York's newspapers.

No one could know, of course, that DiMaggio was now embarked on two months of the hottest batting in baseball history. In the seventh game of his streak, he went to the plate against the Detroit Tigers in the ninth inning with the winning run on third base and none out. In this situation, with a batter of his credentials, the baseball book usually dictates an intentional walk—all the more so since he had got two hits in the early innings. Now a long fly ball would be enough to bring in the winning run. But on this day Del Baker, the Tiger manager, did not hold him in such esteem. He ordered Al Benton, a right-hander, to pitch to DiMaggio, who grounded out.

The Yankees eventually won the game, in the tenth inning, but as the fans walked down the Stadium exit ramps, the prevailing sentiment was, "They're not afraid of the Jolter anymore."

Baker was not alone in his strategy. Against the Boston Red Sox a few days later, the Yankees were trailing, 6–5, in the seventh inning. They had runners on second and third, DiMaggio going to bat.

"You can get him; don't walk him," Manager Joe Cronin told his left-hander Earl Johnson.

DiMaggio lined Johnson's first pitch for a single, driving in two runs for the victory. Now he had hit in 10 straight games. A mini-streak, nothing to be greatly excited about. It received only perfunctory mention in the sports pages.

Always prone to injuries and mild illnesses, DiMaggio had developed swelling in the neck that gave him enormous pain. He did not report it to Manager Joe McCarthy, for fear he would be taken out of the lineup.

"This damn swollen neck is driving me crazy," he said to the pitcher Lefty Gomez, his roommate, a few days later. "But don't say anything about it."

The pain continued for two weeks, and, in a double-header on Memorial Day in Boston, DiMaggio made four woeful errors, dropping a fly ball, bobbling a grounder, and throwing wildly twice. A defensive performer of consummate grace and superb reflexes, he was dismayed over his lapse in the field.

"If you're not going to say anything about that neck, then I will," Gomez said to him.

"I get it every year," DiMaggio said. "It'll go away."

Finally the problem came to McCarthy's attention, and DiMaggio received treatment for it. On June 7, when the Yankees were in Sportsman's Park in St. Louis for a weekend series with the Browns, the pain disappeared. McCarthy, who always worried about the condition of his star player, sat back in the dugout and said, "The boys are just waiting for Joe to show 'em how to do it."

DiMaggio showed the way that day, with three hits. The next afternoon he belted three home runs and a double as the Yankees swept a double-header. Now they were riding an eight-game winning streak.

In mid-June, after DiMaggio had pushed his own streak to 25 games, the writers covering the Yankees began researching the record books. Forty-four years before, in 1897, a player named Willie Keeler, a trolley conductor's son from Brooklyn, had hit safely in 44 straight games. No other big-league player had matched Keeler's streak, although in 1922 George Sisler of the St. Louis Browns had produced a string of 41, breaking Ty Cobb's American League record of 40, set in 1911.

The Yankee team record in this category was 29, held by Earle Combs and Roger Peckinpaugh. DiMaggio passed this milestone with a bad-hop single that struck the shoulder of Luke Appling, the White Sox shortstop. Lady Luck had not only kept his streak alive but also helped transform him into a national celebrity, not just another high-salaried, big-named ballplayer. She had helped him invade the nation's consciousness. He would become a symbol of cosmic masculinity; a creature of animal magnetism desired by women, approved by men; a subject to salute in song.

The drama of the hitting streak grew more intense with each game. Every pitcher worthy of his trade yearned for a chance to confront and defeat DiMaggio. Those who faced him summoned extra energy and grit and bore down on him even more than they did on other batters.

In his singleness of purpose, DiMaggio, too, summoned greater strength and tenacity. The central characters appeared to be waging a concentrated battle involving body, mind, and spirit.

Bob Muncrief, a 25-year-old rookie right-hander from the Texas League, became one of the first pitchers to get personally involved in the streak. It was in the 36th game. Muncrief, pitching for the Browns, had DiMaggio in trouble, having retired him three times in a row without a hit. But in the eighth inning, in what would have been his last time up, DiMaggio saved himself with a single.

Luke Sewell, the Browns' manager, was a hard-bitten competitor who hated to lose, a characteristic made more intense because the Browns were chronic losers. That DiMaggio got a hit his last time up incensed Sewell and he pursued Muncrief after the game.

"Why didn't you walk him the last time up to stop him?" Sewell barked, glaring at the rookie.

Muncrief answered brusquely. "I wasn't going to walk him," he said. "That wouldn't have been fair—to him or me. Hell, he's the greatest player I ever saw."

That generosity of spirit was not shared by Johnny Babich of the Athletics, a right-hander who tried to derail DiMaggio in game 40 of his streak at Shibe Park in Philadelphia on June 28. Babich had acquired his early baseball knowledge in the Yankee farm system. Like most players he dreamed of being a Yankee. But whatever he had learned, the Yankees apparently did not think too highly of it and they traded him out of their system.

Babich never forgave them. He hooked on with the A's and in a short time he developed a reputation for being particularly tough on the New York team. In 1940, he had beaten the Yankees five times, contributing in a significant way to their failure to win the league title.

In the third inning DiMaggio had taken three wide pitches for a 3-and-0 count. Most batters would normally be given the take sign at 3 and 0, but DiMaggio was given the sign to swing away.

"He was out to get me," recalled DiMaggio, referring to Babich, "even if it meant walking me every time up. The next pitch was outside, too, but I caught it good and lined it right past Babich into center field for a hit."

The next stop was a double-header against the Washington Senators on a Sunday at Griffith Stadium. A crowd of 31,000 turned out to see whether DiMaggio could tie and break George Sisler's 41-game record.

During the between-games rest period, a fan jumped onto the field near the Yankee dugout and took DiMaggio's favorite bat as a souvenir. Tracked down in the stands with the bat, the fan adamantly refused to return it.

"Don't let it bother you, Joe," said Tommy Henrich, "you can use the one I've been using that you let me borrow. I've been doing pretty good with it."

Arnold Anderson, off whom DiMaggio had made two hits in a four-hit performance on May 27, was the Senators' pitcher for the second game. DiMaggio lined out twice and drove a long fly ball for another out his third time up.

When he went to bat in the seventh, the crowd sensed that the streak was in jeopardy. Anderson's first pitch almost knocked DiMaggio down. It is the ploy of every pitcher to brush back the batter, to make him so wary and tense that he will eventually defeat himself. The stands rumbled with boos. Even the Senators' rooters were backing DiMaggio.

DiMaggio moved into the batter's box again, his wide stance and bat creating a picture of power and concentration. Anderson's next pitch was a fastball. DiMaggio swung and sent a whistling liner into left field for a single. The fans stood and cheered DiMaggio for five minutes.

On the train back to New York, DiMaggio was in an expansive mood. He ordered beer for all of his teammates. But he was still worried about the loss of his favorite bat.

"I wish that guy would return that bat," he said to a reporter. "I need it more than he does. Most of my models are 32 inches long and weigh 36 ounces, but I had sandpapered the handle of this one to take off a half to three-quarters of an ounce. It was just right."

The next day, a Monday, was an off day for the teams. DiMaggio learned that the fan who had taken his bat came from Newark, New Jersey. An ardent DiMaggio rooter, the fan had made the trip from New Jersey to Washington especially to see DiMaggio break the record. Having returned to Newark, he was boasting around town that he had the bat. DiMaggio had friends in Newark and made a few phone calls. They contacted the fan and persuaded him to give up the bat. It was returned to DiMaggio in time for his next assault, on Wee Willie Keeler's 44-game record.

The following day, a Tuesday afternoon at the height of summer, DiMaggio was the magnetic force that attracted 52,832 paying customers into Yankee Stadium for a double-header against the Boston Red Sox. When he failed to get a hit his first two times up in the first game, the silence that settled over the Stadium blended with the heat and humidity.

His third time up DiMaggio sent a choppy grounder, a tricky ball to handle, at Jim Tabor, the Boston third baseman. Tabor was known for his strong throwing arm. He had often thrown out runners from deep behind third, almost from short left field. This time Tabor rushed the play and threw a wild peg past first base. DiMaggio wound up at second base. Again the crowd became silent.

The official scorer of the game was Dan Daniel, a baseball authority who wrote for *The New York World-Telegram*. He had been the scorer at the Stadium for virtually all of the home games involving DiMaggio's streak, and the pressure on him to call the borderline plays was as intense as the pressure on DiMaggio to get a hit.

Daniel, aware that too long a delay in making a decision would place doubts in everyone's mind, shot up his right arm, indicating that DiMaggio was on second by virtue of a double. It was one of the few times DiMaggio had been given the benefit of a doubt during the streak. The crowd roared. He was one game from tying Keeler's record.

The next time DiMaggio went to bat in the first game, he dispelled all doubts about whether his previous hit would taint his streak. He slammed a ringing single into left field for his second hit of the game.

Before the second game was an inning old, DiMaggio lifted the suspense. He belted a screaming liner for a hit to center field. Now only he and Keeler stood upon a baseball Everest that Ruth, Cobb, Gehrig, Hornsby, and even the great Sisler had not been able to reach.

The next day, in 95-degree heat, DiMaggio took sole possession of the record with his 18th home run of the season, his 13th of the streak, and his 100th hit of the campaign.

DiMaggio seemed to be hitting like a man possessed. In the next 11 games of the streak he rapped 23 hits in 44 times at bat for a .523 average, and in the first 5 of those 11 games he extended his streak in the first inning of each game.

Then on July 16, the Yankees arrived in Cleveland. Its huge stadium was foreboding. If DiMaggio was to meet his Waterloo, this could be the place. In the series opener DiMaggio notched No. 56 swiftly, slashing a first-inning single off Al Milnar's first pitch, and in the eighth, against Joe Krakauskas, he drove a 400-foot double.

Now with an advance reserved-seat ticket sale of 40,000 already in the till, a large crowd for the July 17 night game was assured. The starting pitcher for the Indians was Al Smith, a veteran left-hander who had been cast off by the New York Giants.

By game time the crowd had swelled to 67,468, the largest to see a night game in the major leagues. DiMaggio had not bunted during the entire streak. But in the first inning Ken Keltner, the Indians' third baseman, was playing his position so deep, back to the edge of the outfield grass, that he seemed to dare DiMaggio to bunt his way to first base. With a 1-and-0 count, DiMaggio drove Smith's next pitch past the third-base bag. Keltner made a leaping lunge to his right for the ball, stopped it backhanded, and threw out DiMaggio from foul territory. Smith walked DiMaggio in the fourth, but in the seventh DiMaggio again sent a steaming grounder to Keltner, who again made a fine play and throw to nail him at first.

The tension heightened in the eighth as the Yankees staged a rally. They drove Smith to the showers with four hits and two runs, and as DiMaggio strode to the plate with the bases filled and one out, the Indians' manager, Roger Peckinpaugh, who had held the Yankee record for streak hitting at 29 games until DiMaggio broke it, brought in Jim Bagby Jr., a right-hander whose father had posted 128 victories as a big-league pitcher with Cincinnati, Cleveland, and Pittsburgh.

DiMaggio worked Bagby for a ball and a strike and then slammed a grounder to Lou Boudreau at shortstop. The ball flitted on a bad hop to Boudreau, who picked it off his shoulder and threw to Ray Mack, who threw to Oscar Grimes for a double play. A roar went up in the stadium—DiMaggio's streak had finally come to an end.

2

From North Beach
to the
Big Apple

*O*N A SCENE in Hemingway's saga *The Old Man and the Sea,* Santiago, the old Cuban fisherman who is the protagonist in the story, is talking to Manolin, his young companion, about baseball. The boy has brought stew for supper to fortify the old man, who will soon go off on his great sea challenge. The boy wants to hear more about baseball and the old man brings up the name of Joe DiMaggio, the New York Yankees' star center fielder.

"I would like to take the great DiMaggio fishing," he says. "They say his father was a fisherman. Maybe he was as poor as we are and would understand."

The old man has been a baseball fan all his life, and now he is touting the New York team to his young friend. "The Yankees cannot lose," he says. Manolin says he fears "the Indians of Cleveland." But Santiago reassures him. "Have faith in the Yankees my son. Think of the great DiMaggio."

The boy, strongly influenced by and immensely loyal to the old man, whom he regards as the greatest of all fishermen, accepts Santiago's appraisal that DiMaggio is the greatest of all players. By extension, it is Hemingway's appraisal, too. Isolated though the reference is, it tells of the magnitude of Joe DiMaggio's appeal during the three decades—the 1930s, 1940s and two years in the 1950s—that spanned his 13-year playing career.

Joseph Paul DiMaggio was born in Martinez, California, on November 25, 1914. He was the eighth of nine children of Joseph (Giuseppe) and Rosalie DiMaggio, a Sicilian couple who emigrated to the United States at the height of the European exodus at the turn of the century.

The father arrived in 1902, a year before his wife and infant daughter, and set out for the West because friends and relatives had already settled in California. He had been assured that the climate was sunny and agreeable, much as it was in the old country. He had been a fisherman in Sicily and had served in the Italian Army. But like most disillusioned Europeans undergoing hard times, he thought America and its ideal of opportunity for all would enable him to raise a family and give his children a better place to start. A man of uncomplicated desires and tastes, he simply hoped for a chance to work hard and keep his family intact. He had never dreamed that one day three of his sons would earn their livings as major league baseball players—an occupation anathema to his concept of the work ethic—and that one of them would be heralded as the greatest player of his generation.

When DiMaggio was a few years old, the family moved to San Francisco, settling in the bay community of North Beach, thickly populated with Italian crab fishermen who made their livelihoods working out of small skiffs on bay waters of the blue Pacific.

As a boy, DiMaggio did not take to his father's trade—in fact, he detested it. The father had hoped that his son, to whom he had given his name, would become a sterling fisherman. In addition, he had hoped to expand, with the help of his other sons, the family's small fishing enterprise. But DiMaggio had little stomach for the roll of the sea or the pungent aromas that emanated from a boat filled with crabs.

When DiMaggio was a young ballplayer with the Yankees, he often told of his inability to cope with the problem of going to sea with his father and older brothers.

"I never could take the smells aboard the boat and I always got seasick," he said. "My father just gave up on me. He figured I'd really never make it as a fisherman so he decided I didn't have to go along. I guess it was disappointing to him at the time, but he always wished the best for his children."

In his early years DiMaggio seemed overly endowed with a restlessness bordering on recalcitrance. His father, though disappointed that his son did not take to fishing, had eight other children to worry about; there simply wasn't enough time to dwell on only one of them. So DiMaggio gravitated naturally to his own pursuits, enjoying a mildly rebellious adolescence. Occasionally he helped out, preparing and cleaning the netting for his father's fishing boat, but otherwise he was free to develop his own interests.

The North Beach section of San Francisco, where the family lived on a high, ski-slope-like hill overlooking the bay, was a small town inside a big city. It encompassed a few blocks of row houses and flats, some stores and bars. They occupied a ground floor flat on Taylor Street. At the foot of the hill beckoned Fisherman's Wharf with its tourist trade, restaurants and shops, and the hundreds of small fishing boats that came into the wharf with loads of fish and crabs. DiMaggio's geographical vantage point was confined to the immediate neighborhood and what it had to offer. In his case he was fortunate. The resources did not differ greatly, except in setting, from those available to boys growing up in small rural communities. There was the Church of Saints

Peter and Paul, the playgrounds, and the local Boys' Club. While attending Galileo High School, named after the Italian astronomer, he held odd jobs to earn spending money, but none lasted for very long. They did, however, allow him the experiences of hawking newspapers and discovering what work was like—peeling oranges, for example, in an orange juice factory. For the most part his time was spent indulging in sports at the Boys' Club.

DiMaggio's first experience with baseball came in the playgrounds of North Beach, where he played with a softball on an asphalt diamond, or what passed for a baseball diamond. He was 10 years old, tall and lean, but strong for his age. He attended the Hancock Grammar School at Filbert and Taylor Streets. Virtually all of his activities centered on the few blocks in the neighborhood. The church where he was to be married for the first time and where he took his early Roman Catholic sacraments, was on Filbert and Powell Streets. The San Francisco Boys' Club, where he spent most of his time away from home, was on Stockton Street, near Filbert. It was a hotbed of baseball activity and competition with teams in all age groups.

"Through the club I became interested in real baseball, played on a real field with a regulation ball," he recalled later. He was a third baseman on the first team he played for in the Boys' Club league.

"We won the championship of our division of the club league," he said later. "They spotted me for a good hitter and the next thing I knew I was being approached by managers and independent teams, and I played a lot of Saturday and Sunday pickup games."

DiMaggio also participated in those days in what was called "horse-lot baseball"—a creation of the youngsters in the neighborhood; it toughened them for the more organized forms of baseball they would play later on.

"We used rocks for bases," DiMaggio recalled, "and it was quite a scramble among 20 of us kids to scrape up a nickel to buy a roll of bicycle tape to patch up the ball each day."

The hill above the bay was also home for the families of the 250 members of the crab-fishing fleet who moored their skiffs on Fisherman's Wharf. Half a mile from the wharf was a sand patch, nicknamed the "horse lot" because a dairy company used it as a parking lot for its horse-drawn milk wagons. The youngsters would scare off the horses by throwing rocks at them and then would improvise a baseball diamond by placing rocks for bases and home plate, thus converting the parking space into a playing field. They had no regulation equipment. They played bare-handed, used a taped ball, and for a bat they made do with an old oar. It was not too different from the improvisation American youngsters in small towns in other rural and urban areas resorted to for playing baseball.

In later years DiMaggio would say that he had grown up in a poor but happy family; that while there was little money for extras in such a large brood, "we never went cold or hungry." He was at no more of a disadvantage than most American youngsters growing up in the middle of the Depression.

San Francisco, of course, rebuilt after a devastating fire and earthquake in 1906, was a diverse city, a miniature New York. It had known extremes of poverty and wealth. It had grown into a center for shipping, transportation, industry, and finance. Culturally, it had attained a reputation as a patron of the arts and education. Its politics were lively, and its cable cars and bridges gave it a sophistication all its own. In such a city even the residents of North Beach, most of them children of poor immigrants, could harbor dreams and aspirations of grandeur.

DiMaggio's large family included Nellie, Mamie, Thomas, Marie, Michael, Frances, Vincent, Joseph, and Dominic, born in that order roughly at two-year intervals. His oldest brother, Tom, had dabbled in baseball as a youngster. He was considered very talented, good enough to have been a professional, according to Joe. But in a large family in financial straits, oldest sons usually were needed to help make ends meet. He found time to become proficient at playing squash racquets as a diversion, but his laboring hours were spent on the fishing skiff and any serious attempt at baseball had to be put aside. He was, however, the family spokesman on virtually all serious matters. He was one of Joe's advisers when it came time to sign a contract with the Yankees early in his career. He was also instrumental in developing, with funds provided by Joe, the family's restaurant business on Fisherman's Wharf, and for several years was vice-president of the Fisherman's Union in the bay area.

The DiMaggio household was typically Italianate. Neither mother nor father spoke English—broken English, of course, crept in frequently. The children communicated in Italian and English. The mother, Rosalie, enjoyed keeping house and cooking large meals. One of her entrees, cioppino, a delicacy made of crabs, tomatoes, sherry wine, and garlic, became a specialty of the restaurant.

The father's leisure time away from his boat—which he had named *The Rosalie* in affection for his wife—was spent with cronies on the Wharf or at the local lodge, where talk about fishing, card games, and bocci, a type of Italian bowling, were staple pastimes. The younger boys stayed occupied with sports. One brother, Vince, had already started to perfect his baseball skills, to the extent that he earned money on weekends playing in semiprofessional games. The girls helped their mother with household chores and their father with his fishing nets, which had to be cleaned and made ready for the next day's catch. If funds were short, they didn't give way to despair, but held an abiding belief that things would eventually get better.

DiMaggio remembers that even having enough money to go to a movie was a luxury, and he had already become accustomed to wearing hand-me-down clothes from his older brothers. He recalled later that he had been especially disappointed as a youngster over not being able to afford the 25 cents admission fee to see "The Jazz Singer," the first full-length talking motion picture, made in 1927 and starring Al Jolson. "You might as well have been talking about $10," DiMaggio said when he came to the big leagues. The sisters enjoyed dating and bringing their boyfriends home. Traffic in the ground floor North Beach flat was always heavy with friends. Three of Joe's sisters had already married and made him an uncle when he moved up to the Yankees.

DiMaggio's recalcitrant mood, or what passed for it, lingered with him throughout his high school days. At 16, although he had played a lot of baseball, he became seriously interested in tennis. His tall, lean frame seemed to lend itself to the sport, and for a year and a half he tried to perfect his game. But the long hours of isolated drills necessary to perfect those skills did not appeal to him and he abandoned the sport almost as quickly as he had taken it up. In the aftermath, he dropped out of high school at the age of 17, choosing a job in an orange juice factory so he could do his part, he thought, as a family breadwinner. His father, who had had high hopes for his namesake (he had also given all his sons the middle name of Paul, after his favorite saint), was angered when Joe dropped out of school,and was perplexed over what he thought was his son's lack of motivation.

By this time, Joe's brother Vince was establishing a reputation as a skilled semi-pro player, with a possible big-league future, earning as much as $25 a game on weekends. With this earning power in mind, Joe's thoughts and energies turned to baseball, too.

In 1932 Vince signed as an outfielder with the San Francisco Seals, who farmed him out to the Tucson club of the Arizona-Texas League. He was recalled late in the season and when the Seals discovered a manpower shortage in their infield, Vince suggested that they take a look at his younger brother, Joe. DiMaggio played three games with the Seals that year as a shortstop. He got a couple of hits and was told to report back for spring training the next season.

Joe DiMaggio had committed himself to his first love and it would be a lifelong romance. The next year, 1933, Joe was so outstanding as an outfielder with the Seals that his older brother became expendable and was shipped to the Hollywood team.

The Pacific Coast League at the time was considered one of the strongest minor leagues in baseball. There had been rumors of expanding the major leagues to the West Coast. The Seals were among the teams mentioned for possible franchises, but the ongoing Depression plus adamant official opposition put the rumors quickly to rest.

San Francisco had been a fertile breeding ground or conduit through which many topflight players eventually made it to the majors. Scouts had an easy time of it there, having picked off the vines such stars as Lefty O'Doul, Joe Cronin, Tony Lazzeri, Frank Crosetti, and Harry Heilmann.

DiMaggio's first full season in organized baseball provided statistics that couldn't be ignored by anyone in the market for big-league talent. He set a Pacific Coast League record by hitting safely in 61 consecutive games, a mark that still stands. He finished the season with a .340 batting average for 187 games. He hit safely 259 times, including 28 home runs, 45 doubles, and 13 triples, drove in 169 runs, and scored 129. All 16 major league teams sent scouts to look him over. Almost overnight he had become the most talked-about minor-league player in the country.

Club owners began to send out feelers to see how much it would cost them to purchase DiMaggio from the Seals' owner, Charles Graham, a shrewd manipulator of talent who realized that his price could escalate depending on how well his young star performed. By the end of the 1933 season, the asking price for DiMaggio was $75,000. The Yankees were in the forefront of the bidding. They had had luck with players from San Francisco, notably Lazzeri and Crosetti. Their chief scout in the area, Bill Essick, was told to be alert against the possibility of another team making a firmer bid for the young DiMaggio.

In 1934 DiMaggio was slugging along with a .360 batting average, hitting home runs and making dazzling catches in the outfield. The Seals were playing in Seattle in the middle of the season. The manager of the Seattle team, Dutch Ruether, who had been a big-league pitcher with a 137–95 record for 11 seasons, noticed that DiMaggio seemed to favor his left leg, sort of dragging it, when he ran.

"What's wrong with your leg?" DiMaggio was asked by the Seattle trainer. "Dutch says he's noticed there's something wrong with it."

"Tell Dutch he's nuts," DiMaggio said.

Ruether's keen eye had indeed detected a hitch in DiMaggio's stride, but DiMaggio had been trying to conceal it. The last thing he and Graham wanted now was for the scouts to get wind that he had been injured. Reports of injuries to players spread like California brush fires and in DiMaggio's case it might seriously damage his chances of getting to the big leagues. But it couldn't be concealed indefinitely. Ruether began to spread the word.

DiMaggio admitted later that he had injured his leg after a game in San Francisco earlier in the season. He had a date for dinner at his sister's house one Sunday night after a double-header. He had hopped on a crowded bus and had to sit with his left leg in a cramped position all the way.

"When I got off, I jumped out and my left knee popped like a pistol. I swear you could have heard it down the block," DiMaggio said.

He had collapsed in pain and had to be helped to his sister's house. He showed up at the park the next day, but he couldn't run. He went with the team on a trip to Los Angeles, but had to be sent home. His leg was put into an aluminum cast and he was out for six weeks. He played in only 101 games that season, batting .341. It was the start of a medical log that would be watched as if he were a political candidate or a movie star.

The word was out about his vulnerable leg and the major league clubs recalled their scouts. To buy damaged goods was the one unforgivable sin a baseball team could commit and the scout who would recommend such a purchase might not be a scout for long afterward. DiMaggio was not yet 20 years old. His ability to heal and recover quickly from injury was a function of his youth, and when Joe returned to the lineup he was still limber and strong, and hitting and fielding as well as before the injury.

Essick, a determined scout and a neighbor of the DiMaggios in

North Beach, kept a watchful eye on Joe. Essick noticed that he hadn't lost his speed and that the all-important pivotal movement at the plate was just as smooth as ever. His throwing arm still had its old snap and accuracy.

Essick phoned Edward G. Barrow, the Yankees' business and general manager in New York. "Don't give up on DiMaggio," he said. "He's still looking good out there."

Barrow, astute in business ventures, listened with profit aforethought. If, despite the injury, DiMaggio was still as good as he was before, now Barrow could bargain for him at a lower price—say $25,000 instead of $75,000.

Two weeks later, with DiMaggio still maintaining a .350 batting average, Essick called Barrow again.

"Buy DiMaggio," he said. "I think you can get him cheap. They're all laughing at me, but I know I'm right."

The Yankees hadn't won the pennant in 1933 or 1934 and Colonel Jacob Ruppert, the beer baron who owned the Yankees, was in the market for new talent. Babe Ruth had come full circle and had played his last game for the Yankees. Lou Gehrig was still busting down fences, but the Bombers needed young power in the outfield, someone to take up where Ruth had left off.

Ruppert and Captain Tillinghast L'Hommedieu Huston had purchased the Yankees for $460,000 in 1915, taking over an indigent, debt-and-dissension-ridden team that was an embarrassment to the league. Ruppert had been strictly a New York Giants fan, having been a friend of John McGraw, the Giants' manager, whom he had visited often in the dugout at the Polo Grounds and had accompanied many times to the race tracks. In 1900, when he was 37 years old, Ruppert had been offered a chance to buy the Giants, but his interests at the time leaned to more sophisticated pastimes than baseball. A short time later he had an opportunity to purchase the Chicago Cubs, but ever the New Yorker, he refused, saying he "didn"t want any part of Chicago."

By contrast, Huston was born into modest circumstances in a small town in Ohio and grew up in Cincinnati. During the Spanish-American War he joined the Army and went to Cuba as a captain. (In World War I he won the rank of Colonel.) He stayed in Cuba for 10 years, and had become an engineer. He had also made a lot of money. McGraw often spent winters in Cuba, either with the Giants, who played exhibition games there, or vacationing there with his wife. He met Huston and they became friends. When Huston left Cuba to live in New York, their friendship continued and McGraw eventually introduced Huston to Ruppert.

Ruppert and Huston frequently rooted together at Giants games and they struck upon the idea of buying a baseball team. They wanted the Giants, but McGraw said it was out of the question. The hapless Yankees, he suggested, might be for sale. So they struck the partnership, brought Barrow and Ruth from the Red Sox, and enjoyed a great deal of prosperity. Unlike Ruppert, who had a valet to select his suits from a vast wardrobe, Huston was happy wearing the same blue serge suit seven days a week and he was seldom seen, even in 90-degree weather, without his derby. He was described by W. O. McGeehan, a newspaper columnist and one of Huston's companions, as "The Man in the Iron Hat." In 1923, Ruppert bought out Huston's share in the Yankees for $1,500,000.

So the Yankees swung the deal for DiMaggio for $25,000 and five players. Owner Graham of the Seals attached one proviso, that DiMaggio remain with the Seals for the 1935 season. Barrow agreed. The purchase of the young slugger would be one of Barrow's best investments and it would reap profits not only for Ruppert but for subsequent owners of the New York club. Years later, in describing the deal, Barrow said, "It was the best deal I ever made."

Meanwhile, DiMaggio finished the 1935 season with a .398 batting average, missing the seasonal league title by a point. He slammed 270 hits in 172 games, but his 456 total bases were unbelievable. He hit 34 home runs, 48 doubles, and 18 triples, batted in 154 runs, scored 173, and stole 24 bases in 25 attempts. In New York, Barrow and Ruppert were wringing their hands in dismay that they had not insisted on bringing him up right away. The Yankees struggled through another disappointing campaign, losing the pennant to the Detroit Tigers.

DiMaggio would go to spring training in 1936 as the most publicized rookie in many years, and there were even predictions that he would replace Ruth someday as the greatest of all Yankees. For the dark-haired Italian youth now it would be the Big Apple—New York and Yankee Stadium—and he would become the apple of its eye.

It meant, too, a chance to move into the big money and DiMaggio was well aware of that from the start. The Seals had provided him with experience, but not much money. He and his brother Vince had each earned $250 a month for their labors. Now Tom, already a negotiator for the bay fishermen, advised his brother to bargain hard before signing with the Yankees. They decided to ask for $8,000, top money for a rookie. After a brief correspondence DiMaggio got what he was asking for.

Through the years, the Yankees attracted ballplayers of Italian heritage—Lazzeri, Crosetti, Rizzuto, Berra, Raschi—and DiMaggio was the most illustrious of them. San Francisco seemed to be the place to find them. The first San Franciscan with an Italian background to wear a Yankee uniform was Ping Bodie, whose real name was Francesco Stephano Pezzolo. He was a journeyman outfielder who had played with the Chicago White Sox and Philadelphia Athletics before he put in a four-year hitch with the Yankees from 1918 to 1921. Over nine seasons his batting average was .275, but his chief claim to status was that while a member of the Yankees he was Babe Ruth's roommate. Bodie's legacy to baseball was a remark, made in innocence, but for which he was better remembered than for anything he did to embellish the record book. In his heyday, Ruth was the playboy of the western world. He was a free spirit—rules existed for other players. He loved the high life after dark and a spontaneous soirée on the town was a common occurrence for him and his companions.

The writers who covered the Yankees repeatedly set up Bodie for his classic line, knowing he would deliver on cue.

"Who do you room with?" the writers asked.

Bodie's inevitable reply was: "With a suitcase."

It always got a laugh and assured Bodie a place in baseball's gag book.

Lazzeri and Crosetti were star regulars in the Yankee infield when DiMaggio was purchased. Like DiMaggio, both were products of the sandlots. All three had similar family backgrounds and because of this the two older players were eager to take the hometown boy under their wings, show him the big-league ropes, and offer some big-brother advice. Crosetti would be his first roommate for a brief time.

Lazzeri, a veteran Yankee who had been a star in the Ruth era (in his rookie year at Salt Lake City he had hit 60 home runs), especially wanted to see DiMaggio make good and get off on the right foot. Lazzeri was a spirited player, imbued with the Yankee style and traditions, and he was well aware that press clippings taken too literally could tilt a young player's ego. He and Crosetti wanted their fellow paisano from San Francisco to avoid that.

They invited DiMaggio to join them on their motor trip to Florida for the start of spring training. Lazzeri owned the car and he was the driver on the first leg of the 3,000-mile journey. Crosetti went behind the wheel for the second leg.

By most accounts it was not a momentous voyage. Aggressive players on the field, none was a garrulous personality in his private life. DiMaggio fit the mold of his two friends. He slept through most of the trip until they reached Alabama.

"O.K., champ, it's your turn to drive," Lazzeri said to DiMaggio when they pulled up at a filling station for gas.

"I don't drive," DiMaggio answered. Lazzeri and Crosetti were aghast.

"Let's throw the bum out," Lazzeri said, "and let him walk the rest of the way."

Unfazed, DiMaggio laughed and settled back in the rear seat. "C'mon, you guys," he said, "let's get going, you know I've got a date with the Yankees."

Lazzeri drove the rest of the way, but by previous plan he had decided to slow the pace so that they would arrive late in the evening of March 1, the opening day of camp at St. Petersburg, Florida. They stopped for coffee often, trying to kill time. All had agreed that because of the big buildup DiMaggio had received in the press, it would be better for him if he avoided the sportswriters on his arrival. They figured that by the time they got there the writers would have already filed their stories for the day.

DiMaggio had been warned by Tommy Laird, a San Francisco sports editor, to keep a low profile.

"You're a great ballplayer right now," Laird had told DiMaggio before he left the Coast, "and you'll be a greater one in the big leagues. But don't let those newspaper guys who are going to grab hold of you as soon as you arrive put a lot of words in your mouth and make you sound like a big blowhard before the fans in New York ever get a look at you. Don't say a word. Don't put yourself on the spot. And don't let them put you on the spot."

Lazzeri and Crosetti were also aware of Manager Joe McCarthy's desire for his players to keep a low-key image of themselves with reporters. They knew that DiMaggio's attitude about this at the start would have a bearing on McCarthy's estimate of him.

Among ballplayers, the Yankees were sophisticated. Many of them had already savored the fruits of championships. They were ribald, sharp-tongued, and quick-witted in many ways the young DiMaggio could not fathom.

When he was introduced to the team the next day by Lazzeri, the players were cordial and he smiled and shook hands with them.

Red Ruffing was the only one who went out of his way to make a comment. "So you're the great DiMaggio," the veteran pitcher said sarcastically. DiMaggio just nodded with a deadpan expression.

The New York press was usually brash and aggressive, eager to get to the nub of any personality who came to town so highly touted. DiMaggio kept his distance. Unlike many rookies he did not fawn over the veteran players, or seek out interviews with reporters. He adopted a conservative, tight-lipped attitude, almost a defense.

"His shyness was mistaken for sullenness by some and for swell-headedness by others," wrote Arthur Daley of *The New York Times.* "The DiMaggio of 1936 was silent and uncomfortable. He was monosyllabic and uncommunicative with writers. He was ill at ease with all strangers."

One of the first friendships DiMaggio made when he joined the Yankees was with a photographer, Ernie Sisto, who worked for *The New York Times.* Sisto's assignments included covering the New York team and although he was 10 years older than DiMaggio, they developed an affinity. In general, photographers got along with ballplayers better than reporters and the reason seemed obvious. The fewer questions asked, the better the players got along with the press. After all, it was true, as far as the players were concerned, that one picture is worth 1,000 words.

"The photographers always got along well with the players," Sisto recalled in an interview later. "I guess sometimes reporters rubbed the players the wrong way, asking them to comment on things they didn't want to talk about. We mostly flattered them by taking their pictures. I think for that reason a player would put more trust in a photographer than a reporter. I know a lot of reporters then thought Joe did that with me. They thought I was a shield for Joe. I'd be in the clubhouse and if Joe wanted to avoid the reporters and didn't want to say anything for the papers about signing a contract or a slump or something, he'd come over and sit with me at a table. Even if I was a member of the press, Joe knew that I would never say anything that would hurt him."

DiMaggio, after all, was only 21 years old—no longer in the confines of North Beach where he was the local hero surrounded and protected by family and friends who accepted him on his own terms. Now, for better or worse, his manners and deportment and his remarks would be measured in the public eye.

With the ballyhoo quieting down, DiMaggio would have to prove he was as good as the experts said he was. He worked hard in the first three weeks of training. Then in the fifth exhibition game against the Boston Braves, he injured his left foot sliding into second base. It appeared to be only a slight injury, but the next day the foot stiffened and he was sidelined. The team trainer advised diathermy heat treatments. Inexplicably, his exposure to the heat lamp burned his skin and the injury was worse. It threw a scare into Yankee management.

On April 7, two weeks from opening day, the Yankees' team physician, Dr. Harry G. Jacobi, examined the foot and described the problem. "DiMaggio has an area of ulceration of the dorsum of the left foot, quite similar to that seen following burns," he said. "With proper care he will be able to play again within 10 to 14 days."

DiMaggio would miss opening day and the big publicity buildup for his debut fizzled. He had had a good spring at St. Petersburg and his appearance was eagerly awaited in New York. John Kieran, the originator of the "Sports of the Times" column for *The New York Times,* had been impressed by DiMaggio during a visit to the spring camps. "Possibly he fooled all observers in Florida," Kieran wrote, "but down there Joe looked like a real addition to high life in the big leagues. Until they left his foot in the oven too long, Joe was going about in lively fashion, living up to all the advance notices about him from the California area. He was fast in the field, turned loose a good throwing arm and was lining sharp hits to all corners of the Florida ball parks."

DiMaggio finally took the field three weeks later on May 3 against the St. Louis Browns. He started in left field, the sun field at Yankee Stadium, which many players did not like to play because of the strong glare of the sun early in the day and the shadows later in the afternoon during the late innings of a game. Babe Ruth, on his own insistence, would never play the sun field at the Stadium for those reasons, demanding that he stay in right field even when managerial lineup strategy might have deemed his presence in left field more valuable to the team.

For the opener DiMaggio would bat third in the order, ahead of Lou Gehrig. The center fielder was Ben Chapman, a strong hitter who was in the twilight of his Yankee career and who would be traded before the year ended. Center field was the position that Manager McCarthy, in his mind's eye, saw eventually as DiMaggio's domain.

The Yankee lineup was a powerful one. The day DiMaggio played his first game, Gehrig and Chapman slammed four hits each in a 17-hit attack that routed the Browns by a score of 14–5. DiMaggio's contribution was not meager. He connected for a triple and two singles and by all measurements seemed capable of living up to his press clippings.

At Detroit on May 8, Bill Dickey clouted a three-run homer in the eighth inning for a 6–5 Yankee lead. In the ninth, the Tigers staged a rally. Ervin Fox was walked by Bump Hadley and Mickey Cochrane, the Tigers' great catcher and manager, singled him to third. Charlie Gehringer, the next batter, sent a high fly to DiMaggio, "whose work afield was sparkling all afternoon." DiMaggio made the put-out, his seventh of the game, and Kingsley Childs, a New York writer, described it:

"As soon as DiMaggio made the catch, Fox headed for home, but he was out at the plate trying to register what would have been the deadlocking marker when DiMaggio whipped the ball to Dickey for a brilliant double play."

DiMaggio hit his first major league home run in the first inning on May 10 against the Athletics, drove in three runs, and produced "a glittering catch in left field in the sixth inning." Tom Yawkey, the youthful owner of the Boston Red Sox, was a guest in Barrow's box seat in the Stadium mezzanine and looked "more than mildly interested" in DiMaggio's style. For much of his early career, and in his final year, there would be rumors that DiMaggio would be traded to Boston, where his right-handed hitting power could be unleashed on Fenway Park's short left-field wall, known as the "Green Monster." Yawkey would keep the name DiMaggio in mind. DiMaggio's younger brother, Dom, would begin his pro career with San Francisco the next season and in four years he, too, would be playing in the big leagues—for Yawkey at Boston and in center field.

On May 14 against the Browns, DiMaggio cracked three doubles and a single. On Memorial Day before a crowd of 41,781, including New York's Mayor Fiorello La Guardia, an ardent DiMaggio fan, he tied the score at 4–4 with a two-run single in the ninth, then broke up the game with a winning triple that scored Red Rolfe in the 12th.

He got his first taste of a big-league slump in the next few games, going hitless 12 straight times. On June 8 he broke out of it with a home run, a triple, and a single, knocking in five runs. He continued to excel in the field. "Caught flatfooted by Harland Clift's fly to left in the third," wrote Louis Effrat of *The New York Times,* "DiMaggio made a circus catch, twisting his gloved hand over his right shoulder. In the fifth he raced to the cinder track to pull down Beau Bell's towering drive."

In Chicago on June 24, with his batting average hovering at the .360 mark, he hit two home runs in one inning, tying a record, and added two doubles. Only four other men had previously hit two home runs in an inning and although it was a record in which luck played a large role, DiMaggio had nudged his way into consideration for a berth on the American League All-Star team in his first season.

DiMaggio was the right fielder in the All-Star Game played on July 6 in Boston. The American League had swept the first three All-Star classics since it became a baseball tradition in 1933. The fans turned out to see how the 21-year-old rookie slugger would fare against the best pitching the National League had to offer. The game was a grim experience for DiMaggio. In his first turn at bat against the fabulous Dizzy Dean, he slammed into a double play, the beginning of five hitless trips against the pitching of Dean, Carl Hubbell, Curt Davis, and Lon Warneke. The National League took a 4–0 lead and DiMaggio's fielding, in part, contributed to their edge. He had made an attempt for a shoestring catch of a liner hit by Gabby Hartnett, but the ball went through for a triple that produced a pair of runs. In the fifth inning Billy Herman lined a single to right and DiMaggio bobbled the ball for the only error of the game. Herman moved to second on the error and scored what proved to be the deciding run on Joe Medwick's single.

The American League struck back for three runs in the seventh inning, including a home run by Lou Gehrig. Then with the bases loaded and two out, DiMaggio went to bat against Warneke with a chance to help win or tie the game and make up for his earlier misplays. He lashed a sharp line drive between second and shortstop. Leo Durocher, the shortstop, made a leaping stab at the ball for the out and the National League went on to win by a score of 4–3 and capture its first All-Star victory.

A career as a baseball player, such as DiMaggio had attained, might easily have been a dream of many American youngsters at the height of the Depression, but it could only turn into reality for a gifted few. Unemployment was enormously high—more than 8 million—in 1936.

In November of that year President Roosevelt would try for his second term and already his New Deal had become virtually a part of everyone's daily life. The opportunities open to a young man just reaching his maturity and with limited education were not very great. Among some of the programs created to help alleviate unemployment were the Civilian Conservation Corps (CCC) and the Work Progress Administration (WPA). Enlistment in the armed forces was another option. Even if the DiMaggio offspring had aspired to a college education—undoubtedly they possessed the native intelligence to earn one—it's hard to believe that money would have been available for the purpose. In the depressed economy even persons with college degrees could not find work. Under these sets of options, DiMaggio was fortunate that he had the gifts and that his time was right to reach out and grab the gold ring.

Until he had driven to Florida with Lazzeri and Crosetti, DiMaggio had never been east of the Rocky Mountains. The only big cities he had known were those in the Pacific Coast League, Los Angeles being the largest besides his home town.

"I saw New York in the movies," he said later, "and as I got glimpses of the skyline, of all those tall buildings, of big crowds hurrying through busy streets, I got a little scared."

He adapted, of course, but throughout his career and for years afterward, he was never fond of being caught in a large crowd. Ironically, despite his doubts about the hurly-burly of New York, he became so indelibly linked with the city's mystique that he was never able to divorce it from his identity. Decades later President Kennedy became identified with the citizens of Berlin by proclaiming, "I am a Berliner" in his famous speech after visiting the Berlin Wall. In a similar way, DiMaggio, in having become associated with the daily vicissitudes of the Big Apple, would have had to say, "I am a New Yorker" whether he thought it was true or not. New York's baseball fans simply would not have had it any other way.

As a rookie, DiMaggio's sole interest seemed to center on the main chance baseball afforded him for making money, and for getting his family out from under their financial struggle. He linked this directly to how he performed on the field.

"Right now baseball, and the Yankees, and the absolute necessity of making good, are the most important things in my life," he said after only a few months with the team.

He received many invitations to attend dinners and other social events, some in his honor, others as a guest, but he turned down most of them.

"I don't want to be dined because I have done nothing to be dined about," he said. "Besides, I'm a ballplayer. I have my career in front of me. I cannot afford to stay out late and I can't neglect my diet. If I decline invitations, I hope my friends will realize the situation I'm in and not feel that I'm putting on a high hat or going Hollywood on Broadway."

Family loyalty was always at the heart of his relationships. He typified the striving of many ethnic groups in the 1930s—reaching out for an identity, proving that they could make contributions to the establishment in their own fashion even if the establishment disdained them or offered opportunity only grudgingly. Major league baseball certainly was an establishment sport, one in which no black man would perform until 1947.

DiMaggio's roots, for the time being at least, were in San Francisco with his parents, his brothers and sisters, and the friends who, for whatever reasons, remained in the circumscribed world of North Beach. It would always be home to DiMaggio despite the wealth and fame he would accumulate along the way. It would always be the place to which he would return after the long, weary trips or the emotional upheavals of his two broken marriages. It was the safest harbor, snug and secure in the remembrance of the earliest days with Mama and Papa.

"Every man thinks of his own parents as the best, the kindest, the most loving in the world," he said. "Well, that's how I think of my folks. And with plenty of reasons. They weren't very well fixed financially."

As a teenager his refusal to turn to fishing, as his father had done, for his livelihood was undoubtedly motivated by a strong streak of pragmatism in his nature. Where there might have seemed to be something ultimately romantic in the notion of fishing for one's living—a kind of macho bravado, man against the sea—the young DiMaggio saw no such romance in crab fishing. To him it was a simple, hard day's work that did not reap many dollars at the fish market each pay day. In an uncomplicated way, as he might have seen it, he wanted to become a singularly outstanding athlete and through that medium a wealthy person. Coldly appraising his own talent, he knew he was good enough to attain his goal. Analyzing all the options, it was the only direction he could go. Now he was getting his chance. Overriding all this was his strong sense of roots, and he intended to hold on to them no matter what happened.

"Ma and Papa had little eduation," DiMaggio said. "They were from Sicily. They are great believers in learning. I wasn't asked to quit school and sell papers or to go on a truck. They sent me through three years of high school, and if it had been up to them I would have gone right on. But baseball got me before I could finish my high school courses.

"Let me say this about my Pop. Until three years ago he didn't know what baseball was. Then he became a violent fan, started to go to the games every day, and acquired a surprising knowledge of the finer points. In fact, he got so he could criticize the official scorer. He couldn't read English, but he learned to identify names in a box score."

DiMaggio's father was in his sixties when his son broke in as a rookie. The gap in age between Joe, the eighth child, and his father didn't seem to bother the ballplayer, nor did the age difference concern his younger brothers and sisters. If the generation gap existed, the camaraderie of a large family made up for it.

"It has been a happy life," Joe said, describing his parents' outlook, "full of kids and troubles—but happy just the same. Pop doesn't have to go out fishing anymore. He sits on Fisherman's Wharf, four blocks from our house, and talks fish, and, I have no doubt, about his boy Joe. If your own Pop won't puff you up, who will? In everything I do, I hope that I won't disappoint him when he brags about his boy Joe on Fisherman's Wharf."

Ernie Sisto attests even today to DiMaggio's deep-rooted fondness for the place where he grew up.

"He still has the house he bought years ago in San Francisco," Sisto said. "I think he's a wealthy man, but he doesn't have a lot of cars and homes. I used to say to him, 'Why don't you invest in real estate?' But he didn't seem to want to do that. He's got a big 36-foot boat he takes out when the water's right. He doesn't like to go out when the water's rough. I don't think he'd ever move from the Coast. That's his whole life there."

Indeed, Santiago's words in *The Old Man and the Sea*—"Maybe he was as poor as we are and would understand"—set the tone for a fitting dénouement. Certainly DiMaggio could understand, and his mother and father, who had traveled steerage class from Sicily more than 30 years before, could understand, too.

Rosalie DiMaggio accepted her son's newly won fame in a simple, unaffected, almost stoic manner. He had had a brilliant season, a .323 batting average, 206 hits, 29 home runs, 44 doubles, 15 triples, 125 runs batted in, and his 132 runs scored had sparked the Yankees to their first pennant since 1932. He had made arrangements for his brother Tom to bring his mother to New York for the 1936 World Series. The Yankees made her a guest of honor with a front-row box seat at all games. Only once before had she been to New York—a brief encounter after landing at Ellis Island and passing through by train en route to the West Coast.

The 3,000-mile journey east in a Pullman drawing room took four days and four nights, and her arrival, with little packages of Italian cookies and sausage treats for her son, at the Mayflower Hotel, where she would spend her two-week holiday, was a welcome rest stop. It was September 28. The Yankees had clinched the American League pennant by 19½ games and the Series would open in a day or two against Bill Terry's New York Giants at the Polo Grounds.

"I don't know what to do here," Mama DiMaggio said in Italian as reporters interviewed her. "Yesterday we drove all over and saw the city. Today there is nothing for me to do but sit by the window and think about the games. There is no work. I wish there was some cleaning to do here or some dishes I could wash and dry."

Her requirements for relaxation seemed to reflect a kind of plain, simple, uncomplicated attitude toward the refinements of life. At the age of 57 she was a comfortably stout, cheerful woman, quiet and placid, accepting her role as mother and homemaker for her husband and family without anxiety.

It was a matter of fact to her that her son had achieved something outstanding. It did not surprise her. Yet she was oblivious to the impending fame and fortune he would attain by making a living through the playing of a game—a phenomenon made possible through the complexity of life in a country not yet 200 years old.

"I do not know much about baseball, but I understand what is going on," she said. "I know what it is to make a hit or a home run or a put-out."

She had learned quickly the facets of the game her son did so well. During the Series she paid close attention and kept tabulations of all her son's moves.

It was a big Series for DiMaggio and made up for his poor showing in the All-Star Game. He rapped out nine hits, including three doubles, drove in three runs and batted .346. The Yankees were awesome, taking the Series, four games to two. Twice they crushed Giant pitching with 17 hits, and took the second game by an 18–4 score, the most one-sided contest in Series history.

President Roosevelt threw out the first ball for the second game at the Polo Grounds and he stayed until the last out. Had he left earlier, he would have missed one of the most spectacular catches of DiMaggio's career.

The Giants, of course, had no chance to overtake the Bombers as they batted in the ninth. DiMaggio had already retired the first two men in the inning. Hank Leiber, a long-ball hitter, faced Lefty Gomez, who had been coasting with his huge lead. Leiber connected for a towering shot that sent DiMaggio back to the Eddie Grant monument, almost 500 feet from the plate. DiMaggio ran between the two flights of stairs that led to the clubhouse dressing rooms and caught the ball.

Instead of rushing up the steps after he had made the catch, DiMaggio stood calmly at attention, while the President was driven from the boxes behind the Giants' dugout to the center field exit gates. The crowd remained at attention, too. As he passed DiMaggio, the President threw him a salute, amid the cheers of the fans. Then DiMaggio dashed for the clubhouse to join the Yankees in their first World Series celebration since 1932, when home runs by Ruth, Gehrig, and Lazzeri had crushed the Cubs in four straight.

After the deciding game, Terry sat in the clubhouse wondering what the Giants might have done differently to overcome the Yankees. He was beyond alibis.

"I'd like to add one thing," Terry said, "I've always heard that one player could make the difference between a losing team and a winner and I never believed it. Now I know it's true."

He was talking about DiMaggio.

After the Yankee victory DiMaggio's mother cried. "Maybe because I'm the mother of Joe that they treat me so nice," she said, wondering why reporters and photographers were showering so much attention on her. She wiped her tears and smoothed her green dress. "I don't know, the people are so lovely. I never had anything like this happen before."

She was entranced by the warm-heartedness of the fans. She had seen Bill Terry play in pain with a wrenched left knee and display physical courage. Terry's knee had swollen to twice its normal size. His pain was obvious to all. Terry was not always popular with the press, but throughout the Series the writers filed accounts about his injury and his pain. He was without peer as a fielder at first base; as a hitter he was the last big-leaguer to attain a .400 average. To compound his problem, Terry felt obligated to stay in the lineup because there was no replacement for him at first base; the Giants' other first baseman was out with an injury, too. After each game, Terry returned immediately to his hotel room to rest his leg, putting it up on a pillow on his bed. He would leave his room the next day with only time enough to reach the ball park for batting practice. It had become a daily ritual. The injury forced him to retire as a player at the end of the Series.

Mama DiMaggio's experience at the Series had taken on some of the emotional range, subliminally at least, of Terry's ordeal. She felt sorry that the Giants had been beaten. Terry's courage had won her admiration.

"I feel awfully sorry about the Giants losing," she said. "Every time I think about it I feel hurt about the whole thing. But somebody's got to win, and the Yankees were much superior. What can I say about the games? They were so fine. The boys surely worked so hard. When you see them running, falling, and jumping they surely worked hard."

She had come away with an innocent appreciation for a part of American life, its generosity of spirit, despite all the scams and promotions, to make heroes of even the humblest citizens.

"Only one thing I want to see," she said. "I want to see the Statue of Liberty. I saw it 33 years ago when I came here from Palermo. To see it again will bring back those days."

Among the things she had missed while in New York was Italian food.

"For days I have been begging my son Tom to take me to an Italian restaurant," she said. "I do not like this American-type food. So last night he took me to Papa Moneta's, down on the East Side. Oh, it was wonderful! I had all the Italian food there is. All kinds of it.

"And the minute Papa Moneta found out who I was he went crazy. He ran around telling everyone I was there and everybody came over to shake my hand. I wanted to eat my dinner, but every time I tried to eat something someone would want to shake my hand. It took me almost three hours to finish my dinner."

When Mama DiMaggio and her son Tom finished dinner, the Monetas and their friends piled into three taxi cabs and took her on a sightseeing tour of Little Italy, South Street, the East River, and other city landmarks. It was a time in New York when a visitor could say, as Mama DiMaggio declared, "It was so beautiful."

"Finally, it was 12 o'clock and I wanted to go home," she said as if her Cinderella story had come to an end. "So Tom brought me back here to the hotel and then he went out again. He didn't get back until 5 in the morning. He went to all the nightclubs."

Joe didn't accompany his mother and brother that night. She had no misgivings about that. It was a manner, a custom of the family. Her sons had treated her with respect and kindness and generosity and if they had to keep previous engagements she understood. She knew how to fend for herself when she was alone.

"Joe told me, 'Mama, I got to go out with the boys tonight,' and I understand," she said.

Perhaps it was an old-world attitude—the female acceptance of male preference. In later years, the influence of this unquestioning familial pampering undoubtedly played a role in the attitudes DiMaggio adopted in his two marriages that ended in divorce.

The next day, before she and Tom departed by Pullman on the 3,000-mile trip back to San Francisco and North Beach, Mama DiMaggio visited the Statue of Liberty. In a few days, her son Joe would go home again, too, and receive the keys to the city of St. Francis.

3

Taken in Tow
by a
Left-Handed Joker

*A*T ABOUT THE time President Roosevelt was being inaugurated for his second term, the world champion Yankees were receiving their contracts in the mail for the 1937 season. There was speculation that DiMaggio, who had won rookie-of-the-year honors with a .323 batting average, 29 home runs, and 125 runs batted in, would hold out for more money. The same was said about Lou Gehrig, who had driven in 152 runs (the sixth time he had batted in 150 or more in a season), hit 49 home runs, batted .354, and had won the most valuable player award. Red Ruffing, the star right-hander with 20 victories the previous season, was also unsatisfied with his contract. The Yankees faced a possible three-pronged holdout.

Major league teams shrewdly calculated their payroll plans each winter. In their modus operandi they sent contracts to players with the previous year's salary as the first offer; in many cases the contracts called for a cut in pay. No matter how fine a season a player might have had, a raise was not automatic, and he had to marshal his business advisers to guide him. Agreement with the journeymen players was reached rather quickly. Star players, those who brought out the fans to the box office, haggled longer, often consulting lawyers before accepting terms. A short holdout caused little stir, but a protracted one became a cause célèbre and slowed down a team's spring training plans. Generally, the manager and club owners entered the picture trying to sway the player after the general manager or business manager indicated that he had made no headway and needed help.

In 1936, DiMaggio had used his brilliant minor-league record and the publicity it received to get Barrow to agree to an $8,000 salary. Now he had major-league credentials—top rookie, selection to the All-Star team, and fine slugging statistics—to speak for him as bargaining points. He returned his contract unsigned on January 29.

"I received as nice a letter from Joe as anybody could get," Barrow said diplomatically. "I don't anticipate any difficulty whatever in signing Joe because I know we're not very far apart on terms. He is ready to continue playing ball for us and we're certainly willing to have him do so."

Two weeks later Barrow sent DiMaggio a new contract, offering him $15,000. On the surface it looked like a substantial raise. Barrow and Colonel Ruppert could not deny DiMaggio's strong drawing power, especially in thickly Italian-populated sections of New York and the surrounding metropolitan areas, where baseball was the most popular sport. DiMaggio had in fact become a stronger drawing card than Gehrig, who had been the Yankee leader and team captain for many years.

DiMaggio cautiously acknowledged Barrow's offer.

"We haven't got together yet," he said, "but things look favorable. I think everything will be straightened out next week."

When the Yankees opened spring camp in St. Petersburg, Florida, all the regulars except Gehrig, DiMaggio, and Ruffing were on hand. On March 8, Manager McCarthy showed his first signs of apprehension and phoned the home office in New York for news about his three holdouts.

"Gehrig has just returned to New York," Barrow told McCarthy. "He has had no chance to see Colonel Ruppert yet. And we have no word from Ruffing or DiMaggio. I consider all three holdouts."

With two veterans like Gehrig and Ruffing seeking more money, DiMaggio sensed his timing had been bad. Four days later the Yankees received his signed contract. He had accepted $15,000. It had made him the highest paid second-year player in major-league history, and this time on his way to spring camp there would be no 3,000-mile auto trip with Lazzeri and Crosetti. In a single season he had established himself as a star in his own right who could write his own transportation ticket.

"This holdout business is tougher than playing," DiMaggio said as he arrived in Florida. "All I want to do is get back to work."

On March 20, Gehrig arrived in camp and talked with Ruppert. They reached agreement quickly and then Gehrig and DiMaggio, flanking the colonel, formally signed, giving the Yankees an opportunity to publicize the appearance of harmony in the family. Gehrig received $36,000, the highest salary in the big leagues in 1937. Ruffing had remained a holdout—and it would cost him a day's pay for each day he extended it.

DiMaggio put the money problem behind, but he was soon to fall victim to physical ailments. His late start in training put his conditioning behind schedule. He played in only nine exhibition games. At Tallahassee, Florida, on April 2, he pulled up lame. He was sidelined with acute pain in his right shoulder. When he threw or lifted his arms above his head, the pain persisted. Through April 13 he did not start a game, although he pinch hit 12 times and made six hits. The cause of the pain was a mystery. The team had broken camp in Florida and was in the middle of the southern swing at Knoxville, Tennessee, en route home, when McCarthy decided to have DiMaggio see Dr. Reese Patterson, a Knoxville specialist, to get to the root of the ailment.

Dr. Patterson's examination revealed that DiMaggio was suffering from abnormally swollen and infected tonsils. A decaying tooth also contributed to the pain. The tonsils and the tooth would have to be removed as soon as possible. McCarthy put DiMaggio on the overnight train from Knoxville to New York and told him to report to Barrow as soon as he arrived.

"If the doctor thinks the tonsils should come out," he said, "it's all right with me. The sooner the better."

Barrow had arranged for DiMaggio to see Dr. Girard Oberrender, Colonel Ruppert's personal physician. When he arrived at Pennsylvania Station he was whisked to the doctor's office. On April 16, his tonsils and adenoids were removed at Lenox Hill Hospital by Dr. Oberrender. He missed the season's opening game for the second straight year and was out of action for two weeks.

Returning to the lineup on May 1, DiMaggio signaled the start of another electrifying season. He cracked three hits off Rube Walberg of the Red Sox and figured in all the Yankee runs in a 3–2 victory. By June 11 he had hit 11 home runs, reaching that total with two in one game against the Browns in St. Louis. He had hit five in his last six times at bat and had hit safely in 12 straight games. He continued the hot pace through June and connected for No. 20 on the Fourth of July with a bases-loaded drive off Walberg again, breaking a 4–4 tie and giving the Yankees a double-header sweep.

The grand slam, his first of three during the season, brought DiMaggio unusual accolades from the 61,146 fans at the game and from his teammates. The *New York Times* reporter took pains to describe the reaction:

> Countless homers have been struck at Yankee Stadium. Many with the bases loaded. But few in the history of the Bronx park surpassed this for dramatic appeal and distance. The stands shook with shouts and stomping, a deafening crescendo of shrieks, cheers, whistling and handclapping. At the plate there began a demonstration of affectionate mobbing that continued on the bench as every player pummeled and thumped the youth.

DiMaggio drew a lot of Italians to the Stadium. In the outfield stands and bleachers they waved red-white-and-green tricolor flags and cheered every move he made. They brought their lunch in paper bags—big hero sandwiches and cheese and wine. When he hit a home run they cheered as if he were Caruso delivering an aria from the stage of the Metropolitan Opera. At first it was a source of embarrassment for DiMaggio, but he learned not to let it bother him. While he seemed not to show it, he loved the adulation and he was always aware that he owed the fans his best performance.

In two seasons DiMaggio had come a long way from the shy and reserved poker-faced rookie who had never been east of the Rockies. He minded his business, avoiding clubhouse politics and long gossip sessions. He knew what he was capable of doing on the field and that mattered most. This was often regarded as conceit by teammates and critics among the press. The Yankees had wisely assigned him to room with Vernon "Lefty" Gomez, the team's star left-handed pitcher—a wit and raconteur and a good judge of ballplayers. From the start Gomez saw star qualities in DiMaggio, but his job as Joe's roommate was to keep him from letting the cheers of the fans inflate his ego.

Barrow was aware of this, too. Fans everywhere were inviting him to parties and banquets, showering him with gifts. He called the young DiMaggio to his office one day.

"Joe, I know you've started off at a tremendous pace and the fans are all for you," Barrow said, "but don't take the applause too seriously."

"Don't worry about me, Mr. Barrow," DiMaggio said, "I never get excited."

With the departure of Babe Ruth, who had dominated the Yankee scene on the field and in the clubhouse, Gomez and Gehrig had become the central characters to whom the players gravitated for counsel and leadership. Gehrig was an avid bridge player and Gomez's specialty was casino. Before games, at home and on the road, the Yankee clubhouse invariably had two card games going at the same time. Gehrig drew the bridge brigade and the casino aficionados fell in line with Gomez. DiMaggio naturally joined the casino clique.

It was inevitable that DiMaggio and Gomez should become chums. Both were born in California, Gomez on Nov. 26, 1909, in Rodeo, a small town of 5,400 population southeast of San Francisco, DiMaggio on Nov. 25, 1914 (five years less a day separated them in age). Both had been sent to the Yankees by the same scout, Bill Essick, who started out hoping to be a musician. Gomez very nearly became a New York Giant, but Essick snared him at the last minute.

Gomez's Spanish background and DiMaggio's Italian stock gave them another link, although by nature they were different on the surface. Gomez loved to pull practical jokes; DiMaggio was quiet, often stoical. Still, DiMaggio appreciated his friend's humor and was relaxed around him. He admired Gomez's easygoing, gregarious ways, seeing in him what he could not bring out of himself. Gomez entertained the whole club.

When Gomez married the actress June O'Dea and went off for a short honeymoon, the players ribbed him when he returned.

"Did you have fun, Lefty?" one of them asked him. "Did you try it a lot of different ways?"

"Yeah, sure," Gomez retorted, "even standing in a hammock."

DiMaggio, of course, also admired Gomez as a pitcher.

In 1934 Gomez had won 26 games and lost only 5 for an .839 percentage, one of the highest in baseball history. He had won 21 games in 1931 and 24 the next year. He was, after all, one of baseball's finest pitchers.

His appetite for the practical joke, however, was colossal. He never passed up an opportunity.

After DiMaggio became a regular in center field midway in the 1936 season, whenever Gomez was on the mound, he invariably had the support of an Italian triumvirate of Tony Lazzeri at second base, Frank Crosetti at shortstop, and DiMaggio in center protecting him up the middle. The efficacy of this did not go unnoticed by Lefty.

During a game earlier in the season at the Stadium, Gomez was coasting along with a big lead against the hapless Browns. Late in the game, with one out and a runner on first, Gomez threw to the next batter. The ball was lashed directly back to him. He snared the ball, quickly whirled around and threw it into center field straight at DiMaggio, who was racing in to back up the play.

DiMaggio and the other Yankees were dumbfounded. The baserunner, standing on second, wore a perplexed smile as he brushed himself off after his slide.

In the Yankee dugout, Manager McCarthy went into a slow burn. When the inning ended, he was furious with Gomez.

"Why did you throw to DiMaggio in center field?" he growled, incredulously. "We should have had a double play."

"Someone shouted, 'Throw it to the dago,'" Gomez replied, sheepishly. "But nobody said which dago."

McCarthy lost control, his temper rose to fever pitch, and his voice several decibels. He hollered to the players on the bench: "After this, you've got to specify which dago, you hear?"

The players roared with laughter and McCarthy, suddenly aware of his laugh-provoking gem, doubled up laughing, too.

DiMaggio took delight in repeating the story many times afterward to illustrate Gomez's zaniness and to point up the good-natured ethnic humor that from time to time enlivened a dull afternoon.

Gomez also liked to tell jokes. He would corner a player or a reporter or a photographer and go into his spiel. One photographer who made a good listener was Ernie Sisto.

"Lefty liked to tell a blue joke once in a while," Sisto recalled. "He always cracked me up when he told this one. This guy is out there pitching and all of a sudden he stops and starts fishing around the mound. The manager comes out of the dugout and says, 'What are you looking for?' The pitcher says, 'I dropped my glass eye and I can't find it.' The manager says, 'Well, don't worry about it. We got an extra glass eye in the locker room. We'll send it out to you.' The batboy goes to the locker room to get the glass eye and then runs out to the mound to give it to the pitcher. The pitcher puts it in his eye socket and continues pitching. After a couple of pitches he bends over and is reaching around the mound again. The manager storms out to the mound again. 'What's the matter now?' he says. 'I found the other eye,' the pitcher says. 'Well shove it up your ass and you can keep an eye on that guy on second base at the same time,' the manager says. 'Now let's get on with this ball game.'"

The Yankees, who had taken the 1936 title by 19½ games, were on another tear with Gehrig, Bill Dickey, DiMaggio, and a newcomer, Tommy Henrich, setting a hot pace. Henrich was acquired by the Yankees as a free agent when Commissioner Kenesaw Mountain Landis had ruled that the Cleveland club was preventing him from moving up to the majors by keeping him too long with their New Orleans farm team. As soon as Henrich went on the market, the Yankees got him by signing him for $20,000. They sent him to Newark, but he was there only a week. George Selkirk got hurt and Henrich embarked on a Yankee career that made him a favorite with the fans for many seasons.

He brought a boyish charm and a tenor voice he enjoyed using on numerous light occasions in the clubhouse.

After a good game, in which they had made a cornucopia of hits,

Henrich would lead a group of players in a barbershop rendition of "That Old Gang of Mine" or some other favorite.

"Break it up you guys," McCarthy would shout. "What do you think I'm running here, a singing school?"

DiMaggio had one of his biggest days on July 18 against Bob Feller, Cleveland's 18-year-old fastball sensation, before 58,884 at Municipal Stadium. He slammed a 415-foot triple and a double, then hit his second bases-loaded home run of the season with two out and two strikes on him in the ninth. It was his 24th homer and he had batted in all five Yankee runs in the 5–1 triumph. He had also extended a hitting streak to 17 games.

In 1927 Babe Ruth had set the most glamourous of all slugging records when he hit 60 home runs, a record 17 in September. Only two players had approached the record. Hack Wilson of the Chicago Cubs hit 56 in 1930 to set the National League standard and in 1932 Jimmie Foxx of the Philadelphia A's walloped 58.

On the weekend of July 31–August 1 at the Stadium, DiMaggio hit three home runs, two in one game, to reach a total of 31. The pace he was setting was one game better than Ruth's at that stage of the season. Writers scurried to the record book to make comparisons. Could the 22-year-old DiMaggio, in only his second season in the big leagues, match the most matchless of all of Ruth's records? DiMaggio had hit No. 31 in the Yankees' 89th game; Ruth had attained that figure in the Yankees' 90th game.

The home run mania reached a high point on Tuesday, August 3, with a crowd of 66,767, the biggest weekday crowd of the year, celebrating Lou Gehrig Appreciation Day. The Yankees made it memorable by bombarding the White Sox in the double-header, accounting for all their runs with home runs—all of them over 400 feet. The occasion also marked the 1,900th consecutive game in which Gehrig had played and he received a pocket watch, presented to him by George M. Cohan, the producer, playwright, actor, and songwriter, for having won the 1936 Most Valuable Player honors. Gehrig and DiMaggio hit three-run homers in the first game and Tony Lazzeri also connected in a 7–2 victory. Lazzeri walloped a homer in the second inning of the nightcap and with the Yankees trailing, 3–1, in the eighth, Bill Dickey cleared the bases for four runs, causing the fans to shower the field with pop bottles, streams of torn programs and newspapers, and straw hats. Two days later, DiMaggio extended a new hitting streak to 15 games with a 10th-inning double to beat the Indians, 7–6. On August 18 he got four hits against the Senators, ending the game with his 35th homer in the ninth.

By the last week in August, DiMaggio had realistically assessed his chances of catching Ruth's record. He knew he could no longer make the challenge.

"Confidentially, I don't think I'll be able to beat Ruth's record this season," he told a reporter, "but I would like to hit 50. With about 40 games to go I might make it."

As a right-handed hitter and playing in Yankee Stadium, DiMaggio was at a disadvantage in pursuing home run records. The distance down the left-field line was 301 feet and then it veered sharply to 402 feet in straightaway left. Left-handers were in a better position, since the right-field corner fence was 296 feet down the foul line and took a more gradual angle with a range of 344 to 367 feet approaching the bull pen.

While it may not have sounded like modesty, false or honest, DiMaggio said at the end of his career that he might have broken Ruth's record if he had played in parks that had favored right-handed hitters.

"I could have hit 70 in a field which favored right-handers," he said. "In addition to the 46 homers I got that year, I hit 15 triples that could have been homers. It seemed that every long ball I got hold of that season was a 400-footer, even the outs."

He did indeed have an exceptional season. He won the home run crown with 46. He played in 151 games and had a .346 batting average. He batted in 167 runs and scored 151. In 621 times at bat he produced 215 hits, the second year in a row he attained 200 or more. But the most impressive figures were his slugging average of .673 and total bases. Besides the 46 homers, he hit 35 doubles and 15 triples for a total-base count of 418, unsurpassed by any American League hitter since. Only Jim Rice of the Boston Red Sox, with an output of 406 total bases in 1978, has approached it, doing most of it as a designated hitter.

Gehrig and Dickey each had brilliant seasons. Gehrig batted .351, with 37 homers and 159 runs batted in, and Dickey finished at .332, with 29 homers and 133 runs batted in. Selkirk and Henrich, each playing about half the season, wound up at .328 and .320, respectively. Ruffing, after he came to terms, posted 20 victories and Lefty Gomez notched 21. In the last game of the season, DiMaggio hit his 46th homer, his third with the bases loaded, lifting the team to its second straight campaign with 102 triumphs as they won the pennant by 13 games.

When the balloting was in for the league's Most Valuable Player award, DiMaggio was edged out by Charlie Gehringer, Detroit's marvelous second baseman who had won the batting title with .371. DiMaggio had lost by four votes, 78–74. But the writers in Philadelphia and New York had named him the league's player of the year, ample ammunition for him to fire at Yankee management for negotiating his 1938 contract.

In so doing they had provided him, in his estimation at least, with enough effrontery to challenge Colonel Ruppert and Barrow. He had not taken into account, however, the business wizardry and experience both gentlemen had stored away from past skirmishes, including some classic ones with Babe Ruth. He spent the winter resting on his newly won laurels in San Francisco, plotting his strategy with his brother Tom. Ruppert and Barrow went about their business as usual. They anticipated a skirmish, but they never dreamed of the scope it would assume or the publicity it would generate. DiMaggio didn't either.

4

Ruppert and the Destiny of a Holdout

*M*AJOR LEAGUE BASEBALL changed DiMaggio's life style almost overnight. In two years with the Yankees he had got a taste of the big money—a rookie-year salary of $8,000, then $15,000 for his sophomore year. In each of those seasons he had received a $6,000 share of World Series money—in all a bonanza of $35,000. It sent him almost instantly into an income bracket that only a small percentage of Americans had attained. It was enough money to start him and his family in the restaurant business on Fisherman's Wharf in San Francisco, and he purchased a new home in North Beach for his mother and father.

With all this, he had also become an instant celebrity. Bit parts in movies, a stint in a vaudeville act, speaking engagements at banquets, barnstorming tours after the season, and advertising endorsements came his way and added to his income. His list of friends and acquaintances grew rapidly, too. He attracted all types, and as it frequently happened with most celebrities, they all wanted to join his entourage.

It was a time when advice would come to him from entrepreneurs of all descriptions and stripes, every one eager to snatch a piece of the action through association with a sports figure whose capacity for earning money seemed unlimited.

Whether the seed was planted by these new-found acquaintances or whether it germinated naturally with some family persuasion, DiMaggio's estimate of his financial value as a baseball player took a drastic turn. Perhaps what Lazzeri and Crosetti had hoped to warn him about—taking too much stock of his press clippings—was working its inevitable way into his ego.

The fact that he had been named player of the year by the New York and Philadelphia baseball writers, two prestigious groups, and missed by a narrow margin in winning the Most Valuable Player award obviously were points he weighed in his favor. He could have reasoned that he was at least the second most valuable player in the American League and by extension, since the Yankees had won the pennant largely because of his performance, he could also reason that he was indeed the most valuable Yankee.

Armed with this ego-swelling portfolio, DiMaggio decided to ask for $40,000 for the 1938 campaign. He was heading East in mid-January ostensibly to pick up his trophies from the New York and Philadelphia writers and to see the Jimmy Braddock–Tommy Farr heavyweight fight at Madison Square Garden. He made it known that if he could he would like to talk with Colonel Ruppert and Barrow about his next contract. He had become friendly with people in the boxing business, notably Joe Gould, the manager of Braddock, who had lost the heavyweight title to Joe Louis the previous year. DiMaggio had spent several days visiting Louis's training camp at Pompton Lakes, New Jersey, the previous summer while Louis was preparing for the first defense of his title against Farr, a rugged Welshman who endured a merciless beating by Louis for 15 rounds but refused to be knocked down by the Brown Bomber. DiMaggio enjoyed mingling with boxing people. He had gone to grammar school with Freddie Apostoli, who held the world middleweight boxing title in 1938 and 1939, moved up in weight class and lost twice to Billy Conn in nontitle light-heavyweight bouts. DiMaggio's restaurant business in San Francisco was booming and had become a stopover for tourists as well as sports figures. He had found a lure, a way to promote himself as a sports personality, and it was paying off.

There were at the same time reports, later denied, and perhaps only figments of an imaginative press, that DiMaggio and the Yankees had reached a secret agreement following the 1937 World Series on terms of his next contract and that his current exclamations demanding a big pay increase were camouflage put up to dissuade other Yankees from seeking similar emoluments.

He arrived in New York to keep his appointments and was immediately taken in tow by Gould. DiMaggio, however, strongly denied there had been a secret deal the previous fall with the Yankees.

"To tell you the truth," he said, "and strange as it may sound, I never saw Barrow once to talk to all last season until just before the World Series, when I went to see him about buying two extra World Series tickets. I have signed no contract up to now, haven't even seen one, and have no idea what the Yankees intend to offer me.

"I understand they are sending the contracts out this week, and I hope they don't send mine all the way out to San Francisco because if they would ask me over to see them, I'd go at once and maybe settle the whole business without any further delay."

It was the start of a day-to-day colloquy that became more heated as the days passed and showed both parties in a mercenary light. The Yankees, and particularly Barrow, grew aggravated by what they deemed to be intervention in negotiations by the press, as if DiMaggio one day and the Yankees the next were manipulating the news media to gain public sympathy for their respective postures.

Phone calls were made to Barrow by unknown persons using DiMaggio's name and asking for appointments to discuss his contract. The hoax was reported in the press. DiMaggio found it amusing, but it angered Barrow.

"After that," DiMaggio said, "I'm afraid Barrow would tell me to go to hell if I told him I was Joe DiMaggio on the phone."

Still, DiMaggio would not name a specific figure that he would bargain for and he was stern when asked if his demands would depend on what the Yankees offered Lou Gehrig, the Yankee captain and their highest paid player.

"Lou's figure doesn't enter into this thing at all," DiMaggio said, "and frankly I don't even know what Lou is getting beyond what has been mentioned in the press. That's really none of my business and my negotiations with the Yankees will be carried on entirely apart from what they pay Lou. While I naturally have an idea what I'm worth, I don't think it's up to me to say anything about that now. I'd rather wait until the club has made an offer."

Gehrig's salary in 1937 was $36,000, the highest in the major leagues.

On January 18, Barrow said he planned no preliminary talks with DiMaggio and that the center fielder's contract "would be put in the mail, just like everybody else's."

But Barrow had a change of heart, undoubtedly through the intervention of Colonel Ruppert. Two days later the Yankees invited DiMaggio for a 10 A.M. conference on January 21 at the Ruppert Brewery where Barrow and the colonel himself would be present.

Gould's association with DiMaggio had not gone unnoticed, either to members of the Fourth Estate or to Yankee and baseball officials. *The New York Times* reported:

> By reason of Joe DiMaggio's close association with Joe Gould, the fight manager, who seems to be taking more than a friendly interest in the young player's financial affairs, it is quite certain DiMaggio will enter today's conference with the Yankee warloads well coached in setting forth his demands. Gould, however, emphatically denied yesterday that he was Joe's 'manager' or had any financial interest in the player.

At the brewery offices the next morning, Barrow and Ruppert let DiMaggio cool his heels in the foyer for 45 minutes before they invited him into the colonel's plush, well-appointed surroundings. He had plenty of company, talking to reporters and posing for pictures for news photographers. He took it all good-naturedly, posing for one picture by rapping lightly on the colonel's office door. Whether Barrow and the colonel heard the rap or not, there was no immediate response. Finally, DiMaggio was called in. A half hour later he came out looking grim and unsmiling. Barrow and Ruppert flanked him and looked just as grim.

Ruppert was first to respond to questions and said the difference between what DiMaggio was asking for and what the Yankees were prepared to pay him was "considerable." It hadn't taken DiMaggio very long to refuse the offer. Reports had indicated that he had gone into the conference adamantly determined to stick to an opening figure of $40,000.

"I promised the colonel," DiMaggio said, "I would not mention any of the amounts we are discussing. So all information will have to come from him. All I can say is that I have not signed and that their offer is quite a way off from what I think I'm worth."

Ruppert was a man of much bravura, a dandy dresser who favored tailor-made suits, expensive stick pins, and handmade ties. (His valet made the color selections each morning.) He sported a mustache and considered himself a gentleman and a sportsman in all respects. His annual trip to Florida to the Yankees' spring training camp was always taken in a special private railroad car.

Ruppert was to the manor born on the Upper East Side of Manhattan—Lexington Avenue and 93rd Street—on August 5, 1867. His father had already acquired wealth through ownership of the brewery. He attended the prestigious Columbia Grammar School and was bright enough to pass the entrance exams to the School of Mining at Columbia University. But he had a maverick streak as a youth and chose not to attend college, deciding to join his father's brewery instead of becoming a mining engineer.

The move delighted his father, who denied the young Ruppert nothing that was within his means to provide. From the outset, Ruppert was "the most eligible bachelor in town" and he enjoyed the distinction so much he never married. By the time he was 22 years old he had been appointed a colonel in the New York National Guard, having joined Company B, Seventh Regiment, a silk-stocking outfit, as a private two years earlier. He milked the title for all its accruing benefits throughout his life.

After a good deal of coaxing from reporters, Ruppert decided to clear the air and tell what figure the Yankees had offered DiMaggio.

"I suppose there'll be no end of wild guessing among you fellows," Ruppert said, "so I might as well tell. It's $25,000 and I think that is a very fair salary. I don't intend to go any higher. I want to say to you on my honor as a gentleman that this is the first time that I or anyone connected with the Yankees has spoken to DiMaggio about his salary for 1938."

During his trip to New York, the Yankees had arranged for DiMaggio to take a physical examination so they could insure him for $100,000 as protection for the club against the loss of his services due to any physical accident that he might have on or off the field. This was not disclosed at the news conference and was only made public by DiMaggio on February 6 in a moment of pique in response to queries about his holdout status. No doubt, DiMaggio made the disclosure to bolster his position.

Throughout February DiMaggio stuck by his statement that he wouldn't sign "until I get what I think I'm worth." Now he spent most of his time managing his restaurant, but he did make arrangements to work out with the Seals in their spring camp. He had no plans to report to the Yankees' training camp, scheduled to open on March 1.

If he had accepted advice from Gould it must have been strong advice indeed, but now members of his family and some intimate friends were growing weary of his hard line. There had been no harsh words exchanged to this point, however, between DiMaggio and the Yankee front office, unlike the atmosphere that permeated Babe Ruth's last years with the club when Ruth virtually demanded that Ruppert fire Joe McCarthy and make him the team's manager.

As March and spring training wore on, cool heads no longer prevailed and the remarks from both sides carried harsh stings.

On March 8, the Yankees offered Gehrig a $39,000 contract, which he refused.

From St. Petersburg, McCarthy, who was now becoming part of the the Yankees' official team of spokesmen in the negotiations, said: "Colonel Ruppert met with Gehrig yesterday and offered him $39,000. The colonel said this was his maximum and absolutely his last offer to Lou, who can take it or leave it as he sees fit."

The Yankees were obviously using their negotiations with Gehrig as a buffer to thwart DiMaggio. After all, Gehrig had batted .351 in 1937 and had hit 37 homers and driven in 159 runs. If they could offer such an accomplished star only a $3,000 raise, why should they comply with DiMaggio's asking price of a $25,000 increase?

That same day, told of what Gehrig had been offered, DiMaggio displayed testiness when it was suggested that Ruppert had indicated he had been "reasonable" in negotiations with DiMaggio.

"That's what he thinks," DiMaggio said. "I won't accept $25,000 and I'll stick right here until I get the salary I want." He said he had his 1938 contract "in my pocket" and would mail it back to the Yankees "when I get around to it." But in an offhand remark made while he was working out with the Seals at their camp in Hanford, California, DiMaggio seemed on the verge of accepting the fact that he was playing a losing hand. "I suppose it will wind up with the ballplayer signing the contract, as he usually does," he said.

If he were on the verge that day of capitulating, he gave no evidence of it during the next few days. On March 12 Gehrig accepted the Yankee terms and signed for $39,000.

"It makes no difference to me Gehrig signed," DiMaggio said. "I'm still dickering with Colonel Ruppert and I'm waiting for a satisfactory contract. I have returned my contract unsigned."

The next morning in response to DiMaggio, in a lavishly worded statement aimed at winning public sympathy and made at the Pennsylvania Station before he left for his annual spring training visit, Ruppert told the press:

"DiMaggio is an ungrateful young man and is very unfair to his teammates, to say the least. He wants $40,000 and I've offered $25,000 and he won't get a button over that amount. Why, how many men his age earn that much? As far as I'm concerned, that's all he's worth to the ball club and if he doesn't sign we'll win the pennant without him.

"DiMaggio should have reported to Joe McCarthy by now. Instead, he's still sulking in San Francisco, carrying around in his pocket the contract we sent him three weeks ago. If he's smart he'll sign for $25,000 and report immediately. Judging from what I hear from St. Petersburg we can very well go along without him, although we'd like to have him, of course.

"Oh, he'll undoubtedly see things the right way before long, but is it fair for him to remain home, while the other boys are training down

South? No! Absolutely no! I think he's trying to escape spring training. That's all. I read a story which said he was working out with the Seals to keep in shape. That's O.K. by me, but he should be with his team in St. Petersburg."

Asked if it were true that Gehrig had accepted the Yankees' terms without haggling for more, Ruppert answered in one word: "Positively!"

But Gehrig had been invited by Ruppert to join him that morning as his guest in his private railroad car to make the trip to Florida. At the last minute Gehrig begged off, saying he was too busy moving from his apartment in New Rochelle, New York, to a new one in Larchmont, New York. That night, however, Gehrig and his wife, Eleanor, left Pennsylvania Station for St. Petersburg on a 10 o'clock train.

By the end of March the scenario almost reached the name-calling stage and DiMaggio's image was rapidly deteriorating; now he was cast as the ungrateful 23-year-old athlete who was trying to extract one more pound of flesh from the bleeding establishment, which had already been quite generous.

His repeated refrain, "I won't play for the Yankees until they meet my demands for more money," made him sound like a money-changer. In newspapers throughout the country, the fans were reading all about it.

McCarthy, too, joined the blunt language brigade and fired off his harshest fusillade to date from St. Petersburg. "The Yankees can get along without DiMaggio," he said, "and that $25,000 is final."

DiMaggio was taken aback by what seemed like an ultimatum from McCarthy. He wondered why his manager, of all people, should intrude and inject himself so one-sidedly into the dispute. Worst of all, DiMaggio was hurt that McCarthy could think the Yankees could get along without him.

From San Francisco he issued what sounded like his own ultimatum. "Well, maybe McCarthy knows what he's talking about. Maybe he doesn't," DiMaggio said. "But the contract for $25,000 they sent me is gone with the wind. Just say I've lost it. They're going to pay my price or else."

Ruppert had also been a politician, a Tammany Hall man who had served four terms in Congress and had run for Vice Mayor of New York. He had wide social connections through his memberships in the

Jockey Club, the New York Athletic Club, the Manhattan Club, the Catholic Club, and the New York, Larchmont, and Atlantic Yacht Clubs.

There was hardly anything of value that Ruppert did not collect, including pretty women. He was a connoisseur of fine wines and food, a frequent patron at Delmonico's and Luchow's. He collected jade and porcelain and Indian relics; first editions gathered dust on the book shelves of his study. He was an excellent dancer and owned a box in the dress circle at the Metropolitan Opera. He owned a town house on Fifth Avenue and an estate in Garrrison, New York, overlooking the Hudson River.

In virtually a repetition of his soliloquy rendered at Pennsylvania Station on March 13 when he left for the Yankees' camp, Ruppert took the rostrum again on March 31, after ending his Florida vacation. He was heading back to New York and this time he pontificated as if he were a political candidate running for office as he fired broadsides at his youthful star.

"The boys look in good condition and we should win another American League pennant," he said. "I have nothing new on DiMaggio. I have forgotten all about him. Presidents go into eclipse, kings have their thrones moved from under them, business leaders go into retirement, great ballplayers pass on, but still everything moves in its accustomed stride. If DiMaggio isn't out there, we have Hoag for center field. He's a fighting ballplayer. He's a good fielder and he hits all right. We'll get along."

In 1931 the Yankees paid $65,000 to buy Myril Hoag from Sacramento of the Pacific Coast League. Hoag, like DiMaggio, was a Californian and his father, Tracy Hoag, had been a pitcher in the same minor league but never made it to the majors. Hoag's father had great aspirations for him and discouraged him from becoming a pitcher because he thought his son would have a bigger career as a hitter. Hoag had a difficult time trying to break into the Murderers' Row lineup in his first big-league season and spent most of it on the bench. But in 1932, he compiled a handsome .370 batting average in 45 games. He turned in several journeyman-like seasons afterward, but when the Yankees brought up DiMaggio from the Seals, Hoag's career went into eclipse and he never got the chance to develop into the outfield star the Yankees needed to replace Ruth.

In 1936, Hoag and DiMaggio collided head-on while fielding a ball hit to the outfield by Leon "Goose" Goslin in a game at Detroit. Hoag suffered a concussion and blood clot in the head. It was feared his career was ended, but he recovered and stayed two more seasons with the Yankees before he was traded to the Browns. Now once again he was inextricably involved in DiMaggio's future.

DiMaggio's statements grew more terse and monotonous; he wasn't getting what he wanted and he refused to change his position. He was still talking to Gould and to his brother Tom, now the vice-president of the Fishermen's Union on the Bay Shore and advising him strongly to hold out for all he could get. Tom DiMaggio argued that the salary the Yankees paid his brother was only a small percentage of the gross revenues they brought in and it was only fair that Joe should get a just share since he was responsible, in large measure, for drawing the fans to the games. It was as simple as that, to him.

On April 7, DiMaggio's mood seemed less defiant. "I'm not satisfied, that's all. I think I'm worth more money and I want it," he said. He appeared to be softening, seeking sympathy more than victory.

Ruppert, always ready to capitalize on a chink in the armor, saw that he might be able to jar open the door and make some headway in the impasse.

"That is slightly different from the declaration DiMaggio made the other day," he said, "when he said the contract we sent him was 'gone with the wind' and that we would have to meet his demands 'or else.'

"This statement isn't quite as defiant. I have wondered what he meant by 'or else.' If he means he will not play baseball this year, then we must accept his decision. But I have gone as far as I can with him in the way of salary. He will play for $25,000 or not at all. It is for him to make the choice.

"There will be no more negotiating," Ruppert added. "The time for that has passed. Not a single dollar will be added to our offer. I have made up my mind and will stand pat."

Then Ruppert went on to appraise DiMaggio's career in monetary terms, casting the Yankees as benevolent employers who had done very well by the young upstart from the West Coast who came from humble origins.

"As I view the career of the young man," Ruppert said, "he has done remarkably well with the Yankees as to pay. For the first season he was paid $8,000, top price for a player from a minor league. He was increased to $15,000 last season, his second with us. Then he shares in the World Series at an amount, roughly speaking, of $12,000.

"If he accepts the $25,000 I have offered for this season, at the end of

1938, even if we do not get in the Series again, he will have received at the rate of $20,000 a year for three seasons. I should say that he is a well-paid young man and I can't see where he has any cause to be dissatisfied."

Ruppert did not say it, and possibly he was tempted to, but in 1938 the salary of the President of the United States was $25,000 a year.

By now McCarthy had the Yankees tuned for their exhibition schedule and Hoag was patrolling center field. They worked their way north on their annual tour of southern way stations and appeared ready for the season opener at Boston against the Red Sox on April 18. But DiMaggio was nowhere in sight.

Whatever hope they held out that he would have a change of heart and decide to report for opening day disappeared on April 14 when DiMaggio missed the deadline to book a coast-to-coast train reservation for New York. By then it was too late for him to travel on a three-day train trip and make the opener on time. It was Yankee team policy at that time not to allow their players to fly.

The Yankees lost their first game in Boston and DiMaggio was now losing $167 a day in salary for each day after the start of the season that he was a holdout. With the season under way he apparently, in sentiment at least, refused to cloak himself in the garb of a bona fide holdout. His comments about the Yankees' first-game defeat seemed to bring him back to the playing field. "It's too bad," he said, "but we'll do it again this year." He still obviously regarded himself as part of the Yankees. He said it would take him only about five days to a week to round into shape to play once the holdout issue was settled.

Meanwhile, Barrow stayed close to his office, where he kept a close watch on the wire-service ticker he had installed in his headquarters to monitor sports and news reports. The ticker would bring him word from the West Coast in case there was a change in DiMaggio's state of mind. But no reports trickled in and mention of DiMaggio brought a grim silence.

One dispatch, premature at best, that DiMaggio had reversed his position and was ready to come to terms, brought only a stern denial from Barrow.

"I know nothing about that at all," Barrow said. "We have received no communication from DiMaggio that he has changed his mind and we have made no new overtures to him. What is more, we are not going to make any and so the whole thing rests. All I can add to this is that if he doesn't accept terms 10 days from today [April 19] he will, under baseball law, become automatically suspended."

On the same day, however, there was a report from St. Louis that Donald Barnes, the president of the St. Louis Browns, had offered Ruppert $150,000 to buy DiMaggio. Barnes said Ruppert had turned it down, saying, "DiMaggio is not for sale at any price."

Perhaps it was the talk of his being traded to another team, especially the woeful Browns, or the yearning to play again once the season got started, or Ruppert's tribute to him that he wasn't for sale at any price, or his fear of being suspended—whatever it was that did the trick, DiMaggio capitulated two days later on April 20. He did it without fanfare, notifying Ruppert from San Francisco that he accepted the Yankee terms. Barrow made the announcement and the holdout, one of the longest in Yankee history, was ended.

There were a few conditions to the agreement, however, and they favored the club. DiMaggio's capitulation left Ruppert beaming with self-approval over his victory.

The terms prescribed that DiMaggio's salary would start only when he was pronounced fit and ready to play, and Manager McCarthy would be the sole judge of that. It meant that DiMaggio would have to get back into condition at his own expense—at the rate of $167 a day.

Ruppert could not resist flinging one more verbal brickbat at DiMaggio.

"I hope the young man has learned his lesson," Ruppert said. "His pay will be $25,000, no more, no less, and it won't start until McCarthy says it should."

McCarthy played the arbiter in a similar situation the previous year when Red Ruffing was a holdout. But that time McCarthy started paying Ruffing the day he arrived in camp and thus set a precedent. McCarthy's logic then went like this: "I don't want to be unfair to a player. And I don't want him hustling too fast to get in shape. He may tell me he is ready before he actually is and only harm may result."

McCarthy's logic seemed foolproof, but Barrow said he wasn't certain whether McCarthy would adopt the same policy again in DiMaggio's case. After all, Ruffing was a pitcher who could do irreparable damage to his pitching arm by starting before he was ready.

Before he joined the Yankees, DiMaggio's pay with the San Francisco Seals under a six-month contract was $1,800 and now in three seasons he had attained a $25,000 salary. Whether he was worth it or not, it made him the third highest player in baseball and the highest paid third-year man in the history of the game. By contrast, Carl Hubbell, the great New York Giants left-hander who had turned in five straight seasons with 20 or more triumphs in accounting for 115 victories and had won 24 straight games over two seasons (still the major league record), received $22,500 in 1938, his 11th season in baseball.

DiMaggio booked passage on the 3:40 P.M. train for New York on April 20, a Wednesday, and was due to arrive at Pennsylvania Station at 7:30 A.M. on the following Saturday. He was expected to be in uniform for a game against the Washington Senators at the Stadium.

Before he boarded the train, he said: "I'm all excited about getting back there and rapping the ball again. It's going to be a good season. There won't be any chance of an argument over salary next year. Naturally, I thought I was worth more this year, but I'd rather play ball than hold out. I can't get back quick enough now and I'm rarin' to go. I think the Yankees will win the pennant again. Not because I'm through holding out, though. It is a championship club anyhow. My teammates are a swell bunch of fellows and I'd rather play with the Yankees than any other team in baseball."

They were words of truce, couched in diplomacy aimed as much for the ears of his teammates as for Ruppert and Barrow. Obviously, the 23-year-old DiMaggio had learned more than the lessons Ruppert hoped he had taught him. The emphasis given to his acceptance of the "club's terms" led many reporters close to the Yankees, however, to speculate that DiMaggio had received private assurances of a bonus provided he turned in another spectacular season. But there was relief among members of his family that he had given in and would be leaving at last to rejoin his teammates.

On April 23, DiMaggio was once again in Yankee pinstripes. He sat on the bench at the Stadium as the Senators posted a 7–4 victory in a game in which Lou Gehrig broke out of an 0 for 17 slump with a 400-foot double.

Two days later DiMaggio was formally signed and Ruppert made it plain that he would have to get into condition at his own expense.

"The contract specifies a $25,000 salary which DiMaggio has agreed we shall begin to pay him when he is in condition to play," Ruppert said. "There is no bonus stipulation. Everything is hunky-dory now. I hope DiMaggio has a good season and that the Yankees win the pennant."

The idea that he would have to pay his own freight did not rest well with DiMaggio. McCarthy had not made the exception for him that he had made for Ruffing by putting him on the payroll as soon as he got back. If it meant money out of his pocket he wanted to get into shape as quickly as possible. He had actually worked out only three days with the Seals during his holdout. He suggested that he not make the club's next trip, to Philadelphia, and that he be allowed instead to work out alone and at his own pace at the Stadium. He reasoned that he could not get in enough batting practice time with the club on the road—the six to 10 pregame swings he might get would do nothing for him—and that he could make more progress on his own if he were permitted to practice at the Stadium. Barrow and McCarthy agreed.

So DiMaggio brought his troop of friends with him to shag his flies while he batted. The pitcher was Al Schacht, a former hurler who compiled a 14–10 won-lost record with Washington in a three-year career from 1919 to 1921. Schacht developed a new career for himself as a trick artist with a baseball, hiring his act out to the major league clubs. The act caught on and Schacht became known as the "Clown Prince of Baseball." Gould, the boxing manager whose propensity for catching baseballs was at best suspect and at worst hilarious, was among the group, which included Walter Woods, a middleweight boxer in Gould's stable. Some wore spiked shoes, some wore sneakers. All wore baseball caps of different sizes and shapes and colors. They created a picture of baseball tomfoolery that would have been grist for the Marx Brothers. One wondered how DiMaggio had got himself tangled up with such a group, and even more whether he was taking his training seriously.

DiMaggio's swing lacked its old snap, his eye was inaccurate, and his hands blistered easily. It was clear he was not in any condition for a starting assignment and that the long layoff had softened him. It took him almost two weeks to round into a semblance of his old sharpness. In all he was docked 11 days' pay—a loss in salary of $1,850 that he would not get back directly even during the next season. He resented the Yankees for this show of employer discipline, but he was helpless to retaliate.

He was back in the lineup again on April 30 in Washington and contributed a fluke single to the Yankees' 8–4 triumph that put them over the .500 mark for the first time. But more significantly he was involved in an almost tragic collision with Joe Gordon and both players wound up in the hospital. It did much to point up to DiMaggio the necessity for being in top condition and seemed to remain with him the rest of the season as a bitter reminder of his holdout.

In the sixth inning, Taft Wright of the Senators lofted a high fly into shallow left-center field. DiMaggio, in center field, and Hoag, the left fielder, went for the ball. So did Gordon, who drifted over from second base. DiMaggio and Gordon collided head-on and went down in their tracks. Hoag made the catch. Gordon lay unconscious for fully five minutes and DiMaggio was briefly unconscious. Both were taken by ambulance to Garfield Hospital, where they remained overnight with suspected possible concussions. DiMaggio was hit on the left side of the head and suffered severe swelling. Gordon was struck on the right side of the head and body. His cheek and jawbone were bruised and swollen and his right arm and shoulder were jarred. X-rays showed no fractures for either player and luckily they were discharged the next morning. Gordon, however, was in no shape to play and was sidelined with shoulder pains.

DiMaggio was well enough to take the field and belted his first home run of the season and a single in a 4–3 defeat. Then, on May 2, in a move that was to become an omen, McCarthy juggled his lineup because Gehrig had once again fallen into a batting slump, going hitless 11 straight times in four games. For the first time, McCarthy placed DiMaggio in the No. 4 hitting slot and dropped Gehrig to sixth. It was Gehrig's 1,980th consecutive game and he responded with a single in the sixth inning. DiMaggio unloaded his second home run and the Yankees won 3–2.

On May 12, after hitting safely in all nine previous games in which he had played, DiMaggio failed to get a hit. But he exploded for two homers and five runs batted in on May 18 at St. Louis in an 11–7 victory and the Yankees moved into the American League lead.

Despite his return to top form, DiMaggio had not bargained for what amounted to fan resentment over his holdout. In St. Louis, where a heavy Italian population sent many fans to the ball park when he came to town, and elsewhere throughout the league, he was loudly booed at the plate and when he took the field. It happened to him at the Stadium, too, and half in jest and half in seriousness, his teammates suggested that he wear a catcher's mask on the back of his head to protect himself from the assorted gadgets and debris the fans threw at him from the bleachers.

His sudden loss of popularity was puzzling at first to DiMaggio, but it soon dawned on him what had happened. Usually, in arguments over money between players and employers, baseball fans sided with the players. But these were unusual times, with unemployment still hovering near the 8 million mark. In DiMaggio's case the fans felt that a young man in only his third season in the major leagues should have been satisfied and grateful for having the chance to earn $25,000 a year—to say nothing of having a job at all.

Colonel Ruppert's pronouncements from his employer's lectern about DiMaggio's ungratefulness at the height of the holdout apparently had not fallen on deaf ears.

5

Rings
on
His Fingers

*I*N THE SPRING of 1939 New York was filled with anticipation. The World's Fair was about to open. Mayor Fiorello La Guardia had helped get the city through a bitter winter by giving the town an upbeat rhythm, lifting morale with provocative appeals and his Sunday morning readings of the comic pages on the radio. The Yankees had swept the Chicago Cubs in four games the previous fall in the World Series, and there were signs that the nation and the city might finally begin to pull out of the Depression.

Even DiMaggio seemed eager to get on with the job. He looked askance at a possible prolonged squabble over his next contract. His holdout in 1938 had left him exhausted and out of shape. It had cost him $1,850 in lost salary. Still, despite the holdout, he had a brilliant season, with a .324 batting average, 32 home runs, and 140 runs batted in. He was the bulwark who helped buttress the Yankees on their way to a third straight pennant and World Series championship. As an advocate of the merit system, he felt he was not overstepping bounds to seek a raise in salary of say $5,000.

"I think that is a reasonable request," he said. "We had a championship team last year, one that walked home in the American League and took the World Series in four straight. Being as I led the club in hitting and runs batted in I figure I have a raise coming.

"I have been with the Yankees three years," he continued, "and have yet to play an opening-day game. The first year I had a bad foot that kept me out. This year I want to start from scratch. In 1937 it was my tonsils and last year I was holding out."

After his holdout DiMaggio took a softer stance whenever he tried to justify it, especially when he realized how unpopular it had been with the fans and how debilitating an effect it might have had on his career. But he would not yield on the logic of his overriding philosophy regarding professionalism. He believed strongly that professionals in athletics, or any field, should always opt for maximim compensation because of the short-lived and precarious nature of their occupations. Many athletes had had their careers cut from under them by tragic, untimely accidents. DiMaggio, prone to injury, was constantly aware that this could happen to him at any moment. Monte Stratton, a promising pitching prospect with the Chicago White Sox, had his career abruptly ended in 1938 after a tragic hunting accident in which he lost a leg.

"You can never tell when something is going to happen," DiMaggio said, "something that will end your career. I don't believe in a player being selfish or placing too high a price on his services, but a fellow's a sucker not to try and get all he can. He may be a star one day and a cripple the next."

DiMaggio still rankled over the Yankees' failure to make good on the $1,850 he had been docked during the holdout.

"Everybody kept telling me all year that I would get it back, and not to worry," he said, "but here it is January of the next year and the eighteen hundred and fifty bucks is still missing. I can't kick because I had it coming to me, but I wish everybody hadn't got my hopes up for nothing."

On January 13 Jacob Ruppert died at the age of 71. Curiously, the man who had put the Yankees at the pinnacle of baseball and built a reputation as a raconteur, bon vivant, and Beau Brummel, had for most of his life maintained a reserve that kept him at arm's length from close personal friendships. Still, he was held in a profound respect by baseball people and all of the major league club owners. His funeral at St. Patrick's Cathedral attracted thousands of New Yorkers, who had to be restrained by police barricades from pushing into the church, as if they were overcome with grief for the passing of a Yankee symbol. In tribute to the old colonel, Mayor La Guardia ordered the flags at City Hall to be flown at half staff.

Ruppert's death signaled an immediate revamping of the Yankee front office. Barrow was elevated to the presidency. Although he was 71 years old, he had logged 45 years as a baseball executive and was the logical choice to guide the richest and most successful team in baseball. He took over on January 19. The Yankees' executive offices at the team's headquarters on 42nd Street were filled with commotion as reporters and photographers stormed in for interviews and pictures to record the age-old ritual of one old order changing and yielding place to new. But in Barrow's case it was more of a continuum. Flowers and telegrams poured in from all types of well-wishers—obeisance to baseball's corporate giant.

An admirer of sound fiscal policies, Barrow indicated he would handle his newly acquired prestige and power in a businesslike fashion. His administration would be tough and efficient, as always.

"Business will go along as usual," he said. "We will miss the colonel, of course. But we'll try to carry on the way we know he would want us to carry on. Right now, I'm busy getting things ready to mail contracts to the Yankee players. This is no mean job. You know, a personal letter accompanies each contract. Each document must be reviewed and carefully gone over. It takes time. But I hope to have contracts and letters ready for the mails in a few days. Then we will have to await results."

Barrow usually ignored unpleasantries and disagreements. His cudgel was forceful diplomacy. When he became aware that DiMaggio had hinted that he would ask for a $5,000 raise, he made no comment. Those who knew Barrow's inner workings considered him a tougher bargainer than Colonel Ruppert. He was not about to be dragged into a debate about DiMaggio, who had not yet received an offer from the Yankees. Barrow disliked negotiations through the press. He felt the Yankees had suffered from news media pressure during DiMaggio's holdout. All concerned had learned a bitter lesson.

DiMaggio and his advisers had second thoughts, too. He would keep a low profile and make no comment. On February 4 in San Francisco, however, DiMaggio's brother, Tom, who was no longer DiMaggio's official adviser, said DiMaggio was not planning to open talks with the Yankees to recover the $1,850 he had lost during the holdout.

"Joe hasn't even been in touch with the club," he said. "He hasn't even talked with anybody outside the family about his contract. He's going to let the club give out any announcements about him this year."

On March 4, three days before he could be officially listed as a holdout, DiMaggio's signed contract arrived at the Yankee headquarters in New York. Manager McCarthy made the official announcement at training camp in St. Petersburg, Fla., describing the talks between the player and the new president as friendly and informing the Internal Revenue Service that DiMaggio's salary for 1939 would be $27,500. It was a compromise pact and DiMaggio seemed to have salvaged some of the $1,850 he sorely missed.

DiMaggio's eagerness to sign quickly seemed uncharacteristic. But it stemmed, in part, from the knowledge that the Yankees had acquired several promising rookies, Charlie Keller, Joe Gallagher, and Walt Judnich—all outfielders. The outfield roster already included such highly respected regulars as Jake Powell and George Selkirk, with Tommy Henrich, who had been acquired as a free agent for $20,000 in 1937, certain to hold down one outfield spot. Barrow was reappraising his personnel. DiMaggio had had a fine season in 1938, but his holdout had annoyed Barrow, if not more, at least as much as it had annoyed

Ruppert. Now with abundant rookie talent on the way up, DiMaggio could possibly find himself expendable. One other factor which may have contributed to his quick signing was his romance with a movie actress; it looked like it would lead to the altar.

DiMaggio had met Dorothy Arnold in 1937, not long after she had left Duluth, Minnesota, her hometown, to seek a career in show business. She was singing in a New York nightclub and had a stock movie contract with Universal Studios. They met while DiMaggio was making a movie in the Bronx at the Biograph Studio. "I was just sort of scenery," Miss Arnold, who had a bit part in the movie, said in recalling the meeting later on.

She had taken an interest in DiMaggio even before she knew who he was. "I remember saying, 'That's a nice looking fellow. Who is he?' on the studio lot one day. Everybody looked startled and somebody said, 'Why, that's Joe DiMaggio,' and I said, 'So what?' So, you see, I fell in love with him before I knew he was a celebrity. We started going around together and the first thing we knew—at least I knew—it was getting hotter."

In April, shortly after the start of the baseball season, Dorothy Arnoldine Olson announced her engagement to Joseph Paul DiMaggio Jr. in Hollywood. The announcement said the wedding would take place some time in the summer, with a honeymoon trip planned for after the baseball season. In New York, the news seemed to catch DiMaggio out of position, but he confirmed the report and added his own postscript.

"The wedding will positively not be this summer," he said. "We may be married next winter or the following winter, but the wedding definitely will not take place while the baseball season is on." DiMaggio's insistence that nothing or no one should interfere with his professionalism as a ballplayer covered wide and delicate territory.

Four days later, on April 29, DiMaggio almost suffered the kind of tragic accident he had talked about earlier. In a game at Yankee Stadium against Washington, while fielding a ball in the outfield in the third inning, he injured his right leg and was taken to St. Elizabeth's Hospital for X rays. Dr. Robert Emmett Walsh, the Yankees' team physician, at first thought that DiMaggio might have snapped a leg bone. The X rays showed "torn muscles from the leg from the right fibula and tibia." Although the injury was very painful, DiMaggio luckily had escaped a broken leg that might have ended his career. The doctor indicated that Joe would be sidelined for at least 10 days.

The injury occurred when Bobby Estalella, a rookie outfielder, hit a hard liner to center field. DiMaggio, racing in the muddy outfield grass to his left for the ball, stopped suddenly when the ball took an unexpected bounce away from his right side. The spikes on DiMaggio's right shoe stuck in the mud. He was thrown solidly, as if from a horse. He lay writhing in pain on the grass for eight minutes. When he was helped off the field he looked, according to Dr. Walsh, "pale as a ghost and with hardly any pulse."

"I felt something crack," DiMaggio said. "I thought for a minute the bone was gone."

Discharged from the hospital, he returned to his room in the Hotel New Yorker in midtown. The leg was still painful. Dr. Walsh ordered him not to go on the Yankees' next road trip and sent him back to the hospital instead for rest. At the hotel, he had been receiving so many visitors, phone calls, and telegrams that Dr. Walsh thought it was best for him to get out of harm's way as a precaution.

DiMaggio had had an outstanding spring, giving Barrow reason to believe his star would have another noteworthy season. Barrow, however, was inclined to keep something in reserve in case of an emergency. He had brought up a crop of good, hard-hitting rookie outfielders and thought he could make trades with those who eventually might not fit into the Yankee picture. The injury to DiMaggio forced Barrow to alter his plans. Barrow had virtually cleared a deal that would have sent Jake Powell to the Boston Red Sox. Now he held up on it until he was certain of DiMaggio's availability.

On May 2 DiMaggio was still in the hospital and the Yankees were in Detroit. It was a day to mark on the baseball calendar because Lou Gehrig took himself out of the lineup after having played in 2,130 consecutive games, a record that spanned more than 15 seasons.

Manager McCarthy, who had acceded to Gehrig's wishes to be removed from the lineup, said: "Lou just told me he felt it would be best for the club if he took himself out. I asked him if he really felt that way. He told me he was serious. He feels blue. He is dejected. I told him it would be as he wished. Like everybody else I'm sorry to see it happen. Fellows like him come along once in a hundred years."

Gehrig, of course, was deeply saddened. When the announcement was made that Babe Dahlgren, who had been brought up by the Yankees from the Newark Bears in 1938, would replace Gehrig at first base, a hush shrouded Briggs Stadium. Gehrig, who was the team captain, had carried the lineup card to the umpires at home plate. Photographers swarmed onto the field to record the moment. Then he walked back to the dugout and went to the water fountain and took a long drink. He started to weep. Johnny Murphy, noticing Gehrig's state of mind, took a towel and threw it to him. The towel landed on Gehrig's head. He did not move, but stood at the water fountain drinking, his face hidden in the towel with his tears.

After the game, Gehrig explained why he had decided to take himself out. He had gone eight games with only four hits in 28 times at bat.

"I decided last Sunday night on this move," Gehrig said. "I haven't been a bit of good to the team since the season started. It wouldn't be fair to the boys, to Joe, or to myself. It's tough to see your mates on base have a chance to win a ball game and not be able to do anything about it. McCarthy has been swell about it all the time. He'd let me go until the cows came home, he is that considerate of my feelings. But I knew in Sunday's game that I should get out of there. I went up four times with men on base. Once there were two there. A hit would have won the game for the Yankees, but I missed, leaving five stranded. Maybe a rest will do me some good. Maybe it won't. Who knows? Who can tell? I'm just hoping."

Lefty Gomez expressed the feelings of the Yankee players.

"It's tough to see this happen," Gomez said, "even though you know it must come to us all. Lou's a great guy and he's always been a great baseball figure. I hope he'll be back in there."

At the hospital DiMaggio, who with his history of injuries could appreciate Gehrig's iron-man role of playing every day, said, "There's plenty of baseball left in Lou Gehrig and don't count him out because he's taking the first rest he has had in years."

DiMaggio was out of the hospital three days later and indicated "the leg is coming along faster than expected." Still, his absence dragged on and he didn't rejoin the club until June 5. The next day he hit a home run, a double, and a single in a 7–2 rout of the White Sox and signaled the start of another Yankee sleigh ride to a pennant.

At Philadelphia on June 28 the Yankees swept the Athletics in a double-header, 23–2 and 10–0. With DiMaggio leading the way, they blasted eight home runs in the first game and five in the second and set two major league records. The eight homers set a record for the most in one game, and the total of 13 established a record for most in consecutive games. DiMaggio hit two home runs in the first game and one in the second. The Yankees' total bases—53—in the first game became the American League record.

Gehrig, although he continued to travel with the team, had not taken part in the slugging onslaught, of course. When he had presented the lineup card to the umpires before the second game, the Philadelphia crowd, knowing that the great slugger had missed being a part of the record-setting first game, gave him a long, standing ovation. It brought tears to his eyes. Connie Mack, the A's manager, who seldom left the dugout during games, went out to the plate to shake Gehrig's hand.

On the Fourth of July, 61,808 fans turned out to watch the Yankees split a double-header with the Senators at the Stadium. New York was 11½ games in front, on its way to an unprecedented fourth straight American League title. In Europe there were rumblings of war. In the United States there was concern that a European conflict would drag America into it, too. There were some patriotic speeches during pre-game ceremonies at the Stadium and war talk was in the air. For the lighthearted, such as Lefty Gomez, jingoism and baseball did not mix well.

"Here we are 11½ games ahead," Gomez moaned in the dugout, "and they're trying to ring in a war on us. If we were in third place, they wouldn't even mention it."

The Yankees had so dominated the American League through the first half of the season that when the All-Star Game selections were made six Yankees were in the starting lineup—Red Rolfe at third base, DiMaggio in center field, Bill Dickey catching, George Selkirk in left field, Joe Gordon at second base, and Red Ruffing pitching. It was the seventh All-Star Game since the classic was first played in 1933 and it drew a record crowd of 62,892 at Yankee Stadium. DiMaggio connected for a home run off Bill Lee of the Cubs and sparked a 3–1 American League triumph.

For much of the last part of the campaign, DiMaggio's batting average hovered around the .400 mark. On August 3, he got three hits, including two home runs, and drove in five runs in a 12–3 romp over the Tigers. He had hit safely in 12 straight games. He was stopped in the next week, then started a new streak. At Detroit on August 28, he hit homer No. 21 with the bases loaded and No. 22 with two men on and drove in a run with a single for a total of eight runs batted in. He had extended his new hitting streak to 14 games.

By now he had become the hottest thing in baseball and *Life* magazine splashed his face on its cover and described his rise from humble origins to baseball fame and glory. He had become a national human interest story.

However, in its zeal to portray DiMaggio as the idol of the fans, *Life* seemed to be carried away with his appeal to his ethnic minority.

> When in the 1936 season Joe DiMaggio gave unmistakable signs of being the greatest Italian star in the history of baseball [*Life* wrote], the effect upon New York's Italian population was amazing. Subway guards as far away as Coney Island were accosted by recent immigrants who wanted to know 'Which way de Yankee Stadium?' When DiMaggio made a hit, huge Italian flags, smuggled into the bleachers by his admirers, were unfurled and shaken.
>
> Italians, bad at war [the magazine continued], are well suited for milder competition and the number of topnotch Italian prizefighters, golfers and baseball players is out of all proportion to the population.

Life continued to describe DiMaggio in lofty terms as a player, but seemed determined to dress him at least minimally in stereotypical garb.

> Instead of olive oil or smelly bear grease [*Life* went on], he keeps his hair slick with water. He never reeks of garlic and prefers chicken chow mein to spaghetti. Unlike many ballplayers, he does not chew tobacco. His favorite pastimes are listening to the radio and going to the movies. His favorite radio star is Bing Crosby, whom he calls 'Bingeroo.' His favorite movies last year (1938) were *Jesse James, They Made Me a Criminal* and *In Old Chicago*. His favorite star is Gloria Stuart.

In later years with the rise of civil rights legislation in the United States, some of *Life*'s stereotyping of Italians most likely would have had mammoth repercussions, at least in the press, had similar slurs been made about other minorities.

Going into September, DiMaggio lived up to his national press clippings. At Cleveland on September 1, he hit two triples and a single, driving in six runs in an 11–8 triumph that spoiled Bob Feller's bid for his 20th victory of the season. His most recent consecutive-game hitting streak stood at 17 as the Yankees concluded their last road trip against the western teams. In their last 12 games on the road, the Yankees had won 10, lost two. DiMaggio had made 27 hits in 53 times at bat. He had hit five homers and driven in 28 runs. His batting average during that span was .500. The Yankees headed east with 30 games left to play, 10 against Boston, which was still 13½ games behind in second place.

Whatever semblance of a challenge the Red Sox hoped to mount in the next weeks disappeared on the weekend of September 6 and 7. DiMaggio hit his 26th homer off Lefty Grove in the eighth inning for a 2–1 victory in the series opener and the Yankees widened their lead to 15½ games. The next day he hit No. 27 in the first inning to spark a 5–2 victory.

On September 8, DiMaggio's batting average was .408. Experts were giving him a good chance of attaining the charmed .400 mark and becoming the first batter since Bill Terry averaged .401 in 1930 to reach that plateau. For the last three weeks of the season, however, DiMaggio was nagged by a persistent cold. He was kept in the lineup and began to press in his efforts to maintain the pace. He went into a slump, going 0 for 11 over one stretch, and his average plummeted to .380. He had missed his goal of .400, but settled for .381 and the batting championship.

In the 1980 season, George Brett of the Kansas City Royals won the American League batting title with a .390 average, the highest since Ted Williams finished with .406 in 1941. Brett flirted with the elusive .400 mark during the last month of the season. He reached .408, then a case of tendinitis in the wrist sidelined him for several games. He returned to continue his assault, but faltered in the last week of the season.

During Brett's quest, DiMaggio was reminded of his own pursuit of the mark in the 1939 campaign.

"I remember I was batting more than .400," he said. "Then I got this terrible allergy in my left eye, my batting eye, and I could hardly see out of it. Joe McCarthy didn't believe in cheese champions, so he made me play every day. I went into a terrible slump. McCarthy had to know the agony I was going through, but I'll never understand why he didn't give me a couple of days off. I guess it was the rule of the day—you played with anything short of a broken leg."

The Yankees won the American League pennant by 17 games and were made the heavy favorites to win the World Series against the

Cincinnati Reds. Cincinnati had won the National League crown on the strength of the pitching of Bucky Walters and Paul Derringer, who accounted for 52 victories between them, and the hitting of first baseman Frank McCormick and catcher Ernie Lombardi.

It was a good Series for DiMaggio. He batted .313 and turned in some brilliant fielding and baserunning, skills that eventually went into the experts' appraisals of him as one of the finest all-around players in the game. The Yankees easily won the first three games, raising their streak to eight in World Series play. They had eliminated the Chicago Cubs the previous fall in four straight and had won the Series clincher from the Giants in 1937. In the fourth game at Cincinnati they trailed, 4–2, going into the ninth inning. An error, and a single by DiMaggio accounted for two runs and a tie and sent the game into extra innings.

In the 10th, Frank Crosetti led off with a walk. Red Rolfe sacrificed him to second and Charlie Keller was safe on an error by Billy Myers, the shortstop. DiMaggio lined a single to right field, where Ival Goodman fumbled the ball. Crosetti and Keller raced round the bases and scored, Keller making a tremendous slide at the plate that knocked the ball out of Lombardi's glove.

"Then with Lombardi still on the ground beside the ball," *The New York Times* reported, "DiMaggio winged across the plate from third base before the utterly befuddled Lombardi could do anything about it."

DiMaggio's baserunning, a part of his storehouse of skills that was generally overlooked, had brought in the third run. The Yankees won, 7–4, and the play at the plate involving Keller's slide and DiMaggio's alert baserunning became known in baseball's archives of memorable plays as "Lombardi's snooze."

Art Fletcher, the Yankees' third-base coach, who had sent DiMaggio home on the play, said: "I told him nothing but watch the ball. And boy, he watched it. He gave us one of the greatest pieces of sliding I've ever seen. He had to slide over Lombardi's hand and then dig down and touch the plate, and he did it to perfection."

DiMaggio was duly proud of his baserunning skills, but they generally went unnoticed. In 1935, his final season with San Francisco, he stole 24 bases in 25 attempts. Of course, when he joined the Yankees he was the third man in the batting order, followed by Lou Gehrig and Bill Dickey. It made no sense to risk stealing bases with sluggers like that behind him. He had also perfected his sliding and the slickness and gracefulness with which he executed it, as he had done against Lombardi, had several times fooled umpires.

"I had developed a pretty tricky slide, aiming my left foot for the base, then jerking it away as the fielder reached for me, and touching the sack with my hand instead. One time an umpire had called me out when I was really safe. I asked him to hold off his decision in the future until he was really sure I was tagged. He must have passed the word around because I was never called out wrongly on a slide after that," DiMaggio said.

DiMaggio slid hard, hitting the ground with great force. He was never able to find a pair of pads that would give his thighs ample protection. He suffered many painful bruises from it.

The victory over Cincinnati made the Yankees the first team in baseball history to win four straight World Series championships and the first to sweep two in succession in eight straight games.

DiMaggio had been the key figure throughout the season. On October 25, the Baseball Writers Association of America voted him the American League's most valuable player, an award he would win two more times before his career ended.

Now with four World Series championship rings in his jewelry box, he would add one more ring of even greater significance. He had time now to turn his attention and affection to Miss Arnold and make plans for their wedding. The couple got their marriage license in San Francisco City Hall on November 10, after they had put engraved wedding invitations in the mail the previous week. DiMaggio's friends gave him a bachelor party at his restaurant after he had competed with Joe Cronin's major league all-stars against Lefty O'Doul's minor league all-stars in San Francisco's annual benefit game to raise money for the Catholic Youth Organizations.

On November 19, a pleasant Sunday afternoon, after a courtship of almost two years, DiMaggio and Dorothy Arnold were married in the Church of Saints Peter and Paul in downtown San Francisco.

If measured by the enthusiasm it generated among DiMaggio's family and friends, the marriage was an event that seemed to have been made in heaven.

The large Italian-American population of North Beach turned out in raucous, flag-waving splendor, much in the same manner their New York counterparts had turned out waving Italian flags and cheering the "great DiMadge" from the bleachers at Yankee Stadium.

They created a carnival atmosphere. Veterans of many years on the San Francisco police force could not recall a wedding that had created such a stir and commotion. Thousands of invited and uninvited guests jammed the streets. One man brought six members of his family on one invitation. Parking space had run out for blocks around the church. The street in front of the church was so densely packed with pushing and shoving onlookers that the overflow spilled over into Washington Square. The city's health director, himself an invited guest, had taken precautions by ordering an ambulance—the first at a local wedding— to the site in case of injuries. One woman fainted in the crush at the entrance to the church.

Only once before had the Church of Saints Peter and Paul been overrun in a similar manner. It had happened when the church was being built and served as the scenic backdrop for a tragic scene during the filming of the silent movie version of "The Ten Commandments." This time, on DiMaggio's wedding day, the church was once again decked with long scaffolding, undergoing repairs and reconstruction. Workers had covered the scaffolding with green curtains and had erected a marquee to the curb for the wedding.

Curiosity as much as affection and loyalty to a favorite son had brought out the throngs of paisanos. Only a few days before the wedding, Miss Arnold, who had been of the Protestant faith, had been accepted into the Roman Catholic faith after a period of instructions given to her by Rev. F. Parolin, the priest who would perform the marriage ceremony. Her conversion, as much as her status as a beautiful blonde movie actress, made DiMaggio's conquest complete in the eyes of his hardworking blue-collar neighbors. Loyalty to family and church and the winning of a beautiful woman were, in their estimation, the crowning glories that went with fame and fortune. It was machismo of a high order, but along North Beach none would have expected less from their distinguished son. But DiMaggio's wedding was far from a blue-collar affair. Mayor Rossi of San Francisco was an honored guest and sat in a seat in one of the first 10 rows, gazing on his gift of great and small white chrysanthemums that decked the church altar in a snowy cascade. Plainclothes detectives from the city's Hall of Justice, assigned by the mayor, roamed the aisles and ushered guests to their seats while trying to keep a noisy congregation orderly. Except for those pews reserved for members of the family and close relatives, all the seats in the church had been filled long before the ceremony began. The wedding ceremony was scheduled for 2 P.M., but it was already behind schedule. Most of those who had managed to get into the church had already sat through two earlier masses. The naves of the church were crammed with standing spectators, the choir loft was packed and young boys and girls found squatting space perched atop the confession boxes. Standees pressed beyond the communion rail and the altar.

DiMaggio and his brother Tom, who was his best man, had arrived early to avoid the crush of the crowd. They were both a bit nervous when the bride and her father, V. A. Olson, and the matron of honor, Mrs. Irene Morris, Miss Arnold's sister, and DiMaggio's four sisters, all bridesmaids, were nowhere in sight. The crowd outside the church was so dense, the bridal party had been delayed in traffic. Even DiMaggio's brother Vince had been locked out of the church when the police closed the doors to avert a stampede by the crowd. He and his wife eventually got into the church through a side entrance with the assistance of friends who ran interference against the spectators.

Inside the church Father Parolin, eager to have the ceremony go off without a hitch, tried to constrain the noisy crowd as Joe's mother and father came up the aisle, ablaze with candles and stands of gladioli and pompons, to take their seats. Papa DiMaggio was dressed in a formal tuxedo and Mrs. DiMaggio wore a wine-colored chiffon and velvet dress.

"Remember that you are in the house of the Lord," Father Parolin admonished the gathering. "I ask you in His name to be silent."

The noisy murmurs continued as word spread that the bride and her entourage had arrived.

"When the bride appears," Father Parolin admonished again, "let there be no commotion. Please keep your seats."

Then more than half an hour behind schedule, the ceremony began. Joe's four sisters—Nellie, Frances, Marie, and Mamie—all dressed alike, came down the aisle first, followed by the matron of honor. Then came the bride, carrying gardenias and orchids. She wore a gown of white satin of Grecian style with a V neck, sculptured bodice, a five-yard train, and a coronet veil of fingertip length tied with gold metal lace. Her trousseau was designed by Barbara Ross of Hollywood. The ushers who attended Joe were his brother Dom, who only the week before had been sold to the Boston Red Sox by the San Francisco Seals for $50,000; Frank La Rocco, and Sam and Frank Marino.

When the ceremony ended the bridal party was escorted out of the church by the police. They went to a photographer's studio to take wedding pictures, then to a private dinner with the members of the immediate families.

The scene at the reception that followed at DiMaggio's Grotto on Fisherman's Wharf was as tumultuous as the scene at the church. The mood was festive, friendly, and happy with a blend of city dignitaries, the well-to-do, and old family friends mingling together. Dinner jackets and silk gowns rubbed elbows with leather jackets and gingham dresses. A sumptuous buffet Russe, a three-foot wedding cake, and an open bar attracted them all. Outside a throng of well-wishers and admirers waited for a glimpse of the bride and groom. But they gave the numerous plainclothes policemen, hired to control gate-crashers, little chance to exercise their authority.

Well known and well liked in the community, the DiMaggio family had many friends in city government. Among the guests, besides the Mayor, were City Administrator Alfred Cleary, Police Chief Quinn, and Sheriff Murphy. Among the notable baseball people present were Joe Cronin, manager of the Boston Red Sox; Lefty O'Doul, manager of the Seals and a long-time tutor of DiMaggio; and Oscar Vitt, manager of the Cleveland Indians, all San Franciscans.

A three-piece orchestra played popular dance music and a tenor sang Italian songs. Food, drink, and song lasted long into the night, long after the couple left for an undisclosed honeymoon trip.

The *San Francisco Chronicle* made DiMaggio's wedding front-page news the next day. Its two-column headline exclaimed:

MR. AND MRS.
THE TOWN TURNS OUT
FOR DIMAG'S WEDDING
CHURCH FILLED TO OVERFLOWING
AS JOE MARRIES DOROTHY ARNOLD

DiMaggio was 24 years old and his wife 21.

6

Another Batting Title but No World Series Ring

*J*OE DIMAGGIO, IT might be said figuratively at least, was sitting on top of the world when the New Year rang in. He was happily married to a beautiful movie actress, he was the American League batting champion and most valuable player, he was the only player in baseball history to play on four world championship teams in his first four years in the game, and his salary was larger than that of the President of the United States.

For the DiMaggio family, too, 1940 was to be a very good year. Three DiMaggio brothers would be playing in the major leagues for the first time together. Dom DiMaggio would join the Red Sox in Boston as a rookie, and eventually would stay 11 years and distinguish himself in his own right as a center fielder equal in many respects to his brother Joe. Vince DiMaggio, the most outgoing of the three brothers, had already been up to the big leagues, starting with the Boston Braves in 1937. Unlike Joe's and Dom's, his career, all in the National League, was more like a ride on a roller coaster. In 1940, Cincinnati traded him to Pittsburgh after two games and he stayed in the Steel City for five seasons. In all, he played for five teams during his 10-year career and distinguished himself as the league leader in strikeouts in six of those campaigns. His career batting average was .249 and he hit 125 home runs. As an outfielder he was excellent. "If Joe could talk like me and I could hit like Joe," the loquacious Vince once said, "we'd both be worth a million bucks."

Now Papa DiMaggio, who had believed his five sons should be fishermen like himself, was recanting his words that baseball was an unprofitable business. All of his sons had helped out on his crab fishing skiff at one time or another, but most of the time they preferred to play baseball on the sandlots of San Francisco. "Baseball, what is that?" Papa DiMaggio used to shout in Italian. "A bum's game! Whoever makes a living at baseball? All it does is wear out shoes." Now he beamed with pride, and financial comfort, and told stories to his fishing cronies on Fisherman's Wharf of the exploits of his baseball-playing sons.

In the spring DiMaggio would troop back to New York, which would be bulging again with millions of visitors to the World's Fair, entering its second year. War had been declared in Europe, and the city's economy was beginning to take an upward turn. The symbol of the Fair, a globe and spire, and its theme, "World of Tomorrow," gave a hopeful dimension to the city's character.

The Fair, of course, had its entrepreneurs eager to include sports as part of its tapestry. Sportsmen, city officials, and civic-minded business executives had planned ahead and established an Academy of Sports at the Fair. The Academy would select the outstanding athlete in the United States and present him with its award at the start of the Fair each year. To the millions of Americans who came to the Fair, the Academy exhibit offered a nostalgic history of virtually every sport, with its artistic display of murals, photographs, artifacts, and other memorabilia. It was a big hit with visitors. Christy Walsh, a public relations man who had handled many of Babe Ruth's off-the-field appearances and had extricated Ruth from many embarrassing escapades as an intermediary with the press, was the director of the Academy. He had also been Ruth's ghost writer for many articles. Walsh had conceived the Golden Laurel Award, to be given to the country's best athlete. Its first recipient was Don Budge, who in 1938 became the first tennis player to win the Grand Slam—Wimbledon, the United States Open, the French Open, and the Australian Open—in one year.

DiMaggio was the second winner of the award—for his play in the 1939 season. He was the center of attraction at the Academy exhibit as the Fair ushered in its second year. A huge, wall-sized enlargement of a photograph of DiMaggio in his famous, wide-stanced swing was unveiled. Julian W. Curtiss, an octogenarian and influential Yale Old Blue who had been a member of the Yale crew in 1878, presented the award to DiMaggio. The men of influence who sponsored the award and surrounded Curtiss as he made the presentation represented the Eastern establishment at the height of its power and prestige. It was a time in America when even professional sports paid homage to the values perpetuated by the fathers of amateurism.

DiMaggio, who received no monetary award, regarded the Golden Laurel as just one more trophy to add to his collection and accepted it for the public-relations goodwill it would generate for him. He was happy to see the big photo montage of himself adorning the wall for millions of Americans visiting the Fair to admire. "It looks pretty much like me," he said in a temporary betrayal of self-modesty.

DiMaggio's popularity with the fans and sports writers was growing in proportion to his exploits. His confidence was bulging also and he predicted great things for himself on the field. He said he would try to win baseball's most coveted and elusive slugging honors—the Triple

Crown. "I feel I'm going to have a tough battle, but this year I'd like to lead the league in home runs, batting average, and runs batted in," he said. "I've never led the runs-batted-in race. My 46 homers were tops in 1937 and last year I was first in hitting. This year I'm going to work for all three. I think I can do it with a full season's work."

In four years, DiMaggio's credentials in the Triple Crown categories were impressive enough for him to make such predictions. He had hit 137 home runs and driven in 558 runs—averaging out to 36 and 136—and his cumulative batting average was a robust .344.

At the Golden Laurel Award presentation DiMaggio made an impressive, immaculate appearance in a dark blue double-breasted suit and black shoes glistening with a spit polish. Since his early days as a minor-leaguer he had put a great deal of emphasis on his dress and appearance. Now as batting champion and most valuable player he had to live up to the distinction the Custom Tailors Guild of America had bestowed on him in February.

At their annual convention at the Hotel Belmont Plaza, the men who dressed some of America's richest men named him eighth on their list of the 10 best-dressed men in the United States. He joined pretty select company. Joseph E. Davies, special aide to Secretary of State Cordell Hull, and later American Ambassador to the Soviet Union, headed the list. Among the others named were Paul Whiteman, the orchestra leader; Paul V. McNutt, Federal Social Security Administrator; Dr. John R. Gregg, president of the Gregg Shorthand Publishing Company; William Rhinelander Stewart of New York; and Dr. James B. Conant, president of Harvard University.

Neither the Golden Laurel Award nor the citation for his sartorial elegance, however, would enable DiMaggio to get another hit or buy another suit.

Reports reached the baseball grapevine that the Yankees' board of directors had held a secret meeting at which DiMaggio's salary for the 1940 season was the chief topic on the agenda and its limit was a fait accompli. The reports indicated that the board had ordered Barrow to put a $30,000 ceiling on the star's next contract. Barrow, as the club president, was a key man on the board, which now included George Ruppert, the late colonel's brother, who represented the Ruppert heirs, and George Weiss, the club secretary.

Barrow vehemently denied that the board had met secretly or had discussed a ceiling on DiMaggio's salary. He took umbrage at the inference that his authority as the club's chief executive and sole bargainer on salary matters had been challenged.

"In the first place there has been no recent meeting of the board of directors," Barrow said. "In the second place, the board has absolutely nothing to do with determining the players' salaries. As in previous years, the job is left entirely to me and nobody knows what the club will offer DiMaggio because I haven't mentioned it to a soul. What is more, DiMaggio himself doesn't know what he will be offered inasmuch as he has yet to receive his 1940 contract. But I don't think we'll have any trouble."

Manager McCarthy would be leaving his farm in upstate New York in a few days, scheduled to arrive in the city to talk with Weiss about the team's prospects in the farm system. Barrow had hinted that he would like to have McCarthy participate in the talks concerning player salaries, too. McCarthy, who had played a role in DiMaggio's holdout negotiations in 1938, did not like being part of the salary disputes. He felt it was precarious ground for a manager to be on, especially since it could alienate some players. When Barrow had been general manager under Ruppert, McCarthy (except for the incident involving DiMaggio's holdout) had stayed on the sidelines, minding the managerial store. He had won the respect of his players for that and he valued that kind of relationship.

DiMaggio did not take kindly to the reports, especially after he had produced such an outstanding season in 1939. Barrow's denial didn't satisfy him either. His objective this time around was $35,000 and he publicized it.

"I don't call myself a holdout yet," DiMaggio said, "but if that's what you want to call it, it's all right with me. I won't leave San Francisco until I hear from Barrow. There's no sense in my going to Florida without a contract. I'd have to pay living expenses for myself and my wife once I got there and I couldn't work out unless I was signed."

The Yankees' board of directors had worked its influence whether Barrow wished to admit it or not. By March 5, DiMaggio had signed a contract for $30,000, a raise of $2,500 over his 1939 salary and right on target with reports of the board's ceiling, whether its secret meeting had occurred or not. It was obviously a compromise agreement, with DiMaggio unwilling to buck the tide this time. He left for Florida by train with his wife in time for the Yankees' first exhibition game of the spring.

But the opening-day jinx put him on the sidelines again. On April 14, the day before the season opener at Philadelphia, he strained a tendon in his right knee after hitting a double with two out in the ninth inning of a Sunday exhibition game against the Dodgers in Brooklyn. It was the fourth time in five seasons he had missed the Yankees' first game.

The Yankees' team physician, Dr. Emmett Walsh, cautioned DiMaggio on the overuse of the leg and indicated DiMaggio would be out for three or four days. Two weeks later, DiMaggio was still complaining about the injury and had not seen any action. He checked in with Dr. George Bennett of Johns Hopkins Hospital in Baltimore, a noted bone specialist. There seemed to be a difference of opinion between player and doctor about the severity of the injury.

"All I know," DiMaggio said, "is that I can't run and the doctor told me not to try until the leg felt perfectly O.K. I was getting worried, so I decided to find out just what was the matter. It may be some time before I return to action."

Dr. Bennett described the injury this way: "DiMaggio has an ordinary injury that any athlete would suffer from a wrenched knee. His condition warrants no special treatment and if proper care is taken he should be back in the lineup in a very short time."

DiMaggio's $30,000 salary had made him one of the highest paid athletes in America and his popularity as a celebrity was growing as rapidly as his income. Testimonials, vaudeville appearances, cameo parts in movies, advertising endorsements continued to pour in. His entourage of hangers-on was also growing. His superstar status brought him into contact, willingly or not, with movie stars, judges, lawyers, stock brokers, politicians, Broadway columnists, and business executives.

Star players, DiMaggio included, became targets for gamblers and quick-buck schemers. The manipulation of the press could easily bring a mention in a Broadway celebrity column that certain athletes were associated with not-too-reputable characters—whether true or not.

Outside the sports pages DiMaggio tried to avoid celebrity publicity, but it was not easy. He enjoyed making the Broadway scene—he had already married a movie actress whom he had met through his association with the film industry, and he enjoyed attending boxing matches and horse races.

With this in his background it became inevitable that his link to Joe Gould, the boxing manager, would look suspect to some. About this time, reports emanating from New York began to surface and receive wide circulation that DiMaggio had engaged Gould as his agent for 12 percent of Joe's gross income. In addition, the reports alleged, James J. Braddock, the former heavyweight boxing champion managed by Gould, would get a small percent of the fees Gould allegedly received from DiMaggio.

In the wake of the World Series scandal of 1919 involving the Chicago White Sox, baseball's owners had appointed Judge Kenesaw Mountain Landis as commissioner. His task had been to restore public confidence in the sport, conceived as "Simon-pure" by the club owners. The owners had feared that the national pastime as a shining beacon for American youth had been tarnished by the scandal, as indeed it was. The scandal had caused the banishment from the game for life of eight White Sox players, including the great "Shoeless Joe" Jackson, a superb outfielder who in 13 seasons in the major leagues had compiled a .356 batting average, and Eddie Cicotte, a fine right-handed pitcher who had posted 207 victories in 14 campaigns—28 in 1917 and 29 in 1919. They were among the players who conspired to lose the World Series to the Cincinnati Reds. The club owners, in their financial wizardry, reasoned that this blemish on the integrity of the sport would hurt their business, keep fans from ball parks, and leave the suspicion that any game could be fixed and any player could be bought. It had become a national disgrace, not easily put out of mind either by the fans or the penurious owners who felt their livelihoods in jeopardy.

Landis was the force around whom they rallied. His credentials for meting out judicial decisions were impeccable. He seemed to possess a kind of righteous virtue that most Americans, from blue-collar workers to Wall Street brokers, deemed beyond reproach. In effect, the owners had decided to preserve the nation's proclivity for hero worship by selecting a man in the mold of its folk heroes. Landis took his new job seriously, so seriously in fact that an unwritten code of conduct that seemed to supersede baseball's written rules had put every professional baseball player, and every owner for that matter, on his guard. Czar was the appropriate word to describe the commissioner during Landis's tenure. Now a mere mention in the press that a player was associated with unsavory characters brought an inquiring eye from Landis's office. Players who were particularly friendly with persons in horse racing or boxing, the sports most attractive to gambling, automatically fell under such surveillance.

The Yankees, of course, on the strength of four straight pennants and World Series championships, had been chosen as overwhelming favorites to make it five in a row. Among the gambling gentry there would be a lot of money riding on this premise throughout the season. They were strong at all positions; the pitching was sharp and DiMaggio had already testified that he was shooting for the Triple Crown.

But, for the first month, with DiMaggio sidelined, the Yankees plummeted into a tie for last place with the Chicago White Sox. They had lost eight straight home games and were having trouble against left-handed pitchers. On May 7, DiMaggio was back in the lineup against the sensational 18-year-old Detroit southpaw, Hal Newhouser, but his return was conspicuous in that he popped out in foul territory with the bases loaded and none out in the seventh inning. Newhouser became the fourth left-hander in a row to stop the Bombers. There was an explanation for the Yankee tailspin. Lefty Gomez was out with a bad back and their front line pitching was ineffective. Collectively, the team was batting .250—13 points worse than the St. Louis Browns whose batting was ranked seventh in the league. Persistent injuries added to the malaise and made it difficult for McCarthy to field a consistent lineup.

To complicate matters, on May 15 the Yankees received a wire in New York from Landis demanding that DiMaggio and Manager McCarthy appear at his office in Chicago the next morning for questioning about the reports linking DiMaggio to Gould as his agent.

The meeting lasted an hour and DiMaggio denied all allegations.

"No one has been authorized to act as my agent," DiMaggio said. "My salary never has been and never will be shared with a manager or agent."

Strangely, the Yankees were primarily concerned that DiMaggio had been charged with sharing his salary. They felt that a stigma might be attached to money they were paying him and therefore they might be considered collaborators in the way he disposed of it. The Yankees didn't seem to care how he derived or disbursed any other income, but they wanted assurances that no one shared his salary.

McCarthy emerged from the meeting and in language seemingly couched in an attitude protecting the club, said:

"Judge Landis summoned DiMaggio and myself by wire yesterday, to question Joe on reports that he is paying part of his baseball club salary to a manager. Joe assured the judge there was nothing to the report. I advised Mr. Barrow of the denial over the long distance telephone this morning. The club is interested only in whether DiMaggio shares his baseball salary with a manager. We are satisfied with the denial. What money he makes from outside sources, such as testimonials, picture, and radio work is his own business. We are not concerned with that."

James P. Dawson, as a sports reporter for *The New York Times,* was in Chicago that day to follow up on the story and learn what he could about the charges. He revealed through sources not connected with the Yankees or Landis's office that the meeting was not the first one between DiMaggio and Landis concerning his alleged agent. Even before DiMaggio's holdout in 1938 it had been known that he and Gould were friends. At that time, Barrow had warned DiMaggio that the club strongly opposed his engaging Gould or anyone else as his manager, according to Dawson. Gould denied at that time that he was connected in any way with DiMaggio's business affairs. Dawson disclosed that DiMaggio had met secretly with Landis in 1938 to air the charges and receive a warning. McCarthy acknowledged on May 15 that this actually had been the case.

DiMaggio's denials in both instances of the alleged charges had seemed to satisfy Landis and the Yankees. The second meeting received considerable airing in the press. No penalties were involved because DiMaggio had done nothing wrong. The enquiry, however, had put baseball and the commissioner's office in a favorable light. It created the semblance that both were diligent watchdogs who were keeping faith with the fans, on guard to nip "wrongdoing" in the bud.

The enquiry went on, but it produced nothing that was not already known. It tightened club regulations, however. Barrow posted a letter in the Yankee clubhouse reminding all players of the clause in their contracts that forbade them from making commercials endorsing any products that smacked of bad taste—liquor, beer, cigarettes, lotteries, or any form of gambling—while wearing their Yankee pinstripes.

Although the clause was written into the standard baseball contracts for all teams, and still is today, the DiMaggio incident brought it back into focus. DiMaggio severed all association with Gould and the incident was virtually forgotten. But it had served as a reminder that even a hint of scandal was to be anathema—the White Sox scandal was never to be repeated. This attitude did much to create a paranoid atmosphere—the players were, in a sense, not free to capitalize in the marketplace on their fame and exploits on the field. Those who were singled out were touched with the brush of suspicion—a kind of foretaste of McCarthyism in athletics.

Landis's investigation of DiMaggio had not helped the climate in the Yankee clubhouse and on the Fourth of July, the theoretical midpoint of the season, the Bombers were in fourth place, 6½ games behind Cleveland. Their individual statistics read like those of a last-place team: Bill Dickey was batting .224, Red Rolfe .241, Joe Gordon .254, Frank Crosetti .190. The pitching was no better: Red Ruffing had a 7–6 record, Monte Pearson 6–6, Gomez 2–0, Spud Chandler 4–4, Marius Russo 5–3, Marvin Bruer 6–3, Atley Donald 2–2, and Johnny "Fireman" Murphy, baseball's top relief pitcher, 2–4.

Then in the next few weeks their performance improved. A sweep of a three-game series with Cleveland gave them a record of 16 victories in 22 games. They were challenging for the title. But another slump followed and continued with a disastrous road trip, culminating in four losses in five games at Boston. On August 8 their won-lost record was 50–51 and they were 11 games out of first place.

The gamblers revised their estimate of Yankee prowess and began to write them off as champions. McCarthy resorted to drastic shifts in the lineup, moving the slugging second baseman, Gordon, who usually batted sixth, to the leadoff spot.

On August 22, they revived and started a drive that took them briefly to the top of the standings. DiMaggio slammed a bases-loaded home run in a nine-run second inning against Cleveland in a 15–2 rout. Two days later, against Bob Feller, who already had posted 21 victories, he hit a leadoff triple in the ninth inning and scored on a fly ball for a 3–2 triumph. But he pulled a leg muscle running on the triple and was out of the lineup a few days.

He went in as a pinch-hitter on August 29 with two out in the ninth and the Yankees trailing the Browns, 4–1. He hit a homer off Eldon Auker, tying the game. The Yankees went on to win in the 13th inning. By September 10, with DiMaggio back regularly and hitting at a .350 clip, they had won 25 of their last 31 games and only half a game separated them from the first-place Indians. Rainy weather in Cleveland forced a double-header for September 12. In the opener, Ernie Bonham beat Feller, 3–1, sending the Bombers into first place for the first time. But in the second game, on a wet field and with rain a threat throughout, the Indians overcame a 2–0 Yankee lead with a five-run cluster in the third, aided by errors by Babe Dahlgren and Ruffing. In the fourth inning, rain forced a 30-minute delay. Play resumed, and after the Yankees batted in the sixth without scoring, the game was called because of darkness, the Indians winning, 5–3.

The Yankees lost their next two games at Detroit, then moved to St. Louis for three games, including a double-header. They were still very much in contention. Against the woeful Browns they figured they were certain to pick up valuable ground. The Browns, however, beat Bonham, the Yankees' most effective pitcher all season, 2–1, and took the second game, 10–5. The next day, a seven-run first inning by the Browns forged a 16–4 rout, in which Johnny Lucadello became the first American League switch-batter to hit home runs right-handed and left-handed in a game. The Yankees were now four games out of first and they never recovered.

Their record on the road—42 defeats, 36 victories—helped end their quest for a fifth straight pennant. At Yankee Stadium their record was 52–24. In the final standings they finished third, two games off the pace as Detroit won the championship. DiMaggio's slugging had fallen short, but he wound up with a .352 batting average and his second straight hitting title, 31 home runs and 133 runs batted in. He was 10 home runs and 17 runs-batted-in short of fulfilling his prediction, made before the season began, of winning the Triple Crown.

Because of his success DiMaggio was a perennial target of cranks and schemers, as well as mere admirers, throughout his career. Many would have taken advantage of him if they could, and many tried. Once he realized that the demands on him would come from all directions, he was constantly on guard.

During spring training one season, DiMaggio and a group of friends, including Ernie Sisto, were lounging in a hotel lobby in Florida one night.

A well-dressed man approached Sisto.

"Hey Ernie," the man said, "how about taking a picture of me with DiMaggio?"

Sisto did not know the man, but he assumed that the man knew his name because he was a *New York Times* photographer. Sisto thought that the man was a local fan who was staying at the hotel to watch the teams in training. Over the years Sisto had taken hundreds of pictures of DiMaggio requested by fans. Most of them wanted a personalized picture posing with the famous slugger.

DiMaggio had gone to the newsstand for cigarettes. When he returned Sisto went over to him.

"Joe, this fellow wants to have a picture taken with you. Is it O.K.?"

DiMaggio said it was all right. Sisto took the picture.

"Joe was in a good mood that night," Sisto recalled later. "He's a friendly guy if he takes a liking to you and he's in the right mood."

"Geez," DiMaggio said to Sisto and his friends, "I've got a yen for some stone crabs. I haven't had them in a long time. Let's go have some. I know a place that serves them."

Stone crabs are a delicacy caught only in Florida waters and flown to expensive restaurants in New York and other major cities. They are scarce and difficult to catch.

DiMaggio and the four others in his party got a cab and took off for the nightclub he knew that specialized in stone crabs. By this time the well-dressed man who had had his picture taken with DiMaggio considered himself part of the group and he went along, too.

"He had said something friendly in Italian," Sisto recalled later. "He seemed friendly so we figured he was all right, no harm done."

When they arrived, the nightclub was overcrowded. The maître d'hôtel recognized DiMaggio and found the group a table. Within minutes of their arrival, the manager of the club spotted DiMaggio. The manager went to the microphone to announce his presence.

"Ladies and gentlemen, we have a celebrity with us tonight," the manager hollered. "Joe DiMaggio."

"Let's get the hell out of this place," DiMaggio said, as if aware that he would be under the gaze of the crowd, and possibly badgered, all night. At the same time he didn't want to be used as bait by the manager.

"We're here now, Joe," Sisto said, trying to conciliate DiMaggio. "Let's have an inning here and then we'll go."

The crowd broke into applause and cheering. The spotlight from the bandstand focused on DiMaggio, who was finally convinced to stay.

The waiter started to bring out huge trays of stone crabs. DiMaggio and everyone else began to eat and enjoy them. The manager kept a constant eye on the waiter to see that he replenished the trays and drinks and kept DiMaggio's party happy.

"More crabs, more crabs for Joe," the manager exhorted the waiter.

"This is beautiful, it's easy," Sisto said to DiMaggio, thinking the manager had adopted a quid-pro-quo policy and was going to pick up the check in return for the pleasure of DiMaggio's company and the goodwill he brought to the patrons.

When DiMaggio was ready to leave, the manager presented him with the check.

"What's this fuckin' bill?" Sisto said incredulously. "I thought this was on the cuff, Joe. Here Joe, take this, let me chip in, too."

Sisto tried to hand DiMaggio a $10 bill.

"Get outta here. What chip in?" DiMaggio said. "The bill is for $130."

Everyone broke into laughter, except the well-dressed man who had joined the party in the hotel lobby.

"Here, I'll take that," he said, grabbing the check out of DiMaggio's hand. "It's on me."

He paid the check and left a big tip and the group left the club. They piled into a cab, feeling no pain, and laughed and sang songs all the way back to the hotel.

The next day at the ball park, DiMaggio cornered Sisto.

"Ernie," DiMaggio said, "ruin those negatives of the picture you took of me with that guy last night. Throw the goddamned stuff away. Don't ever give that guy another print."

"Why? What's the matter, Joe?" Sisto asked.

"That guy is some kind of hood. He owns a nightclub in Detroit and he's in the rackets. I found out the guy's been in jail. I don't want to get involved."

"Well, I destroyed the negatives," Sisto recalled later, "but I was thinking of this guy who took the check. About a month or so later, I got a letter from him and he said he was sorry and that he had no intention of getting Joe involved in any trouble. Who knows? Joe always had to guard against that stuff."

7

The Anatomy
of a
Hitting Streak

*D*IMAGGIO'S RECORD OF hitting safely in 56 consecutive games in 1941 has been one of the most lasting records in baseball. Many experts believe it is the one unbreakable record. During the 1978 season, Pete Rose, then playing with the Cincinnati Reds, became the most durable and serious challenger to DiMaggio's record in 37 seasons. Rose, a brilliant player in all dimensions of the game, distinguished himself as a hitter, baserunner, fielder, and hustler par excellence. He did not possess DiMaggio's power, but in 17 summers in the big leagues he had made more than 3,000 hits, had surpassed the National League record for most singles in a career set by the legendary Honus Wagner, and had broken Ty Cobb's record of most seasons with 200 or more hits.

As DiMaggio did in 1941, Rose captured the public imagination with his hitting streak. In his quest to overtake the Yankee Clipper's record, he reached 44 straight games before he was stopped. He broke the modern National League standard of 37 set by Tommy Holmes of the Boston Braves in 1948 and tied Willie Keeler's mark of 44 set in 1897, which DiMaggio brought down. Rose fell 12 games short of equaling DiMaggio's standard, but he learned first hand what immense concentration was needed to attain such a record.

The pressure on Rose each day to get a hit undoubtedly was just as great as the pressure on DiMaggio and in many instances they must have lived through parallel situations. For example, during DiMaggio's streak, the possibility that he would not go to bat in the late innings when he had not yet had a hit, a situation that occurred often, created additional pressure as it did for Rose.

At Yankee Stadium, DiMaggio's chances diminished because, as the home team, if the Yankees were winning (and they won often at home) they batted in only eight innings. On the road, they would always go to bat in the ninth.

In the 38th game of the streak the Yankees were leading, 3–1, in the eighth inning at the Stadium and DiMaggio still did not have a hit. He was the fourth batter scheduled in the inning. It meant that at least one of the men ahead of him—Johnny Sturm, Red Rolfe, or Tommy Henrich—had to get on base. Eldon Auker of the Browns, a right-hander who threw a kind of sidearm-underhand submarine ball that often baffled batters, was on the mound.

Sturm flied out and Rolfe drew a walk. If Henrich hit into a double play the inning would be over. Then it would be necessary for the Browns to tie the game or go ahead in the ninth for DiMaggio to swing again.

Henrich, on deck when Rolfe drew his walk, returned to the dugout.

"If I hit into a double play," Henrich said to Manager McCarthy, "Joe won't get up. Is it O.K. if I bunt?"

McCarthy nodded. Henrich went to the plate and laid down a perfect sacrifice bunt. On Auker's first pitch to him, DiMaggio capitalized with a line double to left field.

The day DiMaggio tied and broke George Sisler's American League mark of 41 games the temperature in Washington was 98 degrees. During batting practice, DiMaggio was mobbed by autograph-seekers. The Senators sent their ace, Emil "Dutch" Leonard, against the Yankees in the first game. To this point in his streak, DiMaggio had not faced Leonard, having made hits off 37 other pitchers, some of whom he had faced more than once.

In the sixth inning, DiMaggio fouled off Leonard's first pitch. Then he took a ball. Leonard threw a low fastball and DiMaggio drove it for a double that rolled to the 422-foot sign on the bleacher wall. The hit tied Sisler's record and the fans cheered DiMaggio for five minutes.

Between games in the clubhouse, DiMaggio, who was usually embarrassed when he drew attention to himself, was jubilant. He shook hands with the players and exchanged jokes. He took a shower and put on a fresh uniform.

James Dawson of *The New York Times* walked over to him.

"Well, how do you feel about it, Joe?" Dawson asked.

"I'm tickled," DiMaggio said. "Who wouldn't be? It's a great thing. I've realized an ambition. But I don't deserve the credit all alone. You have to give Mr. McCarthy some of it. I got many a break by being allowed to hit that 3 and 0 pitch. It brought me many a good ball to swing at. You know, he's got to give you the signal on 3 and 0 pitches and he was right with me all the time."

DiMaggio never considered his streak a stroke of luck. He thought of setting the major league record for hitting safely in consecutive games ever since he set a 61-game record for the Seals in the Pacific Coast League in 1933, a record that still stands.

McCarthy was elated over DiMaggio's performance. He stood with his arms folded in front of him, his face breaking into a smile that made him resemble the Irish actor Barry Fitzgerald.

"Joe didn't need any help from me," McCarthy said. "But don't forget we got another ball game in a few minutes."

McCarthy rarely had trouble with his players. They respected his baseball knowledge and integrity. He was affable and good-natured, but his first order of business was winning baseball games.

DiMaggio's single in the seventh inning of the second game, off Arnold Anderson, broke Sisler's record. In the dressing room afterward DiMaggio relaxed with a bottle of beer, as he did after almost every game. He was relieved that the pursuit of Sisler's record was over.

"I'm glad the strain is over," he said. "Now I've got to go after that forty-four game mark. I'll keep on swinging and hitting as long as I can. I never really was concerned about the mark until around the thirty-third game. Yesterday, in Philadelphia, I think, was the first time I was really nervous. I was tense out there today, too."

The day he broke Keeler's record of 44, DiMaggio reported to the Yankee Stadium dressing room and noted that the temperature was about 95 degrees. Hot weather usually drained him physically.

"It's kinda hard to keep from pressing," he said to Lefty Gomez, who was trying to keep DiMaggio calm. "The last few games have been a little hard. I know I mustn't press. If I do I can't hit and you know how much I want to hit. Just holding back trying to be natural is kind of a strain."

"Don't let it choke you, Joe. You'll be all right," Gomez said as he cleaned his spikes.

An attendant brought DiMaggio a hot cup of coffee. He lighted a cigarette and stretched out in front of his locker, his long legs and thighs bulging, his veins rippling his muscles.

On that day *The New York Times* assigned one of its outstanding reporters, Russell Owen, to do a personality profile story about DiMaggio for its Sunday magazine. Owen had won the Pulitzer Prize in 1930 for his news dispatches from the Admiral Byrd Antarctic Expedition, and although sports was not his realm, DiMaggio's streak had caught his and the public's imagination.

"What are you going to look for today, Joe?" Owen asked.

"A nice straight one down the middle," DiMaggio said, with a grin. "But I'll go after anything I can hit, and a change of pace won't bother me."

"How are the nerves?" Owen asked.

"Doesn't pay to get excited in this game," DiMaggio said. "Some guys naturally are more tense than others. They can't help it and today I can understand why. Whether I break that record or not, there will just be a lot of ball games. It's my job. I'll do the best I can."

Gomez was scheduled to pitch against the Boston Red Sox. He seemed more fidgety than DiMaggio. He sat on the edge of a table and examined his spikes.

"Nothing bothers this guy," Gomez said to Owen. "He sleeps like a log. We went to a movie last night and then played some gin rummy. Generally hit the sack about 12 and boy how that fellow can sleep." Gomez nodded toward DiMaggio.

"You don't do so bad either," DiMaggio said. "He's quite a joker. You know what he did to me once in Miami? He gave me a suitcase to carry back to the hotel. I thought it would take my arm off, it was so heavy. I ached for a week. Thought his shoes must be in it. Look at those feet. And what do you think it was? A log of wood. That log would have burned for four days. Nice joke."

DiMaggio welcomed the release from tension. The talk with Owen seemed to relax him. He walked to the water cooler, then stopped to chat with other players.

"He's a good ballplayer because he knows he's good," Gomez said to Owen. "I don't mean he's conceited. He isn't. But he is confident. He knows what he can do and that is why he is relaxed. He's always relaxed."

DiMaggio returned to his locker.

"What's he been saying about me?" DiMaggio asked Owen.

"Nothing good," Gomez said.

Whenever DiMaggio and Gomez were interviewed they knew they could rely on each other to say a good word about the other.

The huge locker room began to rumble and fill with the raucous laughter of the players. As a group the ballplayers always seemed happy. Their ability to pass time and keep themselves occupied with what appeared to be trivia was almost childlike.

The Yankees were big, powerful men. They began to change from street clothes into their uniforms. Stripped to the skin they seemed even more powerful. In a peculiar way only their arms and faces and necks were heavily tanned. The other parts of their bodies were starkly white, untouched by the sun. In full dress, in uniform or street clothes, they always looked richly tanned, giving the impression that they frolicked all summer in a vacationland where they were always bathed in sunshine.

"Lefty was saying that you're always relaxed," Owen said to DiMaggio.

"I guess it just looks that way," DiMaggio said.

"When you're in the outfield, you play it with a kind of indifference," the reporter said.

DiMaggio paused before answering.

"There's a little trick about that," DiMaggio said. "I'm pretty much on my toes, even if it doesn't seem so. I know that when I run, these long legs of mine make me look as if I were loping along. But I can travel fairly well. I'm not as fast as some men, by a long shot. But there is a little trick of leaning in the direction you know the batter is apt to hit the ball, and when he hits you are already on your way. That helps a lot."

DiMaggio got up from the bench and demonstrated how he stood and leaned in the outfield. While he was going through the motions, Tom Connolly, the chief of the American League umpires, walked into the locker room. Connolly saw DiMaggio and went over to him. He grabbed DiMaggio's arm in an affectionate embrace and patted him on the back.

Connolly was an Irishman who still talked with a heavy brogue. He had known Willie Keeler, the man whose record DiMaggio would try to break in the next hour or two.

"Boiy," Connolly said, "I hope you do it. If you do you're breaking the record of the foinest little fellow who ever walked and who never said a mean thing about anyone in his life. Good luck to ye."

DiMaggio broke into a grin. He was warmed by Connolly's remarks. The six-foot-two-inch, 205-pound DiMaggio always got along with umpires. He was never thrown out of a game and rarely argued about a call.

"Yes, sir, thank you," DiMaggio said as Connolly moved on to brief his crew of umpires.

DiMaggio began to put on his playing gear. Gomez started to dress, too.

"You think the crowd will get to you?" Owen asked DiMaggio.

Since his first year as a Yankee in 1936, DiMaggio had drawn thousands of new fans to the Stadium. He loved their adulation. Off the field he was wary of and uncomfortable in large crowds and tried to avoid them. He was a realist, however, and suffered no illusions about popularity.

"This is the way I make my living," he said. "I like to be popular, who doesn't. But I don't pay much attention to the fans. While I give them all I have, and hope I can make good for them, primarily I am out there playing ball for the club—and for myself. You have got to do the best you can while you last in this game, and I want to make what I can while I last."

It was time for the team to move out on the field. Gomez offered another tension-reliever to the reporter.

"Want to know what this guy reads?" he volunteered. "We go into a hotel and get to the newsstand, and he whispers to me, 'Hey, there's a new *Superman.* Get it for me.' Joe doesn't dare buy it himself. They all know him, you know. So he gets me to buy it for him. Superman and Bat Man. That's his favorite reading."

"I like Westerns, too," DiMaggio said, half in self-defense and half in embarrassment. DiMaggio and Gomez and Owen laughed and together they moved out toward the ramp that led to the field.

When DiMaggio reached the dugout he was greeted by a horde of photographers. He didn't like to be photographed but he knew its value. He knew publicity either for himself or the Yankees was one more weapon he could use when it came time to negotiate a new contract.

Ernie Sisto usually was the man New York photographers delegated to arrange a picture-taking session with DiMaggio. Likable and pix-ieish, Sisto had used his camera to charm his way through the 1928 Democratic National Convention in Texas and 13 consecutive runnings of the Kentucky Derby. With Sisto around, DiMaggio felt more at ease when he was asked to pose for photographs on the field.

"Hi, Ernie," DiMaggio said when he saw Sisto. "Howya doing?"

"Joe, the boys want to make a picture," Sisto said. "Just a few shots of you polishing your bat with a beef bone."

Many players used beef bones to keep their bats smooth so they would not splinter. A good bat meant a great deal to a hitter. DiMaggio normally used sandpaper to keep his bats in condition and he wasn't happy about the prop.

"You got to be kidding, Ernie," DiMaggio said.

"That's what they want, Joe," Sisto replied, throwing up his arms as if to say, "What can I do?"

"O.K.," DiMaggio said, "but it's got to be here in the dugout. The crowd will think I'm a regular jerk if they see me out there polishing a bat."

DiMaggio complied with the request and a dozen photographers clicked their cameras. His teammates heckled and teased him about the bat and the beef bone. But DiMaggio remained quiet and relaxed, grinning and polishing the bat. It seemed as if he were concentrating and could not be distracted from the task that would confront him when the game began.

Sisto's colleagues complimented him for getting DiMaggio to cooperate. Then they made one more request. Sisto said he wanted no part of it because he anticipated DiMaggio's reaction. But his job came first.

"There's one more picture they want to make, Joe," Sisto said. "They want to get you on the field standing in front of 45 balls arranged in a 4 and a 5, just in case you break the record. You know you're going to break it anyway, Joe, so you might as well take it and get it over with."

Reluctantly, DiMaggio went out on the field and the pictures were taken. He could not let Sisto lose face with his co-workers.

"Chrissakes, Ernie," he said. "I feel like a real jerk. Making all this fuss."

Yankee Stadium was sun-baked when the game got under way. DiMaggio trotted out to center field, stepping on second base on the way. He did that in every game for good luck. He did it each time he went out to his position and each time he returned to the dugout.

DiMaggio moved into the batter's box for his first chance in the first inning. He was set in a wide stance, feet wide apart, his top-heavy bat slanted across his shoulders almost at port arms. He seemed frozen in concentration.

Heber "Dick" Newsome, a right-hander in his first big-league season, received the starting assignment for Boston. Because of the 95-degree heat, it was too warm for 43-year-old Lefty Grove to take his regular turn even though he was seeking the 299th victory of his major league career. A day in the blistering sun would do him more harm than good.

Newsome kicked dirt on the mound and wiped sweat from his face. He peered at Jake Pytlak, the catcher, for a sign. DiMaggio stood riveted in his stone-like stance. Newsome delivered and DiMaggio lined a sharp drive to right-center field.

Stan Spence, the right fielder, briefly misjudged the ball. He recovered swiftly and made a leaping catch. DiMaggio quietly returned to the dugout.

In the third inning, Jim Tabor, the third baseman, made a quick pickup and throw on a difficult bounding ball to check DiMaggio again.

Gomez was in control with a 2–0 lead in the fourth inning. He went to bat in the Yankee fourth with two out and nobody on base.

Newsome threw a fastball. Gomez swung listlessly and missed. Newsome threw another fastball. Again Gomez swung and missed, by a wide margin. Newsome's third pitch was out of the strike zone, but Gomez struck out on it with another listless swing.

"Boy, it's so hot out there, nobody should be playing ball on a day like this," Gomez said when he went back to the dugout.

In the fifth inning, the Yankees had reached Newsome for two runs and he was kicking dirt again. Red Rolfe lashed a double and Henrich grounded out.

DiMaggio went to bat for the third time. Newsome's first pitch was a ball. He looked for the sign from Pytlak and threw again. DiMaggio swiftly brought his bat around and sent a towering liner into the left-field stands—foul. He took another ball. Then, in a synchronization of eyes, bat, ball, and swing, he drove the next pitch for a record-breaking home run. The ball landed a few feet from where he had hit Newsome's second pitch foul. He had surpassed Keeler's record.

The crowd stood and cheered as he rounded the bases. When he touched home he doffed his cap and headed for the dugout. Rolfe and Timmy Sullivan, the batboy, congratulated him at the plate. He lumbered down the cement steps of the dugout. His teammates surrounded him. They slapped him on the back, whistled, and rapped their gloves against the bench and water cooler. Gomez was ecstatic.

"You not only broke Keeler's record," he said to DiMaggio, "you even used his formula—you hit 'em where they ain't."

Joe Cronin, the Red Sox manager, went to the mound. He signaled to the bull pen. "Black Jack" Wilson started walking in toward the mound. Newsome was finished for the day. The Yankees, however, were not. Charlie Keller, Bill Dickey, and Joe Gordon filled the bases. Gomez got another chance to bat.

Wilson was regarded as a hot-and-cold pitcher. He didn't have tantalizing stuff. Gomez had a genuine ability to deceive. He knew that Wilson must have been watching from the bull pen when Newsome struck him out on three straight pitches his previous trip to the plate.

Gomez was a master of the come-on—a ploy pitchers used to get a fat pitch they could pounce on for their infrequent hits. Whatever

Wilson thought of Gomez as a hitter, he undoubtedly reappraised it moments after he threw a softie across the plate.

Gomez drove it for a single to right center field that sent in two runs. It put the lid on a six-run inning. The Red Sox scored three runs off Gomez in the sixth and he left the game because of the heat.

"How did you like that come-on I gave those guys?" Gomez said in the locker room after the game.

"I guess you're hitting them where they ain't, too," DiMaggio said.

The mood in the Yankee dressing room was happy. Everyone talked about DiMaggio's streak. He sat beside his locker, No. 5, the same number he wore on the field. It was next to locker No. 4, Lou Gehrig's locker and number that would never be used again by any other Yankee player. DiMaggio puffed on a Chesterfield. A ring of reporters stood around him.

"I don't know how far I can go," he said, "but I'm not going to think about it now. I'm glad it's over. It was quite a strain the last ten days. Now I can go back to swinging at good pitches. I was swinging at some bad ones so I wouldn't be walked."

He picked up a bundle of mail.

"The streak has been as tough off the field as on it," he said. "I've been getting all this fan mail, every day, and there's always a good luck charm or something in every letter. It's just too much. I have to turn it all over to the front office to handle. I guess it's a great tribute to me and I appreciate it, but it has its drawbacks."

DiMaggio took a shower and got dressed. He wore an expensive dark gray double-breasted suit, a white shirt and flowered tie, and highly polished black shoes.

The temperature had started to cool. The next day would be an off day before the Fourth of July double-header with the Senators at the Stadium.

"It'll be good to be off," DiMaggio said.

Gomez went over to him. "You ready to go, Joe?" he said. "There'll probably be a mob out there."

Outside the Stadium, several thousand fans waited to get a glimpse of DiMaggio. A police escort got DiMaggio and Gomez through the crowd and into Gomez's car. Slowly the car wound its way through the street for the ride downtown. A group of youngsters ran alongside the car, slapping the fenders and shouting DiMaggio's name.

DiMaggio's feat became the subject for editorial page writers throughout the country. Radio news bulletins interrupted programs to report his day-to-day progress. "Joltin' Joe DiMaggio" became a popular song on juke boxes everywhere.

When DiMaggio had tied Sisler's record, an editorial in the June 30th issue of *The New York Herald Tribune* said:

> The question on every baseball fan's lips as he called up a newspaper office or tuned in on his radio for the scores has been, "Did DiMaggio get a hit today?" Even hardened big-league pitchers "warming up" in the bull pen, have ceased their activities when the great "DiMag" came to bat to turn and watched him, wondering if he could possibly equal this amazing skein—a record which has escaped such hitting stars of all time as Ty Cobb, Babe Ruth, Rogers Hornsby and Lou Gehrig. No such record as this is ever put together without a good deal of help from Lady Luck. But as George Sisler himself said the other day in commenting on DiMaggio's performance, "If anyone does it I hope it's Joe." By that he meant that DiMaggio was the nearest thing, perhaps, that we have seen, to the man with the perfect batting temperament.

The Fourth of July double-header at the Stadium was postponed by rain, but on a Saturday, against the A's in New York, DiMaggio notched No. 46 in the streak when he drove Phil Marchildon's first pitch in the first inning 420 feet to the bull pen for his 19th home run of the season.

With 60,918 fans watching the next day he cracked four hits—three singles and a double—in the first game of a double-header and then cuffed a triple and a single in the second game to send the streak to 48.

"The Sensational Joe DiMaggio Will Attempt to Hit Safely in His 49th Consecutive Game," proclaimed a newspaper advertisement as the Yankees rolled into St. Louis. That night, against the Browns, DiMaggio was lucky to get his hit in the first inning and save his streak. Rain forced the game to be shortened to 5½ innings—an official game. The next day he got four hits, getting his first of three singles in the first inning and capping his performance with his 20th home run as the Yankees posted their 11th straight victory. In the third game of the series the Browns named Eldon Auker as the starter. Auker had turned back DiMaggio three times in the 38th game of the streak without a hit and had set the stage for Tommy Henrich's sacrifice bunt that enabled DiMaggio to preserve the streak with a double in the eighth. Now

Auker had stopped him in the first inning as DiMaggio narrowly missed hitting into a double play. But in the fourth, DiMaggio connected for a double and reached No. 51.

The Yankee caravan moved to Chicago for two games with the White Sox and 50,387 fans streamed through the turnstiles. The streak seemed imperishable, DiMaggio incapable of faltering. He lined three singles in the first game. Against Thornton Lee he grounded out the first time up in the second game, drew a walk in the fourth. Not until the sixth did he preserve the streak, with a low line single to right center field.

On July 14, Johnny Rigney of the White Sox handcuffed DiMaggio into the sixth inning when DiMaggio went to bat for the third time. Swinging heavily, he topped the ball toward third base. Bob Kennedy, playing deep, ran in for the ball at break-neck speed. But the ball rolled so slowly, Kennedy had no chance for a play. By the time he picked up the ball DiMaggio was across first base. It was a clean hit, but perhaps it was the least imposing of all during the streak.

DiMaggio faced Edgar Smith the next day. He had started the streak two months ago to the day against the left-hander. His first time up DiMaggio reached base on Luke Appling's error. In the third, Rolfe singled, Henrich walked, and DiMaggio drove in Rolfe with a single, his first of two hits off Smith. The Chicago fans were so eager to see DiMaggio hit that even with the streak no longer in jeopardy in that game, they booed Smith when he intentionally walked DiMaggio in the seventh with men on second and third and one out.

The streak, of course, came to an end in a night game at Cleveland on July 17. Before the game, after a light supper, DiMaggio and Gomez took a cab together to Municipal Stadium, hard by Lake Erie. The cab driver recognized DiMaggio when they got in.

After a short distance, the cabbie turned to DiMaggio at a stop light and said, "Joe, I have a hunch you're going to be stopped tonight. I just feel it in my bones."

DiMaggio paid little attention to what the cabbie said, but Gomez told him, "Buddy, you're full of bunk."

Al Smith and Jim Bagby Jr. stopped DiMaggio at 56 games, but it was two great fielding plays by Ken Keltner at third base that robbed DiMaggio and kept him from continuing.

When they went back to their hotel room that night, DiMaggio and

Gomez sat around eating sandwiches and drinking milk. Gomez was pacing up and down the room.

"That lousy son of a bitch," Gomez kept saying. "That lousy dirty son of a bitch."

DiMaggio thought at first Gomez was talking about Keltner.

"Heck, Lefty," DiMaggio said, "he was just playing the game. The pressure has been terrific. I'm glad it's finally off."

"The bum jinxed you, Joe," Gomez said. "He put the whammy on you with all that talk about hunches."

"Who the hell are you talking about?" DiMaggio said.

"The cabbie," Gomez said, "that lousy rotten cabbie."

DiMaggio burst into laughter and Gomez joined him. It was the first good laugh they had had in weeks.

The next day DiMaggio embarked on another hitting spree—a new streak that lasted for 16 games. From May 15 to August 3 he had hit safely in 72 of 73 games. In the record-setting streak he went to bat 223 times. He made 91 hits, including 15 home runs, 16 doubles, and four triples. He scored 56 runs and batted in 55. His batting average during that span was .408.

The Yankees were back at the pinnacle of the baseball world. They went on to win the league title by 17 games and defeat the Brooklyn Dodgers in the World Series.

In August, with the club closing in on an early clinching of the pennant, several Yankees held a clubhouse meeting to discuss DiMaggio's role in helping the team win the title. They planned an informal party for the night of August 29. They would have the night off after checking into the Shoreham Hotel in Washington.

George Selkirk sat in his room making phone calls to the players and the reporters who would be invited.

DiMaggio was getting dressed for dinner. Gomez was getting ready to take a shower.

"Say, Joe," Gomez hollered from the shower. "I'm getting tired of tagging along with you to all those banquets you're invited to. How about tonight you and I go to dinner where I want to go? O.K.?"

"O.K. with me," DiMaggio said, "but don't take all day in the shower. I'm hungry and all those good steaks will be gone if you don't hustle."

Gomez dried himself slowly. He began to dress, almost in slow motion. He took several windups. He whistled and hummed. He took 15 minutes to get his shoes in shape.

Finally, they went to an elevator. Gomez pressed the button for the fourth floor instead of the main lobby.

"What the hell are you doing?" DiMaggio said, still unsuspecting.

"I just remembered something," Gomez said. "I got to go to Selkirk's room for a minute."

"O.K.," DiMaggio said, "I'll go down and get us a table."

"You said you'd go where I want tonight," Gomez said quickly. "Stay with me. I'll only be a minute."

"O.K.," DiMaggio said, "but let's not take all night."

Selkirk looked out from behind the door of the suite.

"Here he comes," he said to the players and reporters.

The Yankees had purchased a sterling silver cigar and cigarette humidor from Tiffany's to present to DiMaggio. Manager McCarthy had given the team permission to have champagne. Gomez led DiMaggio into the room and the players broke out in song:

"For he's a jolly good fellow. . . . "

Gomez made the presentation. "Remember, Joe, no cigars, only cigarettes," he said. Gomez intensely disliked cigar smokers.

On the cover of the humidor a statuette depicted DiMaggio in his famous swing. The number 56 was engraved on one side and on the other 91—the numbers for the games in the streak and the hits he made in it. Also engraved on the humidor were the signatures of all his teammates with this inscription: "Presented to Joe DiMaggio by his fellow players on the New York Yankees to express their admiration for his consecutive-game hitting streak, 1941."

DiMaggio, who was recovering from a sprained ankle that had sidelined him the previous week, made an awkward attempt to make a speech. He said something about the Yankee club being his home and every man on the team being more than a teammate—he was a "friend and brother."

8

*War Breaks Up
the Papas
and the Yankees*

*I*N THE SUMMER of 1941, the last before America was plunged into war, DiMaggio's record of hitting safely in 56 consecutive games had made him a subject to be saluted in song. A catchy tune, "Joltin' Joe DiMaggio," was frequently heard on the radio. It gave listeners a welcome relief from news bulletins telling of the war in Europe. The song was written by Alan Courtney, a disc jockey, who scribbled the words on a tablecloth one night in a nightclub not far from New York City. Courtney had shown the lyrics to Les Brown, the band leader and arranger, and Brown turned them over to Ben Homer, a writer who came up with the tune. Together, the three produced a lively hit heard often on the nation's juke boxes:

"Who started baseball's famous streak
    That's got us all aglow?
He's just a man and not a freak,
    Joltin' Joe DiMaggio.
Joe . . . Joe . . . DiMaggio . . . we
    Want you on our side.

From Coast to Coast, that's all you hear
    Of Joe the One-Man-Show.
He's glorified the horsehide sphere,
    Joltin' Joe DiMaggio.
Joe . . . Joe . . . DiMaggio . . . we
    Want you on our side.

He'll live in baseball's Hall of Fame,
    He got there blow-by-blow.
Our kids will tell their kids his name,
    Joltin' Joe DiMaggio."

DiMaggio had helped propel the Yankees to the top once again. In his six years with the Bombers they had won five pennants and world titles. In the fall he was voted the Most Valuable Player in the American League for the second time in three years. He edged Ted Williams of Boston, who had won the batting title with a .406 average, becoming the first man to hit .400 since Bill Terry of the Giants had done it 11 years earlier. In 1947, Williams would win the Triple Crown in batting, but DiMaggio again edged him for the Most Valuable Player award, his third, on the strength of having led the Yankees to another crown. "It took the Big Guy to beat me, didn't it?" Williams scowled then.

DiMaggio had returned home to San Francisco after the 1941 Series, hoping to bask in his latest triumphs and enjoy the quiet leisure of family life. The precious days of fall dwindled down and by the year's end the nation would be cloaked in war and uncertainty. Soon baseball's heroes, and the fans who had cheered them, would be off to fight and serve in remote places of the globe that few Americans had heard of before.

On Fisherman's Wharf, DiMaggio's father and the immigrant old-timers would congregate every morning to talk about fishing and "de beisball." They were called "Papas" by the younger generations and were revered, much as Santiago was revered by Manolin in the Hemingway story, for the skill and stubbornness they had brought to bear in plying their trade in the Pacific Coast waters since the turn of the century.

The Papas had been founders of the Wharf. Singing the Italian seining song, they had launched their small fleet of crab-fishing skiffs into the bay in the early morning mists, returning weary at nightfall with their catch. They had hauled it to market and had sold it from boxes on the street curbs. They had created the local color that had made the Wharf a picturesque marine landmark and tourist attraction, famous throughout the world. Some had fished from the Wharf for 40 and 50 years.

Eventually, the second-generation sons and daughters of the Papas had become proprietors of thriving businesses on the Wharf. Restaurants such as DiMaggio's Grotto, Alioto's, and other seafood emporiums that attracted a select clientele sprang up, giving the Wharf a colorful and prominent place in the San Francisco mosaic.

As a bachelor, and even into his early married life, DiMaggio often had spent the off-season winter months rambling around the spacious new home he had bought for his mother and father for $14,000 in 1937. Business matters at the Grotto had occupied some of his time, but he spent part of each day leisurely walking along the Wharf talking about fishing and baseball with his Papa and the other Papas, now in their 60s and 70s and slowing up. The homecomings were filled with warmth and visits with old friends of the horse-lot days. In the local *Chronicle* he was "Our Joe" in the headlines and accounts of his exploits.

He was somewhat pampered, too, by his sisters and his mother, who cooked his favorite meals and tended to his domestic needs. He and his mother had played a little game, almost a ritual. His routine usually called for sleep until 11 o'clock in the morning. When he got up he raised the Venetian blinds in his room. His mother, on the lookout, peered from the kitchen window, just across the courtyard from his bedroom, waiting for the blinds to go up. When she got the signal she knew he was starting to dress. It was time for her to start his omelette, usually one flavored with onions and potatoes, and get the coffee hot for her son's breakfast.

The Papas had become a legend on the Wharf. They had come in large numbers from tiny fishing villages in Italy and Sicily and had settled on the bay shores of San Francisco. They were robust, strong, lusty, hard-drinking, and hard-working. And they raised large families. they were mostly unschooled, many were illiterate, and every one of them was poor. They kept close ties to the church and to the customs of the old country. While they had been mindful of the opportunities their adopted country could offer their children, many had taken the prospect of citizenship for granted, unaware of the mechanics necessary to become naturalized. They had been carefree fishermen who worked hard and provided as best they could for the needs of families that often included ten and twelve children. They were close-knit and characteristically closemouthed.

For the Sicilians among them, like the DiMaggios, many of the old country roots and values were never severed. Life was best endured by accepting what it had to offer. They had brought with them a basic distrust for authority and a sense of dichotomy steeped in an old culture of a nation that had endured conquest and revolution until conquered once again and united with Italy in 1860.

Giuseppe di Lampedusa, the author of *The Leopard,* a novel about the decline of Sicilian aristocracy, had captured the essence of the country's people and character in his masterpiece. Later he wrote, "We are old, very old. For more than 25 centuries we've been bearing the weight of superb and heterogeneous civilizations, all from the outside, none made by ourselves, none that we could call our own." With this heritage in his background Papa DiMaggio had sustained his family among his neighbors. Now on the Wharf he had become a celebrity among his cronies.

The attack on Pearl Harbor abruptly changed the daily tenor of life for the Papas. Haunting fear, an emotion they had scorned all their lives, gripped their hearts. The same fear gripped the hearts of Japanese-Americans and Japanese aliens living on the West Coast.

Within days of the Japanese attack, the War Department declared that North Beach, so close to the Pacific Ocean, was within a restricted strategic zone. Federal regulations stipulated that "no enemy alien will be permitted to live in a forbidden zone, to work there, or even to visit there." The Wharf was included in the restricted area.

Virtually to a man, the Papas either had never started naturalization proceedings or had failed to pass the English writing and reading requirements of the citizenship test. Those who were aliens under this edict, without exceptions, would be forced to evacuate the area. Their homes, families, and jobs would have to be left behind.

The War Department evacuation orders had been issued on January 31, 1942, and it set a compliance deadline of February 24, 1942.

With this new sobering development DiMaggio's homecoming was tinged with anxiety. His parents would be considered aliens and would have to move from the area. They would have to move in with other members of the family who lived outside the designated zones.

At the end of January the New York Baseball Writers Association held its annual dinner at the Hotel Commodore. DiMaggio, who had been designated their "player of the year," shared the guest-of-honor spotlight with Hank Greenberg and Mel Ott. DiMaggio was to receive his award for an unprecedented second time; Greenberg was cited for "symbolizing the American spirit in sport," and Ott, who had become a New York Giant at the age of 17, was now taking over as manager.

Unlike previous years, a martial tone prevailed, with high-ranking military officers mingling with baseball executives and politicians. Mayor Fiorello La Guardia of New York, an avid baseball and DiMaggio fan who doubled as Federal Director of the Office of Civil Defense, alarmed the gathering by injecting into his speech comments about air-raid precautions at ball games. He had assured the three New York teams that there would be no interruption of "the normal conduct of baseball" in the city and that there would be "no danger at the ball parks in case of air attacks because alarms would come in ample time to give spectators a chance to leave the parks." He failed to mention how the 6 million other residents of the city, to say nothing of the millions on the Atlantic and Pacific seaboards, would receive their ample warnings.

Greenberg, a native New Yorker and a star slugger for the Detroit

Tigers who had hit 58 home runs in 1938 and barely missed equaling Ruth's record of 60 in one season, had raised baseball's patriotic consciousness. Seven months to the day before America had entered the war, May 7, 1941, Greenberg had been inducted into the Army. One of the highest paid players in the sport at $55,000 a year, the 30-year-old Greenberg had drawn a low number—in the 600s—in the Selective Service draft. In the next few months, the age requirements for the draft were changed, providing for the release of draftees already in the service who had reached their 28th birthday. Greenberg was released on December 5, 1941. Two days later the Japanese bombed Hickham Field. Before the year was out, Greenberg, who had led the Tigers to the 1940 pennant and had been selected the American League's most valuable player, voluntarily enlisted, donning his Army uniform once more.

"I'm going back in," he said. "We are in trouble and there is only one thing to do—return to the service. I have not been called back. I am going back of my own accord. Baseball is out the window as far as I'm concerned. I don't know if I'll ever return to baseball. If I do, all right. If not, well, that's all right, too."

The speakers at the dinner, all evoking the spirit-of-patriotism theme, included William Lyon Phelps, professor of English Literature at Yale University, who was a devout baseball rooter, and Oscar Levant, the humorist and pianist, who quipped, "It's like a New Year's Eve party before going off to war."

DiMaggio's thoughts must have wandered back to North Beach and the plight of the Papas. He must have wondered where he fit into all this. He had already been placed in Class 3 in the draft, a class for married men with children, and it assured him of playing out the campaign. The long arm of the draft had already reached out to many players. The Government had not yet imposed travel restrictions on the clubs and the Yankees would still train in Florida in 1942. Wage freezes in all jobs would eventually become law. Many players who figured the 1942 season might be their last planned to hold out now for more money in anticipation of the wage freeze.

While he was in New York DiMaggio had stopped by the Yankee office to talk to Barrow about his next contract.

"This emergency is going to change things, this year," Barrow said to DiMaggio as the two exchanged pleasantries.

"I just thought I had a pretty good season last year," DiMaggio said, "and I think I deserve a raise."

"I was thinking you might have to take a little cut, the way things are," Barrow said. "You know there's a war on."

DiMaggio couldn't believe what he was hearing. He left without any comment.

The next day Barrow sent Mark Roth, the road secretary, to DiMaggio's apartment to deliver a contract calling for $37,500, the same salary he had played for in 1941. This presentation did not go over well with DiMaggio and he resented the club's use of the war emergency as a method to intimidate him into a quick decision on terms.

By mid-February, as the war intensified, a shroud of gloom and apprehension engulfed the aliens on the West Coast. Large segments of the population—workers in defense plants, on farms, and in waterfront areas—were to be displaced and put out of work. California legislators predicted a population shift comparable to the days of the Depression when countless families were tractored off the Dust Bowl of the Midwest wheatlands.

Singapore was under siege and surrendered on February 16, as Britain suffered its worst defeat of the war. Anti-Japanese sentiment was at a high pitch. Sabotage had been uncovered and the California coastline had been shelled by a ship believed to have been Japanese. Agents of the Federal Bureau of Investigation arrested two Japanese Army reserve officers working in a Japanese bank in San Francisco and posing as clerks. By February 20 evacuation proceedings orders had been issued to include, along with the aliens, Japanese-Americans who were native born citizens of the United States. In Washington, the Tolan Investigating Committee on Enemy Aliens heard witnesses testify that it was possible to establish a procedure to judge the loyalty of German and Italian aliens, but in the case of the Japanese, "it was impossible." It was the beginning of a sad chapter of American history in which the government eventually adopted a policy of internment for aliens, with virtually the whole brunt to fall on the Japanese. The climate had grown irrational and racism had shown its ugly face.

On February 24, the shadows of huge troop transports fell like a blight on once picturesque and lively scenes of Fisherman's Wharf, dotted with gay, colorful skiffs moored at the docks. The boats stood idle under the stern watch of armed sentries. In the small shops, the juke boxes that had blared "Joltin' Joe DiMaggio" and "Amapola" were silent and the old Papas, pantaloons drooping over their shoes, stood in clusters venting their frustration with unmistakable Italian gestures.

Papa DiMaggio, now 69 years old, was still one of them, all irretrievably caught in the irony of a world gone mad. His problem was no longer the need to make a living from the sea; his sons had seen to it that he would be comfortable. But he was still one of the Papas who had not become a naturalized citizen and he would be forced to leave.

Luciano Maniscalco, a fisherman for 40 years since he had come from Italy as a young man of 18, pointed to his boat, the one he would not be able to board or even go near after this day.

"I try, try, try to become a citizen," he said in despair. "My head she too hard," he went on, rapping his skull with his fist. "Can't learn, can't write. Go to school. Get first papers in 1921. Go back, get second papers. Can't write. Can't get papers."

He screamed wildly: "My head she too damn hard! Too damn hard! I wanta be citizen, wanta fish. What I do now, monkey around? Can't get job, not a citizen. I can fish good as anybody."

Maniscalco had fathered twelve children. "I got four kids working for Uncle Sam. Buster, he in merchant marine. Tommy in Navy eight years now. Vincent in Army. Mariana, she drive ambulance. Can't fish. I wanta be citizen and fish."

The plight of the Papas would be eased somewhat by their children who lived out of the designated zones and who would take them in. But for many other aliens the displacement would be a horrendous shock and hardship. What gnawed at the Papas most was the off-limits designation of the Wharf and the assumption that they were potentially disloyal.

Anthony Sabella, the owner of a sea-food business and a block of buildings on the Wharf, lamented the plight of his 71-year-old Papa, Luciano. His father had worked the Wharf for 54 years and now in semiretirement he helped his son's business by dunking crabs in boiling water each day. Papa Sabella had fathered twelve children.

"Papa out there, not on the Wharf," his son said, fighting back tears, "after all these years. It'll kill him. But he's not a citizen. He can't write."

"Let's move to Hunter's Point," a Papa said, trying to raise a glimmer of hope.

"The water there is too dead," another said. "Smells bad."

"The Navy has zoned that, too," a third Papa said, conclusively.

"Can't hang around no more," Papa DiMaggio said, speaking for all.

DiMaggio's father had joined this once-happy band of fishermen after he had moved from Martinez, California, a town of 9,000 north of the San Francisco–Oakland area. Seven of the nine DiMaggio children had been born in Martinez, where the father had worked as a section hand on a railroad. When he lost that job he decided to return to fishing, a skill he had mastered before he left his native Isola de Femme in Sicily in 1902. As a teenager he had served in the Italian Army, seeing combat in Italy's expansionist war with Ethiopia (Abyssinia) in 1896 at the Battle of Aduwa, in which the Italians were defeated.

War or no war, and notwithstanding the troubles at home, DiMaggio went off for a Florida vacation of "fishing and loafing." His wife and 4-month-old son would join him in a few days, but already the stress in his domestic life had begun to encroach on his marital life. After his talk with Barrow, and the threat of a pay cut, he was more determined than ever to stand his ground in demanding a raise.

Like other celebrities who had not responded quickly to the call to arms, ballplayers, and particularly the highly paid ones, had become targets for public criticism. As DiMaggio's holdout threats grew stronger, his position with the public became more unpopular, much as it had in 1938.

In Florida, DiMaggio acknowledged the receipt of a second contract from Barrow calling for a raise of $2,500.

"I received a contract in the mail for $40,000," DiMaggio said. "I phoned Mr. Barrow and told him I would not sign. All things considered, I feel justified in looking for an increase. I do not consider $2,500 a fair raise."

He said his timetable for reporting to spring training rested solely in Barrow's lap. He would stay in the vicinity, he said, "but I don't know how soon we'll get together."

Besides DiMaggio, five other Yankees—Red Ruffing, Bill Dickey, Red Rolfe, Joe Gordon, and Charlie Keller—a veritable all-star lineup in itself, were listed as bona fide holdouts.

While DiMaggio and his wife and son were enjoying the sun and beach and their rented Lido Beach penthouse, Barrow ruminated in New York, figuring how to bring his players into line.

One tactic was to announce that he had already offered DiMaggio a raise. On March 6, he phoned Manager Joe McCarthy in St. Petersburg from his 42nd Street headquarters and told him to announce to the press before the Yankee exhibition game with the St. Louis Cardinals that DiMaggio had refused a $40,000 contract and that that was the club's final offer to him.

In later years, even after he had retired as a player, DiMaggio continued to insist that Barrow had suggested a pay cut, after his spectacular 1941 season. Joe had characterized it as "presposterous."

A holdout by six players simply wasn't good business in Barrow's estimation. He had notified McCarthy that he would arrive in St. Petersburg on March 12 specifically to deal with the problem and DiMaggio in particular.

On March 9, however, Barrow got a windfall. Ruffing, Dickey, Gordon, and Keller had come to terms and would report to camp in a day or two. Ruffing and Dickey, who had received $23,000 each in 1941, had been offered pay cuts and had held fast against it. Gordon, who had hit 24 home runs, and Keller, who had led the club with 33, simply wanted a raise, and they each got one.

Barrow arrived in Florida at noon on March 12. He wasted little time setting up the meeting with DiMaggio. It lasted an hour and when the two emerged they had an agreement.

"I talked the matter over at length with Mr. Barrow," DiMaggio said. "We reviewed the situation pleasantly. There were no harsh words exchanged. I am satisfied with the terms we agreed upon and will sign as soon as Mr. Barrow has the papers drawn."

DiMaggio had won his mini-holdout and a $6,000 raise. He would report to camp the next day. Unlike Colonel Ruppert, who gloried in success in negotiations, Barrow had little to say, but a smile betrayed his relief over solving the impasse. As for Rolfe, he had not returned a signed contract because he had been ill. Barrow had thought this suggested he had been holding out, too, but it proved not to be the case.

"Actually, Barrow never offered me a contract calling for a cut," DiMaggio said after his retirement. "Eventually, I signed for $43,750, but while I was battling for it, the Yankee front office put out a lot of propaganda about guys being in the Army at $21 a month, the insinuation being that I was lucky to be playing ball. I don't think anything ever burned me up as much as that did."

DiMaggio was in the lineup every day now, but his batting was sporadic. He got hits in clusters, then slipped into prolonged slumps. April produced two memorable days. At Washington, he made three hits and knocked in five runs, hitting his first homer of the season, a 450-foot blast into the center-field bleachers where it bounced over the fence, traveling more than 500 feet. At the Stadium on April 22, he slugged his 200th career home run and two triples. The homer went more than 400 feet, the first triple soared 430 feet on the fly, bouncing in front of the center-field flagpole, and the second triple to left-center was almost as long. Early in May he brought the Yankees back from a 4–0 deficit with two homers and a game-winning triple in the 10th inning.

In 1938, after his return from his holdout, DiMaggio had been booed in all the towns in the league, and the loudest and longest ones came at the Stadium.

"It got so I couldn't sleep at night," DiMaggio had said then. "I'd wake up with boos ringing in my ears. I'd get up, light a cigarette and walk the floor sometimes till dawn."

During June he was in a protracted slump, struggling to bring his batting average to the .300 level, and once again he was hearing boos all along the circuit, with the loudest ones in New York.

By July, thousands of Japanese had been herded into relocation camps and Nisei, second-generation Americans of Japanese ancestry, were exempted from the draft, the government disavowing their loyalty. Leaders in the Italian-American community in government, politics, and industry had been using their influence to ameliorate the status of Italian aliens. The Japanese had no such recourse.

The nation was on a war footing and baseball had to do its part, too. It scheduled two All-Star Games, with the Army and Navy Relief Funds to be the beneficiaries. To assure a bigger crowd, the regular game between the league all-stars was shifted from Ebbets Field in Brooklyn, with only a 35,000 seating capacity, to the more spacious Polo Grounds, where 54,000 could see the game. It was a routine game, with the American League winning by a score of 3–1. The big show was the next night, July 7, when 62,094 turned out to watch the American League stars against a team of All-Service stars, managed by Lieutenant Mickey Cochrane, at Cleveland. Cochrane's team was made up of former big leaguers now in service and was led by Chief Boatswain's Mate Bob Feller, who gave up four hits and three runs and who was the losing pitcher in a 5–0 decision. But the game, which raised $120,000 for the service relief funds, gave ample evidence that a war was on. While the brass reviewed the pregame festivities, hundreds of military vehicles rumbled across the field. Soldiers, sailors, and marines marched in precision, and the Great Lakes Naval Training Station band played martial music.

The Yankees plodded along and won the pennant easily by nine games that season, but somehow they didn't have the flair of the great teams of earlier years. DiMaggio, although he played in all 154 games for the first time, had seemed lackluster although he had been the main cog in the attack. Besides Joe Gordon, who led the club with a .322 average, DiMaggio was the only regular over the .300 mark, with .305. It was only the second time in seven years that he had failed to lead the league in at last one hitting category. He was the team leader with 114 runs batted in, second to Ted Williams' league-leading 137. Williams had taken the Triple Crown, his first, with a .356 average and 36 home runs. DiMaggio had finished with 21 homers and a .498 slugging average, the first time he had dipped below .500. Charlie Keller, with 26 homers, 108 runs batted in, and a .292 batting average, had compensated in good measure for DiMaggio's reduced slugging efficiency. Pitching had been the bulwark that enabled the Yankees to register 103 victories. Five men on the staff accounted for 10 or more triumphs, with Ernie "Tiny" Bonham, a 215-pound right-hander, posting a 21–5 record. Spud Chandler followed with a 16–5 mark, and veteran Red Ruffing won 14 and lost 7. Hank Borowy, a rookie up from the Newark Bears, had a 15–4 record and Atley Donald, another Newark alumnus, captured 11 games and lost only 3. The staff led the league in complete games pitched, with 88; shutouts, with 18; saves, with 17; earned-run average, with 2.91; and fewest bases on balls allowed, with 431.

Still, the war would go a long way toward breaking up the Yankees, as it already had done in breaking up the Papas on Fisherman's Wharf.

The St. Louis Cardinals, under Manager Billy Southworth, had overtaken Brooklyn with a late-season surge and had won the National League pennant by two games. Their lineup boasted Enos Slaughter and Terry Moore, and a rookie named Stan Musial, in the outfield. They had logged 106 victories and their pitching was good. But as World Series rivals of the Yankees, who had not lost in the postseason classic in 16 years, they were given little chance. Even Cardinal fans were taking odds that their team couldn't dethrone the Yankees.

In the opener at St. Louis, the Cardinals made four errors, as the Yankees routed Mort Cooper, a 22-game winner, and had forged a 7–0 lead going into the home half of the ninth. Red Ruffing had set a Series record with 7 2/3 hitless innings, his bid for a no-hitter spoiled by Moore's single. Then suddenly the Cardinals chipped away with six hits and four runs before Chandler, who saved Ruffing's record seventh Series victory, got Musial on a bases-loaded grounder to first for the third out. The Yankees had won by a score of 7–4, but the Cardinal rally in the ninth had become an omen.

Musial delivered a game-winning single in the second game and a brilliant throw by Slaughter from right field cut down Tuck Stainback at third base in the ninth with the potential tying run. Ernie White shut out the Yankees for the first time in World Series play since 1926, turning them back with only six singles, 2–0. The Cardinals won their third in a row in the fourth game by a score of 9–6 with a three-run rally in the eighth. They needed one more victory to give the Yankees a taste of what it was like to lose four straight World Series games.

The last time the Yankees had lost a World Series had been in 1926, and the Cardinals, led by Rogers Hornsby, had turned the trick after Grover Cleveland Alexander, already the holder of more than 300 big-league triumphs, and the winner the previous day, saved the 3–2 victory for Jesse Haines by striking out Tony Lazzeri with the bases filled in the seventh and deciding game.

The Yankees relied on Ruffing against young Johnny Beazley in the fifth game. They were locked in a 2-all tie going into the ninth with a crowd of 69,052 on the edge of its seats. Walker Cooper opened the ninth with a sharp single to center. Johnny Hopp sacrificed him to second, bringing up George "Whitey" Kurowski, a rookie third baseman, who drove one of Ruffing's pitches deep into the left-field stands inside the foul line for a home run. It was the biggest upset in a World Series since 1914, when the Boston Braves swept the Philadelphia Athletics in four games.

It had been a busy Series for DiMaggio. He batted .333 with three runs batted in and he set a Series fielding record with 20 putouts for five games. But he had been unable to come through with the big, decisive hits that sway the outcome. His seven hits were all singles.

DiMaggio had driven in a run in the fourth with a single off Beazley to put the Yankees ahead, 2–1. In the fifth he got his best chance to get the big hit. Ruffing beat out an infield hit. Phil Rizzuto was safe when Hopp threw away a double-play ball for an error, one of four in the game by the Cardinals. Red Rolfe hit another potential double-play ball to Jimmy Brown at second base. Brown fumbled the ball for his second error and the Yankees had the bases filled with one out.

The 23-year-old Beazley got Roy Cullenbine on a pop fly to shortstop. DiMaggio had been hitting well, but Beazley made him hit on the ground, a sharp bounder to Kurowski at third who gobbled it up and made the force play to end the threat.

In the Cardinal clubhouse after the game the scene was bedlam. "We beat the Yankees. We beat them in their own backyard," the players shouted. They mobbed Kurowski, literally ripping the pants off him. Amid the din there was pushing and shoving, everyone seemed to be hoisted shoulder high; Commissioner K. M. Landis lost his hat and Branch Rickey his overcoat.

"We took 'em and we took 'em good, in clean, honest fashion," said Manager Southworth. "It's an honor to beat a team like the Yankees. If ever a bunch of fellows was typical of American youth this bunch of mine is. I told Beazley to throw breaking balls high and inside to that DiMaggio fellow, and we stopped him with them. We stopped the Yankees, too."

The Yankee dressing room was silent. For Manager McCarthy it was his first Series defeat as the Yankee pilot and his first since Connie Mack's A's beat his Chicago Cubs in 1929. It was the first time, too, that DiMaggio had been on a Series loser.

"They're a good ball club, and they beat a good ball club," McCarthy said. "They deserve all credit, but my boys weren't disgraced. That's what I told Southworth. The spotlight's on him now."

Spud Chandler was among the players who stopped to say goodbye to McCarthy.

"I'm sorry we let you down," Chandler said.

"Maybe I let you fellows down," McCarthy said. "Maybe my judgment was bad."

Someone had broken up the Yankees, at last.

For many of the players now the future was undecided. The war would cut short many careers and rob some, DiMaggio among them, of their prime years.

On October 12, Columbus Day, one heavy burden was lifted from DiMaggio's shoulders. President Roosevelt declared that Italians were no longer to be considered enemy aliens. The Papas could go back to the Wharf, and DiMaggio might choose to stroll with them again.

On December 3, DiMaggio's wife was in Reno, Nevada, where she engaged a lawyer ostensibly to begin filing a divorce suit. They had been married for three years and 14 days. He had already felt the stings of public criticism of high-priced ballplayers who seemed slow to respond to the national emergency. If he were divorced it would change his status in the draft and at 28 make him subject to call at any time. He had returned home this time without a World Series championship ring, but when the New Year rolled in that would seem trivial compared with other matters he would have to think about.

9

Uncle Sam Calls Balls and Strikes

IMAGGIO WAS A man filled with a sense of pressure and urgency in his personal problems after the disappointing 1942 World Series. His marriage, while not yet completely on the rocks, was going through rough water. His wife had already established residence in Reno, Nevada, the divorce capital of the nation, and odds were better than even that she would go through the long process of winning one. The marital strife would also cast a new light on his future classification in the military draft. Like many a spurned lover trying to effect a rapprochement, he followed his wife to Reno.

Early in January the Yankees announced that they would abandon plans to train in Florida for the 1943 season, in compliance with government travel restrictions, and would choose a new site up north. As if by coincidence, Prescott Sullivan, a sports columnist for the *San Francisco Examiner*, and DiMaggio became embroiled in a controversy that pointed up DiMaggio's confused state of mind.

Sullivan, who wanted to write about how training in the cooler North might affect DiMaggio's training regimen, wanted to check with DiMaggio, who was known to abhor the cold. Sullivan had learned that DiMaggio had followed his wife to Reno. Sullivan had started out simply wanting to get DiMaggio's personal reaction to the Yankees' training announcement, but as it developed, the story had grown into one that would now have to include reactions to the marriage breakup. He phoned DiMaggio in Reno.

"What effect is the absence of spring training in Florida likely to have on your play this season?" Sullivan asked DiMaggio.

"Spring training won't concern me this year," DiMaggio said brusquely.

"You mean you're quitting baseball?" Sullivan said, sensing perhaps a bigger story than he had set out to get.

"I'm not saying, you can draw your own conclusions," a perturbed DiMaggio answered, not measuring his words.

"You mean you're going to announce your retirement? Or do you intend to enlist in the Army or Navy?" Sullivan pressed him. "Are you trying to reconcile with your wife?"

"None of your business," DiMaggio said angrily. "I'll be back in town in a couple of days, then I'll tell you what I'm going to do. I'll see you later." DiMaggio banged down the phone.

The next day Sullivan wrote that DiMaggio had decided to enlist, that he would not be back in baseball for the coming season, and that he had gone to Reno to seek a reconciliation with his wife.

Two days later, DiMaggio was back in San Francisco. He said his remarks were misquoted and misrepresented by Sullivan and denied he had implied that he was retiring or enlisting in military service. Sullivan said DiMaggio had used strong language in denying what he had written.

DiMaggio seemed to be wallowing in confusion and indecision. His friends were giving odds that he would ask his draft board to change his classification and grant him permission to enlist in the next few days. His brother Dom had already enlisted in the Coast Guard.

DiMaggio was back in Reno on January 13, apparently just in time to forestall a divorce since his wife had just completed the legal residency requirement.

Arm in arm and smiling for photographers, the couple announced that they had patched up their differences and were back in each other's good graces. DiMaggio said that indeed he planned to enlist for military duty.

"We're very happy about it all," his wife said.

"Everything is straightened out," DiMaggio said. "I'm going to try to get into the armed forces as soon as I can get a few things straightened out. I really don't know which branch I'll try for, but I'll be in somewhere pretty soon."

Most major league clubs issued complimentary statements when their star players left to join the service. The Yankees issued a similar one when they learned about DiMaggio's plans.

"I wish him Godspeed," Barrow said in New York, "and good luck. We are perfectly in accord with anybody who wishes to serve his country. Joe will make a fine soldier."

Then, reverting to business as usual, he added that center field on the Yankees was open to anybody who "could make the grade." Barrow, however, had already thought of the contingency of losing DiMaggio and had acquired Roy Weatherly, a journeyman center fielder, from the Cleveland Indians, as a stopgap.

McCarthy, from his farm in Buffalo, New York, said: "Whatever he does is his affair. I have nothing to say."

A week later, DiMaggio's status once again became unclear and caused embarrassment in many quarters. Enlistments in the Armed Forces had been halted by orders of the Selective Service System. The

North Beach draft board, with which DiMaggio had registered as a resident of that area, became bogged down in red tape. For DiMaggio to get immediate induction into active service, the local board members would have to make a special ruling in his case and reach unanimous agreement on it.

In a story released by The Associated Press, DiMaggio denied that he was going to enlist, saying he was leaving his military status "in the hands of my draft board." Earlier, Barrow had received a letter from Joe Devine, the Yankee scout in California, who said he had talked to DiMaggio's brother Tom, who had indicated that DiMaggio's plans were to enlist as soon as he had received clearance from the draft board.

"I don't know any more about it now than the next guy," an exasperated Barrow said. "What's more, until I hear directly from Joe, I'm through talking about DiMaggio."

Finally, on February 16, the mix-up came to an end. The North Beach draft board had cleared the way for DiMaggio to trade his $43,750-a-year salary for $50 a month and an olive drab Army Air Force uniform.

Neal Callaghan, the chairman of DiMaggio's draft board, said, "He wanted to get into the service right away and this [the special ruling] was the only way open now that enlistments had been stopped. He wanted immediate action and we gave it to him."

"This desire to join the Army isn't anything recently born," DiMaggio said. "I seriously entertained the thought immediately after the World Series last fall, but private and domestic troubles curved my mind a little away from the Army. They can put me where they think I'll do the most good. I haven't asked for anything special. All I know is I'm to report for a physical examination tomorrow morning at 7:30."

He waived the traditional short leave given to new inductees and was sent directly to the Reception Center at Monterey, California. His wife and 16-month-old son would move to the Los Angeles area and live in Hollywood to be near him.

For his first tour of duty he was stationed at the Santa Ana Army Air Field, where he was assigned to Special Services and played for the baseball team. He was the only major leaguer on the team. While he was easily the top attraction, he took a lot of criticism and booing from the airmen when the club was not doing well. Most of the games were against area college teams and the pitching left something to be desired. DiMaggio complained that once he spent more than 45 minutes in the outfield chasing hits. He put up with the mild irritations, realizing his tour at Santa Ana was good duty and allowed him to visit his wife and son often.

Those visits, however, did not help mend his marital problem and the reconciliation foundered. On October 11, 1943, his wife sued for divorce on the grounds of cruelty. She asked for custody of the boy, $500 monthly alimony, and $150 a month for child support. Early in 1944 she was granted the divorce.

For DiMaggio's mother and father, brothers and sisters, who were practicing Catholics, the divorce was a disappointment. They had worked hard to make Dorothy a welcome and loved member of the family. Joe's loss of custody of his son was the hardest blow of all to take. Still, regardless of their religious views, their first loyalty was to their son and brother no matter which party was at fault in the breakup. It had caused tempers to flare, tension, and misunderstanding but the family remained a unit that never wavered in its support of Joe.

DiMaggio was promoted to staff sergeant and was transferred to Honolulu to play for the Seventh Army Air Force team, which was building a powerhouse with former major leaguers and which had its eye on the Far Eastern service title. Among the big leaguers on the base, besides DiMaggio, were Joe Gordon of the Yankees, Walt Judnich of the St. Louis Browns, Dario Lodigiani of the Chicago White Sox, Myron McCormick of the Cincinnati Reds, and Gerry Priddy of the Washington Senators. Judnich and Priddy had been Yankees for a brief time and Lodigiani was a San Franciscan who had played on the same high school team with DiMaggio's brother Dom. Joe had been acquainted with all of them.

On June 3, the day of their arrival in Honolulu, the players were greeted by Brigadier General William F. Flood, chief of staff of the Seventh Army Air Force.

"If any of you men can't make our team," the general said, trying to inject a touch of humor, "we've lots of planes on our line that need shining up. We've also got a lot of small islands around the Pacific."

The brass and servicemen expected great things from this veritable all-star team, but DiMaggio warned them early to "keep your shirts on."

"I've had a baseball uniform on once in the last three months," he said, "and we all need a little time to get into shape."

The team was easily the class of the Far East and DiMaggio set a blistering pace. In 90 games, he batted .401 before he was sidelined with a stomach ailment.

Near the tail end of the 1940 season, DiMaggio had developed a mild case of ulcers. He had been troubled by it off and on, but never required extensive medical treatment. Now the condition seemed to have been aggravated by several factors—his divorce and worry over his son's welfare, the shifting of military assignments, even the change in food and climate. On August 18 he was out of the Seventh Air Force team's lineup and was hospitalized for three weeks. Rumors spread that he might be given a medical discharge. The team's manager, Lieutenant Thomas Winsett, denied the reports and said DiMaggio was "expected back with the team in the near future." But his bout with ulcers and his hospital confinement ended his career as an Army Air Force baseball player.

With only routine duty keeping him occupied now, DiMaggio became a restless soldier. He was still carrying the torch for his former wife, his ulcers were not improving, and he had not seen his son for almost a year.

Late in September he was transferred again, leaving the Special Service assignment to join the Air Transport Command, a duty that included, for those lucky enough to draw it, flying hops between Honolulu and the California mainland. The flights brought wounded troops home and returned with replacements and supplies.

DiMaggio's Air Force friends were saying that he was still in love with his former wife, that if he got a flying assignment he would snap it up quickly so he could get home to see her. He had telephoned her frequently from Honolulu.

"They are really in love," one close friend said. "It seems it took a divorce to straighten out their difficulties and make them realize how much each loved the other. Joe telephoned Dorothy recently. He was anxious to be reunited."

It was as if DiMaggio had refused to accept the divorce, hoping it had all been a bad mistake and that things could be patched up for the sake of his son, for whom there was nothing he wouldn't do.

DiMaggio's style as a husband had some of the ingredients that inevitably might have led to a strain between him and his wife. They were very happy the first year, and the birth of the boy brought them even closer. She had given up her movie career and had concentrated on keeping house, pasting up DiMaggio's scrapbook, and taking lessons from Mama DiMaggio on how to cook some of her husband's favorite Italian dishes. But DiMaggio enjoyed staying out with his buddies into the early morning, too, and his constant traveling as a ballplayer and celebrity kept him away from home for more than six months a year.

The ulcers persisted. In mid-October DiMaggio returned to the Pacific Coast for medical observation and treatment at the Fourth Air Force Hospital. The Air Force, which earlier had described the problem as a stomach ailment, now refused to disclose the nature of his illness. After a three-week stay he received a 21-day furlough. He flew east to New York, where his wife was now living with his son. If possible he would try to patch up their rift. She was now working as a singer on radio and in nightclubs. DiMaggio took a room at the plush Chatham Hotel at 48th Street and Vanderbilt Avenue, not far from the Adams Hotel, where his former wife now lived.

During the furlough he held a news conference at his old haunt, Toots Shor's restaurant, mostly to renew his acquaintances with old friends and cronies and to oblige sportswriters who had helped his career along.

The subject of his rumored medical discharge came up.

"I will not request a medical discharge," he said. "Of course, if the Army decides to release me, that is beyond my control. Like the rest of the G.I.'s, I just do what I'm told."

The Air Force had ordered him to report to the Redistribution Center at Atlantic City, New Jersey, when his furlough time was up, so he would still be within easy reach of New York.

The ulcers had kept him on a rigid diet. He had lost 25 pounds, down to 187, but he appeared trim and well groomed in his tailored, olive drab uniform.

"That G.I. issue looks pretty sharp, Joe," one sportswriter said, "who's your tailor?"

"It's Regular Army issue," DiMaggio said quickly. "But the G.I. uniforms are a little skimpy. I just have them fixed up a little.

"I'm on a strict diet now," he continued. "I have to eat all soft foods. Of course, every once in a while I get a craving for something . . . well, never mind that. But Toots Shor has good food here, wonderful food."

"Will you be looking up your former wife?" a reporter asked.

"I was afraid you'd ask that," he said. "Well, you can say everything is just the same, nothing has changed. Sure, I came here to see her. I have a son, too, don't forget. I haven't seen the baby for over a year."

Was he seeking a reconciliation? Weren't there rumors circulating that he and Dorothy might get remarried?

"It would be sticking my neck out to answer that one, wouldn't it?" DiMaggio said.

It was not an idle question. It would take DiMaggio a long time to make a final break with this woman. Just as there were rumors now that he might remarry her, there were similar ones after his discharge from service when he was seen with her frequently and friends thought for certain they would be reunited. In the summer of 1946, however, DiMaggio lost all chance when his former wife married George Schubert, a stockbroker. He had by this time been allowed alternate weekend visits with his son. After his retirement, and after Dorothy had divorced Schubert, DiMaggio was once again rumored to be considering remarriage to her. His son now was enrolled at the exclusive Black Fox Military Academy and lived with his mother in Los Angeles. DiMaggio visited there often. By 1952, however, the relationship had apparently deteriorated to the point where she had taken him to court to seek an increase in child support.

Dorothy charged that since Joe was now in the six-figure income bracket he was obligated to increase his support for his son, which was then at $300 a month. DiMaggio countered that ex-wife was using the boy's support money personally. She had demanded an increase to $1,000 a month.

At a hearing in Superior Court in Los Angeles on October 16, 1952, Judge Elmer Doyle issued a decision and made comments that would have made a later generation of women's liberation advocates bristle with anger.

Judge Doyle ruled against Miss Arnold, stated that $300 a month was generous by the standards of the day and suggested to her that she had "made a mistake" in divorcing DiMaggio in the first place, and characterized DiMaggio as "a sportsman" and an exemplary father and citizen. She apparently had cooked her own goose when she had testified that she had received $2,000 extra from DiMaggio in the previous year—a gift occasioned when she had told Joe that she intended to sell a mink jacket—a gift he had given her, no doubt in better days. The press pursued the fuss. "DiMag Cracks Another

Homer" and "Miss Arnold Strikes Out in Court" were among the bromides contained in headlines.

But it was still October 1944 and at the news conference at Toots Shor's a waiter went up to DiMaggio and spoke a few words in Italian.

"I lived in San Francisco 35 years ago," the waiter said, "when you were a little boy."

"When I was a little boy?" DiMaggio blurted out to the waiter. "I wasn't even born yet. I won't be 30 until next month. Don't make me older than I am."

The reunion was a happy occasion and reminded everyone of DiMaggio's playing days in New York when things seemed brighter and there was no war.

He found time to pay a visit to Barrow at the Yankees' headquarters and to chat about the Yankees' prospects for the coming season. He had learned that the Yankees would train at Atlantic City for the 1945 campaign and he raised Barrow's beetle eyebrows when he told him that he was going to report to the New Jersey resort city after his furlough had ended.

"Atlantic City?" Barrow said, "but that's where we're training next season."

"I mean the Atlantic City Redistribution Center," DiMaggio said. "I've been transferred there."

They broke into laughter.

DiMaggio's stay at Atlantic City lasted almost six months. He was assigned to the physical training section of Special Services. In August of 1945, with the war in Europe ended, he was sent to the Don Cesar Convalescent Hospital in St. Petersburg, Florida, where his condition was diagnosed as a duodenal ulcer. He had only 85 points toward a discharge, not enough at that stage of the war to get a release from the service. The only way he could make it out of the Army would have to be on a medical discharge or through orders from Washington. With the collapse of the Japanese in mid-August following the atomic bombings of Hiroshima and Nagasaki, his discharge became a routine matter.

On September 14, with two weeks of the regular baseball season still remaining, DiMaggio mustered out of the Army, his medical disorder no doubt helping to hasten his release.

While he had been in the hospital he had received a phone call from Larry MacPhail, the new president of the Yankees who, together with

Dan Topping, a marine captain and a millionaire sportsman, and Del Webb, a construction and hotel tycoon, had bought the team from the Ruppert heirs for $2.8 million. MacPhail, who had been an Army colonel and had been part of a group that had tried to kidnap the German Kaiser after World War I, wanted to be certain that as a part owner and director of the Yankees' operations he would have the services of one of baseball's best known stars when the 1946 season began. He assured DiMaggio that his job was still his and that he could expect a real welcome from the Yankees. A verbal agreement was reached over the phone, with MacPhail offering DiMaggio his prewar salary.

On November 20, dressed once again in his conservative double-breasted suit and highly polished black shoes, DiMaggio formally signed for the 1946 season at Yankee headquarters. This time, MacPhail, not Barrow, was presiding and DiMaggio knew he was to open a new chapter of his career.

10

A
Disappointing
Comeback

*P*RESIDENT ROOSEVELT HAD been dead a year, the guns of World War II had been silent for eight months, and Harry Truman resided in the White House when the 1946 baseball season got under way. Anticipation filled the air. Baseball fans, like the rest of the nation, awaited a return to normalcy. Major league officials set their sights on record attendance and profits. After four wartime years, they predicted a resurgence of interest in the game with the return of the big-name stars.

During the war, baseball solidified its place as G.I. Joe's favorite sport. Makeshift baseball diamonds sprang up in the jungles of New Guinea and Okinawa and the dusty fields of North Africa, France, and Italy. Daily broadcasts of major league games were beamed overseas by the Armed Forces Radio to American outposts and were popular diversions from the danger and monotony of the war. Baseball had kept its old friends and had made many new ones.

At the height of the war, *Yank,* the popular Army weekly newspaper, published a widely circulated humorous cartoon depicting baseball as a morale booster among the troops. It showed a G.I. arguing the decision of an umpire—an officer, naturally.

"Thank you for quoting me the rules, Corporal," the officer-umpire says as he draws a little book from his shirt pocket. "Now let me quote you the Articles of War."

Among the stars who were mustered out of their olive drab government issues and blue-bottoms were Ted Williams, Stan Musial, Bob Feller, Barney McCosky, Dick Wakefield, Johnny Mize, Joe Gordon, Johnny Pesky, Walt Judnich, Tommy Henrich, Charlie Keller, Hank Greenberg, Phil Rizzuto, Pee Wee Reese, Dom DiMaggio, Pete Reiser, Enos Slaughter, Red Ruffing, Warren Spahn, Johnny Sain, Kirby Higbe—and, of course, Joe DiMaggio.

The returning Yankees found the team under new ownership. MacPhail had shifted his allegiance and money from Brooklyn, where he had been vice-president of the Dodgers, to the Bronx. He would run the show for Topping, who also owned the pro football Dodgers and Yankees, and Webb, who had been a semipro pitcher. Topping, who had married and divorced Sonja Henie, the Olympic figure skater, was working on his fourth marriage, and Webb, who belonged to 14 golf clubs across the country, was always on the lookout to develop new businesses. They both had vast amounts of money and the Yankees served them, if not as a plaything, then as a vehicle for publicity and public relations goodwill in bigger enterprises. George Weiss, a master builder of the minor-league farm system, was now the general manager.

DiMaggio had discovered that MacPhail's casual business manner had made it easy for him to come to terms, even though the quick signing of his contract had become a necessity. He owed the Internal Revenue Service three years of back taxes after being in the service.

"I owe Uncle Sam three years in back taxes and he's crowding me," DiMaggio said. "My attorney's trying to work out a deal, but he says, how can you get blood out of a turnip?"

Late in the fall of 1945 and into the new year, DiMaggio trained diligently at the New York Athletic Club—pedaling a stationary bicycle, lifting weights and jogging around the track. Still nursing his ulcers, he was aware that his 31-year-old body needed careful attention and tuning up. He had not played baseball—not even service games—for a year and a half. He saw his return in all its dimensions and ramifications. He had to be certain of what his body could and could not do. It was like starting again as a rookie and he had much to protect. Although his marriage had failed, his 4-year-old-son, Joe Jr., was starting to make demands on his famous father's time. There was also the possibility that with baseball expecting a resurgence and television entering the sports market, he could win more lucrative contracts if he performed at his prewar level. He had to be ready.

Before he entered the Army, DiMaggio had been an unsmiling, poker-faced, colorless personality. His innate shyness seemed to keep people at a distance. It went a long way to characterize him as a loner who was comfortable only among close friends and associates whom he felt he could trust. In the service he had been shifted to several different bases and was forced into contact with many different types of personalities. He saw first hand what his exploits as a famous athlete meant to the average G.I. The experience, he said later, did a lot for him in terms of opening himself up to strangers. He felt more at ease than ever before. He had gained a new insight, a new sense of celebrity he had not been aware of previously. Now instead of seeing himself as revolving simply around his New York circle of friends and acquaintances, he discovered his persona extended beyond the Hudson and East Rivers and the narrow confines of Broadway. He became more vocal and communicative, with both the press and his teammates.

His early association with Joe Gould, the boxing manager, had brought him into a circle of misfits. Gould, a brash, aggressive person who fancied himself an entrepreneur, presumed to speak on some occasions for DiMaggio. His role, whether instrumental or not, in the player's holdout in 1938 left the general impression that Gould did indeed go to bat for DiMaggio. But the time he spent in military service made DiMaggio aware of his own naiveté.

"I was strictly bush in those days," DiMaggio said, "and I guess I liked sitting around with the big shots of Broadway. It took me a long time to realize that Gould and those fellows were using me to dress up their act."

His contract talks with MacPhail were the most genial he had had since he had joined the Yankees.

"This was the first time I ever had business with MacPhail," DiMaggio said, "and in no time at all we had come to terms. Very satisfactory terms, too. This much I can say for sure, MacPhail's easier to do business with than Ed Barrow was. Barrow was always thinking I had a business manager and he'd grumble he had no use for ballplayers who had managers. The fact is I never had a manager in my life, although it was generally supposed I did. Even Landis called me in on that."

With wartime travel embargoes lifted, the Yankees were booked to start training early in February in Panama and DiMaggio had pushed up his training schedule so he could be with the team. The workouts at the New York Athletic Club were designed to get his legs into shape.

"I'm not so concerned about making a comeback," he said, "not if I can get my legs in shape. If your legs are right, your timing is right and everything else falls into line. You know, all those good pitchers are going to be back and it's not going to be easy to get base hits. That's why I want to be in real shape for that opening game."

But 1946 would be a grueling season for DiMaggio. He took the trip to the Canal Zone seriously. He had played his last previous game with a service team in June 1944. On February 19 at Balboa he slugged his first home run since then. He clouted 14 home runs in spring training and everything pointed toward a brilliant comeback.

The Yankees, however, were having internal troubles. Joe McCarthy was not happy with the new ownership. He and MacPhail had irreparable differences. Before the season was two months old McCarthy was out as manager and Bill Dickey had taken over as player-manager. Weiss, eager to find new talent, was scouring the minor leagues, where he knew he could put a finger on many young players fresh out of service and hungry for a chance to break into the major leagues. If it could be said that the Yankees were rebuilding, then it followed that the old-guard players would have to perform outstandingly in order to hold their jobs. Even a player with DiMaggio's status could find his spot in jeopardy.

President Truman was the pitcher of record when the Senators and Boston Red Sox opened the season on April 16 at Griffith Stadium in Washington. Truman, the first southpaw President to throw out the first ball, was an avid baseball fan. He departed from tradition by bringing an entourage of Cabinet members and Justices of the Supreme Court to the park with him. Baseball was to be used by every facet of American life—including politics—to restore the nation to peacetime confidence and tranquillity.

DiMaggio had put in a full spring of training, one of the few times in his career that he had been healthy enough to do it. Of course, in years past several contract disputes had also kept him from joining the team early. But he felt he was not as sharp as he could have been and he got off to a slow start.

He had been nursing a week-old cold when the Yankees met the St. Louis Browns on May 9 at the Stadium. In a woeful experience, which he would avoid talking about later in his career, DiMaggio made two errors in one inning.

The Yankees were trailing 3–1, with one out in the eighth inning, when the Browns' catcher, Frank Mancuso, lofted a fly to center field. DiMaggio drifted under the ball nonchalantly and seemed to have it tucked away. Suddenly, he dropped the ball for a two-base error. Mancuso, running all the way, wound up on second. Nelson Potter, the Browns' pitcher, followed with a double, and the Browns had an unearned run. Glenn McQuillen, the next batter, slashed a single to center field that DiMaggio moved in on, trying to scoop it with his gloved hand. He booted the ball and Potter scored easily from second. The Stadium crowd "booed the Jolter unmercifully."

The Yankees, it seemed, could not untangle their feet. Dickey, who had been manager for a week, didn't get his first victory until the second game of a double-header against the Red Sox on May 26, when DiMaggio hit his 10th home run but little else. Still, despite their lack of sparkle in the field, the Yankees were not short on support from the fans. A crowd of 29,000 turned out on June 4, a Tuesday and usually a day for small crowds. They sent the home attendance to 801,662, the earliest date that figure had been reached by any club in the history of baseball. The postwar resurgence the owners had predicted was coming true. MacPhail had foreseen it all when he phoned DiMaggio in the Florida convalescent hospital late in 1945 and got his agreement to return to the Bronx ball park.

On July 6 DiMaggio rapped a three-run homer, his 17th, and helped beat the Athletics 8–5, but the Yankees were trailing the first-place Red Sox by 6½ games and were hitting poorly. Dickey had dropped DiMaggio behind Charlie Keller to No. 5 in the batting order in an effort to bolster the attack. DiMaggio considered it a demotion and the move did not rest well with him.

Dickey could not recall in his 18 years as a Yankee when so many regulars were hitting below the .250 mark. These included Phil Rizzuto, Snuffy Stirnweiss, Nick Etten, and Joe Gordon—and DiMaggio and Tommy Henrich were not far above that figure.

Then on July 7 in Philadelphia, DiMaggio tore a cartilage in his left knee and sprained his left ankle on a slide into second base. It put him out of the All-Star Game scheduled for Fenway Park in Boston. The game had been suspended in 1945 because of the war and now the fans were eagerly awaiting its renewal and a chance to see the returning stars again. It was the first time since he became a Yankee in 1936 that DiMaggio, who had been selected each year, missed the Dream Game. He was replaced in the lineup in center field by his brother Dom of the Red Sox, who was having a sensational comeback and who finished the season with a .316 batting average.

The knee injury was a recurrence of one DiMaggio had suffered with the San Francisco Seals in 1934. It had almost destroyed his chances of moving up to the Yankees. The ankle injury, not considered serious at the time, was a forerunner of the battles he would wage with bone spurs later in his career.

DiMaggio stayed out of the lineup until August and for all intents and purposes the Yankees were out of the running in the 1946 pennant race. DiMaggio's comeback had been disappointing. He finished with a batting average of .290, his first year below .300. He hit 25 home runs and drove in 95, failing to reach 100 for the first time.

Late in September once again talk of a possible trade of DiMaggio became widespread. But in view of his poor season, many wondered whether any other teams would want him.

Mickey Vernon, a clever hitter and first baseman with the Washington Senators, had won the American League batting title with a .353 average, beating out Ted Williams of the Red Sox, who batted .342. Vernon's hitting had helped the Senators finish in fourth place, a good showing for them. The Red Sox were interested in acquiring Vernon, but the Washington manager, Ossie Bluege, was cool to the deal.

"No, we'll keep Vernon," Bluege said, "but we could get something for him from New York."

"Do you mean Joe DiMaggio?" a reporter asked.

"That's right," Bluege answered. "You could make the deal right now."

No deal for DiMaggio materialized, of course, but MacPhail and the other Yankees owners were not happy. They had gone through the season with three managers, finishing in third place, 17 games off the pace. The Red Sox easily took the championship, by 12 games, with Detroit the runner-up. The Yankees had gone three seasons now without a championship and the fans would have to wait another year to see whether the three-year wartime layoff had indeed robbed DiMaggio of his natural talents.

Joe DiMaggio, right, as a 21-year-old rookie joining shortstop Frank Crosetti, left, and second baseman Tony Lazzeri, already established stars, to give the Yankees an Italian-American triumvirate from San Francisco in 1936.
(The New York Times)

Getting ready for the 1936 World Series against the New York Giants. DiMaggio batted .323, hit 29 homers, and drove in 125 runs during the regular season. *(The New York Times)*

In 1937, his second season in the major leagues, DiMaggio won the home-run title with 46 and established himself as a bona fide star. Wherever he played throughout the league fans of all ages sought his autograph. *(The New York Times)*

After seeking $40,000 for the 1938 season, DiMaggio finally ends one of the longest Yankee holdouts and signs for $25,000. Colonel Jacob Ruppert, owner of the Yankees, beams beside him while business manager Edward G. Barrow smiles from behind. *(The New York Times)*

Dorothy Arnold, the first Mrs. Joe DiMaggio, cuts wedding cake at reception at DiMaggio's Grotto on Fisherman's Warf. The wedding ended a two-year courtship. She was 21 and he was 24. *(The New York Times)*

When the 1939 Yankees swept the Reds in the World Series, they became the first team in baseball history to win four straight pennants and World Series championships. Here the nucleus of their powerful squad takes the field in Cincinnati. From left: Frank Crosetti, Red Rolfe, Charlie Keller, Joe DiMaggio, Bill Dickey, George Selkirk, Joe Gordon, Babe Dahlgren, Jake Powell, Tommy Henrich, Buddy Rosar, and Arndt Jorgens. *(United Press International Photo)*

Joe welcomes his brother Dom, right, to the major leagues before 1940 game at the Stadium with the Red Sox. The "Little Professor" was in his rookie season as Boston's center fielder, and Ted Williams, center, was the Red Sox sophomore left fielder. Dom batted .301 in his rookie campaign, Williams had a glittering .344 average, and Joe won his second straight batting title, with .352. *(The New York Times)*

DiMaggio's wedding didn't go unnoticed. Besides invited guests, it brought out thousands of curious admirers, fans, and gate-crashers. They jammed the streets and tied up traffic for blocks around the Church of Saints Peter and Paul (note scaffolding and canopy, upper left), where they were married in downtown San Francisco. *(The New York Times)*

Mrs. Joe DiMaggio, in 1940, with scorecard and pencil, large brimmed hat, fur, and orchid corsage, in a reflective mood watching the Yankee Clipper perform in a game at the Stadium. *(The New York Times)*

DiMaggio selecting a bat at the Stadium before going to plate on July 2, 1941, to break Wee Willie Keeler's 44-game consecutive hitting streak. The Clipper broke the mark with a home run against the Boston Red Sox. *(United Press International Photo)*

Teammates hoist DiMaggio onto their shoulders in the Yankee dressing room after he breaks Keeler's record. Player wearing cap is Tommy Henrich. *(The New York Times)*

A somber DiMaggio recuperating after bone spur surgery in winter 1948.
(The New York Times)

After his bone spur operation DiMaggio signed a historic pact for the 1949 season. He became the first $100,000-a-year player. Club owner Dan Topping, left, and General Manager George Weiss, look on. *(The New York Times)*

Slow to recover from bone spur surgery, DiMaggio was unable to play in the Yankee opener in 1949 and he would miss the first 65 games. He is escorted to the Stadium dugout by an admiring Casey Stengel, who was making his managerial debut with the Yankees. *(The New York Times)*

"Old Soldiers Never Die..." General and Mrs. Douglas MacArthur
meet the Yankee Clipper at the Stadium in 1951, not long
after the general, a DiMaggio fan, was recalled from the Korean War
and dismissed by President Truman. Casey Stengel is at right.
(Ernie Sisto)

DiMaggio made a great comeback in the 1949 season. Here
his 10-year-old son, Joe Jr., a
frequent guest at the Yankee
clubhouse, gets acquainted with
Johnny Lindell, who helped fill
the gap in center field while
DiMaggio was sidelined. *(The
New York Times)*

Flicking away a speck of dirt from his eye, DiMaggio announces his retirement to reporters in New York on December 11, 1951. Flanked by General Manager George Weiss and Manager Casey Stengel, left, and Yankee owners Del Webb and Dan Topping, DiMaggio presented his glove to the Hall of Fame. *(Wide World Photos)*

"Shine your shoes, Joe?" Years after his retirement DiMaggio was still a star attraction at Old-Timers' Day games at Yankee Stadium. Here, Ernie Sisto, an old friend of DiMaggio's and a prize winning photographer for *The New York Times,* gags it up as Mickey Mantle and Ralph Houk, then the Yankee manager, join the shenanigans. *(Ernie Sisto)*

A youthful Joe DiMaggio, top photo, follows through with his famous swing as he blasts a hit during his record streak in 1941. Below, a middle-aged DiMaggio, with a few pounds added, still retained some of the classic style and form while batting in an Old-Timers' Day game 30 years later at Yankee Stadium. *(Ernie Sisto)*

11

Playing Like a Champion Again

*I*N THE FIRST week of 1947 Babe Ruth took a turn for the worse in French Hospital in New York. The first diagnosis of the throat cancer that would take his life a year and a half later had been made. Edward G. Barrow, who had converted Ruth from star pitcher to a star outfielder and sent the Bambino on his way to baseball immortality, retired from the Yankee organization at the age of 79. The Yankees announced that DiMaggio would soon enter a hospital for an operation to remove a bone spur from his left heel. The spur had been discovered after X rays were taken late in the 1946 season, but the club and DiMaggio had said nothing about it at the time.

Barrow's retirement ended an era in which he had been responsible for directing the team, either as general manager or president, to 14 pennants and 10 World Series championships. For all practical purposes Barrow's influence with the Yankees had ended in 1945 with the purchase of the franchise by MacPhail, Topping, and Webb from the Ruppert heirs. He had, however, retained a link to the team as chairman of the board under a three-year contract. It included a clause permitting cancellation after two years, with the payment of a year's salary. Barrow now exercised this option and not reluctantly. Old age and wavering health had taken their toll. He had actually resigned on November 21, 1946, and the Yankees accepted it on December 1, putting it into effect on December 31.

"We are parting on very friendly terms," said Barrow, one of the last of the rugged individualists. "When a man gets to be as old as I am, well, I'm afraid he's getting pretty old."

The Yankees, under MacPhail, were embarking on a new course to assure that fans would continue to patronize Yankee Stadium. Three years without a pennant was a long time measured by Yankee standards. MacPhail leaned heavily on showmanship. He had introduced the giveaway of nylon stockings at Ladies' Day games, fashion parades, and pregame tennis exhibition matches between professional stars as fan attractions. Barrow had only disdain for these gimmicks.

As the president of the corporate Yankees, MacPhail wished Barrow well on his retirement and assured him "there will always be a box at Yankee Stadium available to you, your family and friends and we hope to see you often."

Barrow had joined the Yankee organization on December 31, 1920, after three years as manager of the Boston Red Sox. In 1918, he led the Sox to the American League pennant, their last one until 1946, and the World Series title. As Yankee general manager, he had taken over a poor, disorganized team, torn by dissension and a problem to the league. An archconservative, Barrow, who was once described by DiMaggio as "a nice guy, but one tough cookie," immediately established the authority of the field manager. Besides Ruth, he brought in other talented players, built Yankee Stadium, and laid the groundwork for a vast farm system.

What became known as "the Yankee type" was really a reflection of "the Barrow type." He was such an astute businessman and sure judge of talent that he always was willing to adapt when he saw the practicality of change. At first he saw little merit in developing a farm system, arguing that it was too costly a venture to keep players tied up. However, once he saw the assembly-line benefits it reaped in resupplying the team with topnotch players he invested in it heavily.

Barrow's retirement closed a 51-year career in baseball. He never played in the major leagues, but broke in as a manager in 1895 at Wheeling, West Virginia, where he led the team to the pennant. Then he moved on to Paterson, New Jersey. Before moving to the Yankees from Boston, he had managed at Indianapolis, Toronto, and Montreal, and in the major leagues at Detroit in 1903 and 1904. As a manager he knew the necessity of independence of judgment and decision-making. When he took over in New York one of his ground rules was to bar the owners from the clubhouse. He himself never stepped into the Yankee clubhouse. It assured not only the success of Miller Huggins and Joe McCarthy, his two great managers, but longevity in their jobs, to say nothing of championship teams.

Had Barrow been a younger man at the time of the death in 1946 of Judge Landis, the baseball commissioner, it is likely he would have succeeded the famous judge in that post. Barrow had been shaped in the same mold as Landis and many of his friends and club owners tried to persuade him to take the job. He declined on the grounds of health and advancing age.

MacPhail, of course, as the originator of major-league night baseball, was hell-bent on making playing at night seem as normal as playing in the sunshine, and he succeeded fabulously. Barrow, however, had an aversion to the night game and would have resisted it—perhaps more because of a personal incident than anything else—at least until he saw its practical, money-making attributes.

When Barrow managed at Paterson, the club had scheduled a night game against Wilmington. The lighting was so poor that the candle power hardly could have exceeded that given off by Japanese lanterns at a lawn party. Going into the late innings, the Wilmington pitcher, a practical joker, substituted a Fourth of July firework for the ball when he faced Barrow's bowlegged cleanup hitter. The pitcher threw and the batter lashed into the ball, exploding the firework in a resounding pyrotechnic eruption. Singed by the explosion, the hitter chased the pitcher to the center-field fence and the game ended in a brawl among players and fans.

The bowlegged hitter, of course, was Honus Wagner, Barrow's first great talent discovery. According to the historians of ancient baseball, Wagner had been discovered by Barrow throwing rocks great distances into the Monongahela River from the banks of the small town of Carnegie, Pennsylvania, not far from Pittsburgh. The Flying Dutchman, as Wagner was known, signed with Barrow for $125 a month, then moved on to star in the big leagues at shortstop with the Pirates. He was among the first five players inducted into Baseball's Hall of Fame.

With Barrow's retirement the last vestige of the Murderers' Row Yankee teams had faded. McCarthy, who had succeeded Huggins, had departed in 1946, giving way to Dickey. Now in 1947, Stanley "Bucky" Harris, who had been the "Boy Wonder" manager of the Washington Senators when he was still only in his twenties, was at the helm, MacPhail's hand-picked choice.

DiMaggio and Dickey were virtually the last links to those great teams. The new owners were relying heavily on DiMaggio's leadership, his return to form, and his drawing power to restore their franchise to preeminence.

On January 7, DiMaggio underwent an operation for the removal of a three-inch bone spur from his left heel at Beth David Hospital in New York. The prognosis by the surgeon, Dr. Jules Gordon, was that the heel would mend rapidly and that DiMaggio could be expected to be in condition to commence spring training when the Yankees headed for Puerto Rico in mid-February.

DiMaggio was with the crew who made the 1,600-mile journey to Puerto Rico on February 14. The trip constituted the longest aerial flight over water ever made by a major league club, another of MacPhail's innovations. The surgical cut in DiMaggio's heel, however, was still open and he was taking considerably longer to recover than expected. Twelve days later, after having been unable to work out and with no noticeable improvement in the heel, DiMaggio left for Johns Hopkins Hospital in Baltimore. He would take further treatments and check out the possibility of having a skin graft operation to close the wound. This was recommended by Dr. Mal Stevens, the Yankees' team physician.

At Johns Hopkins DiMaggio lingered through March 9. Under the care of Dr. George Bennett, he was given penicillin therapy in the hope of avoiding a skin graft. Dr. Bennett inspected Dr. Gordon's surgery and said: "That operation was swell, but you never can tell how long these things will keep a man out. A month is a pretty long time, and he may be ready, but I can't say now how soon he'll play again."

The doctors decided a skin-graft operation was necessary. Dr. Edward M. Hanrahan, a Johns Hopkins plastic surgeon, performed the 45-minute surgery on March 11, removing a piece of skin 2 inches long and 1½ inches wide from the upper part of DiMaggio's right leg and grafting it over the 1½-inch open wound. A special orthopedic shoe was designed for him by Dr. Bennett.

By now the Yankees had pitched camp at St. Petersburg, Florida, after leaving Puerto Rico. DiMaggio left the hospital on March 26, limping and wearing a big bandage over his left foot. He immediately took a train for Florida, arriving in camp looking pale and drawn and underweight. He supported himself with a cane. The doctors would not predict when he would be ready to play, but it was obvious he would miss another season opener—for the sixth time in nine seasons. As March passed, the best DiMaggio could do was go through mild calisthenics, and his leg muscles grew weaker. It bothered him because, humiliated by the decline in his average in 1946, he had signed again at the same salary. MacPhail had promised him a bonus of $10,000 if he had a good season.

Harris, of course, was concerned, too. Without DiMaggio he would have to make extensive adjustments in his lineup. For a new manager it wasn't exactly the right foot on which to step out in quest of a championship season.

MacPhail, who liked to run the team from all vantage points, complicated the situation by telling reporters that he was resigned to DiMaggio's absence from the lineup for at least two months after the season opened. Harris did not like MacPhail's negativism and engaged in his first front-office confrontation as the Yankees were preparing to break camp in Florida and head North on their annual swing through the southern states.

DiMaggio had grown irritated by the endless medical intervention and his disappointment over his heel's slowness to heal made him even more touchy. He insisted that he stay behind in Florida and save the wear and tear on his heel while the team was barnstorming through small towns. Dr. Stevens overruled DiMaggio in this instance, contending that the only way he could keep an eye on the player's condition was to have him along with the rest of the team.

"My one object," DiMaggio said, "is to get in shape to play ball and I want that done as quickly as possible. Up to now I have done everything I was told to do, but I think the time has come when I myself ought to have something to say about it. After all, this is my foot and my career is at stake.

"I think the best interests will be served all around if I remain here, do my special exercises under this Florida sun, and get my arms and leg muscles in the best possible shape until such time as I am ready to run hard and take up regular hitting practice.

"Until I am ready to run I see no sense in getting hauled around from town to town. If this program is followed I am confident I'll get into the best shape of my life and perhaps a lot sooner than some folks seem to believe."

Harris talked to Dr. Stevens in an effort to persuade him to see things DiMaggio's way. He got nowhere at first, then resorted to bringing the matter to MacPhail's attention.

MacPhail interceded and suggested that Dr. Stevens also stay behind with DiMaggio to supervise the player's exercises and to monitor his progress. Under these conditions Dr. Stevens withdrew his objections and agreed to remain in St. Petersburg with DiMaggio for two more weeks. The Yankees, meanwhile, would have a stand-in physician with them to take over Dr. Stevens's normal duties.

Two days later, DiMaggio, wearing a loafer shoe on his left foot, went through a two-hour workout. He did no running, but took batting practice against Spud Chandler. He hit Chandler's first pitch high over the left-field wall—foul. Then he cracked three line drives "that would have been hits in any man's league." A week later he ran in the outfield for the first time. By opening day at the Stadium, April 15, he was in uniform and running at three-quarter speed. But he was unable to do anything but watch from the dugout as the Athletics posted a 6–1 triumph.

With the heel mended, DiMaggio was back in action as a pinch-hitter on April 20, but failed to get a hit. On the train heading for Philadelphia that night, he asked Harris to start him the next day against the A's. In the third inning he unloaded a three-run homer off Jesse Flores, assuring a 6–2 victory. He was running almost at his usual speed now and he began to hit consistently.

Early in May, after losing a double-header to the Chicago White Sox, the Yankees were in fourth place. Rumors began to surface that the team was fragmented by dissension. On May 22, the day after DiMaggio slammed a bases-filled double to spark a 5–0 triumph, MacPhail fined six Yankees a total of $250—DiMaggio drawing the heaviest fine of $100.

The fines and the reasons for them were only part of the strife. MacPhail had fined DiMaggio, Charlie Keller, and Aaron Robinson for failing to cooperate with Army Signal Corps photographers. Mac-Phail had given the Signal Corps permission to take pictures of the players with soldiers and members of the Women's Army Corps who were modeling the proposed new Army uniforms. Johnny Lindell, Don Johnson, and an unidentified player were fined for not keeping dinner engagements to which they had accepted invitations. These were public-relations obligations the club expected the players to honor. These "violations" embarrassed MacPhail, who had many friends among the Army's top brass. He was also acutely aware of the value of a good public image, and knew a good promotion when he saw one. At the same time, the Yankees were disgruntled over reports that if they refused to fly to road games in the club's charter plane and chose train travel instead, they would be charged for the train fare by the club.

"This whole business has been steamed up to a degree of importance it doesn't deserve," MacPhail angrily told reporters. "I haven't received any squawks at all from the players I fined, and generally if there is anything wrong, I hear about it right away. We go to a lot of pains to keep our players from being swamped with unreasonable requests by channeling all their invitations through our office. In return we expect them to cooperate when we do ask them to do something. When these incidents were brought to my attention I got a little mad and decided it was time to lay down the law in a way the players would understand. That was all there was to it."

In the new major league players' contract there was a clause binding them to participate in all promotions by a club. With MacPhail using his keen business sense and influence, the club owners were ready and eager now to embark on wholesale public-relations promotions that would attract new fans. The players received no compensation for their roles in the promotions.

"In these cases, we weren't particularly trying to promote anything," MacPhail said, "but we did feel let down at the way in which the players acted."

MacPhail tried later to make amends and returned the fines to the players.

"Give mine to the Damon Runyon Cancer Fund," DiMaggio told him.

After the 1946 season, MacPhail introduced an air-travel plan for the Yankees. Their preseason trips to Panama and Puerto Rico had been successful and a majority of the players favored airplane travel. The Yankees in the original air-travel squad had voted, 40–8, for it and at the end of the 1946 campaign they reaffirmed their wishes with a 30-8 ballot. This encouraged the club to renew its contract with United Air Lines for air travel for the first half of the 1947 season. When objections among the players increased, however, MacPhail put the problem out in the open and took another poll of the players. This one showed 20 players in favor of flying on all road trips, 8 in favor only for long hops, and 8 exclusively for train travel.

"No one on our ball club ever has been told that he has to fly," MacPhail said, "nor will anyone be told that he must fly. Players who prefer to make trips by plane may do so at any time. It is absolutely untrue that the club charged the players who traveled by train on our last trip. We never have done this and never will."

The rift was settled quickly. MacPhail was the kind of quick-acting executive who disliked prolonged squabbles, especially if they cast him in a villain's role. The Yankees acceded to the minority's wishes and because it was club policy for the players to travel as a group, train travel for all games became the club's standard. MacPhail's innovations were certainly delayed a little, but eventually they came to fruition. He knew the Yankees had to be kept reasonably happy if he intended to have a pennant flying over the Stadium once again.

In late May DiMaggio rapped out four hits against the Red Sox in a 17-hit, 17–2 romp and had lifted his batting average over the .300 mark once again. If it were true that "as DiMaggio goes so go the Yankees," now seemed to be the propitious time for a Yankee surge to take place. MacPhail was in seventh heaven on the night of May 26 as 74,747 fans, the largest single-game crowd in baseball history, jammed into the Stadium for a weekday night game. In the fifth inning, DiMaggio belted a three-run homer to stake the Yankees to a 9–3 victory over the Red Sox and it brought him a $100 bonus. The Yankees had staged a pregame home-run-hitting contest and offered $100 to the right-handed and left-handed batter who stroked the most balls out of the park. The contest had failed to produce a homer by a right-handed batter so the prize carried over to the one who connected in the game.

DiMaggio now was on a hitting streak, connecting safely in 16 games. On June 1 he crashed four hits, including two homers, one with the bases loaded, against the Indians at Cleveland. He had made a safe hit in 25 of his last 27 games, fashioning a .468 average in that span on 29 hits in 62 times at bat.

DiMaggio's blistering pace did not go unnoticed by the fans. In late June, the final balloting for the All-Star Game showed they had voted him the major leagues' top all-star, with more than 700,000 votes. The Yankee home attendance on June 25 had gone over the 1 million mark—1,018,082—as 60,090 watched Frank "Spec" Shea, a rookie from Naugatuck, Connecticut, throw a three-hit, 3–0 shutout against Cleveland for his ninth victory. On July 2, DiMaggio smashed this 10th homer in an 8–1 rout of the Washington Senators. A few days later he hit No. 11 as the Yankees swept a double-header from the A's to send their winning streak to eight games just before the All-Star Game.

The Yankees were on the move again. From mid-June to mid-July they reeled off 19 straight victories and made a shambles of the pennant race. DiMaggio, Tommy Henrich, and another surprising rookie named Yogi Berra did the big hitting; Shea and Allie Reynolds, who had joined the Yankees from Cleveland in a trade for Joe Gordon, supplied the clutch pitching, and Joe Page, an uncanny left-hander and DiMaggio's roommate, set records as their No. 1 relief hurler. They had moved into first place on June 15, then fell back briefly. They regained the lead on June 20 and from that date they were never in trouble on their way to their 15th American League title since 1921.

In preseason forecasts the Yankees had been rated to finish no better than third. They had gone through 1946 in disarray, winding up third, five games out of second and 17 out of first, under three managers—first McCarthy, then Dickey, and for the final 16 games, Johnny Neun.

It was a caretaker managerial atmosphere at best and the players were all too aware of it. No Yankee team had won a pennant without the steady hand of a full-time manager. It had not been easy for the regulars to round into condition after returning from military service and an unstable managerial climate did nothing for their morale. DiMaggio had failed to be the catalyst in 1946, but now he had regained his old form, sparking their 19-game winning streak with his hitting and inspiring the players with his leadership once again.

In August DiMaggio was sidelined twice with strained neck muscles and an injured left ankle, but the Yankees were enjoying a 14-game lead and none of the contending teams could overtake them. In the National League, the Brooklyn Dodgers were outdistancing their rivals, too. They did it with a standout rookie, Jackie Robinson, the first black to play in the major leagues, outstanding relief pitching from Hugh Casey, and 21 victories by Ralph Branca. By the end of August, Brooklyn had built a seven-game lead and a Subway Series, last seen in 1941, once again became the topic of conversation for most New Yorkers.

Back in the lineup on September 4, in Washington, DiMaggio hit his 18th homer. MacPhail, en route to New York after a brief vacation at his nearby farm in Maryland, stopped at the nation's capital to watch his team. He was asked if he intended to scout the Dodgers, too. The Yankee president was in a jocular mood, sensing that in a week or so his team would nail down the championship for him. "Why should I?" MacPhail answered, "I've known most of the Dodger players longer than those on our own club."

On September 15, while rain washed out a Yankee game at the Stadium, the Red Sox were losing the first game of a double-header to the White Sox in Boston. The defeat mathematically clinched the pennant for the Yankees, who were leading by 13½ games. For Mac-Phail and Harris the victory was sweet and historic. MacPhail had achieved a championship in both major leagues as an owner and executive on two different clubs. He had been the mastermind behind the Dodgers' 1941 pennant-winner, when they also faced the Yankees in the World Series. Now he had done it again, having exchanged teams. Harris became the first manager to win pennants in his first year at the helm of two different teams. He had been a much-traveled manager in both major leagues and in the minors. As the "Boy Wonder" with Washington in 1924 he had piloted the Senators to the title. He won it again in 1925, and now 22 years later he had another championship team. His opposing manager in the World Series would be Burt Shotton, also a first-year pilot, who had come out of retirement to replace Leo Durocher after Durocher had been suspended for a season by the new commissioner, A. B. "Happy" Chandler, for "conduct detrimental to baseball."

For DiMaggio it was a comeback season in every sense. His batting average returned to respectability at .315 and his 20 home runs and 97 runs batted in earned for him his third Most Valuable Player award and his seventh championship in nine seasons. It was not achieved without pain—he had played hurt and his heel injury would, in large measure, hasten his departure from the baseball scene.

In the Subway Series, DiMaggio had his high and low moments, but it produced some unforgettable events. The Yankees easily took the first two games at the Stadium and the oddsmakers were predicting a fast conclusion—it would not go beyond five games, they said.

At Ebbets Field, the Dodgers rocked Yankee pitching for six runs in the second inning of the third game and it appeared they would get the victory the bookmakers had alloted them. But the Yankees chipped away to close to within a run, 9–8, with DiMaggio and Berra hitting home runs, Berra's in a pinch-hitting role. It was the first pinch homer in Series history. Then in the eighth inning, with Hugh Casey pitching in relief, Henrich walked, Johnny Lindell singled Henrich to third, and DiMaggio, with none out, strode to the plate. He swung softly as if to poke the ball to right field. The ball trickled to the second baseman, Eddie Stanky, who scooped it up, tagged Lindell and doubled up DiMaggio with his throw to first. George McQuinn grounded out and the Yankees lost, 9–8.

DiMaggio was inconsolable after the game.

"I tried to check myself on a slider," he said, "topped it, and lost the ball game."

The fourth game was one of the most dramatic in Series annals. Bill Bevens, a big Yankee right-hander, held the Dodgers hitless for 8 2/3 innings and was on his way to pitching the first no-hitter in a World Series. The Dodgers had scored a run in the fifth without getting a hit. The Yankees had scored in the first and fourth and Bevens continued to stop the Dodgers, despite yielding 10 bases on balls. Then in the ninth, with two out and two men on base (the second man had reached base when Harris ordered an intentional walk), Harry "Cookie" Lavagetto, a pinch-hitter, tagged Bevens for a long double. It was the Dodgers' only hit of the game and the two runners carried the tying and winning runs home. Bedlam broke out on the field as fans and players mobbed Lavagetto. The Dodgers had tied the Series at two games apiece with a 3–2 triumph and Bevens walked off the field a loser after giving up only one hit.

In the pivotal fifth game at Ebbets Field, DiMaggio provided the blow that meant the difference. He slammed a homer with one out and the count 3 and 2 on him in the fifth inning. It stood up for a 2–1 Yankee victory and supported a gutsy four-hit pitching effort by Spec Shea. Despite the homer, DiMaggio was not happy with his performance. He had struck out in the first inning and grounded twice into double plays.

The combination of DiMaggio's home run and Shea's pitching, however, seemed to spark the Yankees emotionally. The scenario of the old pro and the rookie accounting for the fabric of victory led them to carry Shea off the field into the clubhouse after the game. Reporters had to go back to the days of Earle Combs to recall when a Yankee team displayed such brazen emotion for a player's clutch performance. Even DiMaggio, who was usually placid and who never seemed to get excited, was infected by the mood as he roughed up Shea's hair and slapped him on the back. Shea had won the first game of the Series with relief help from Joe Page and had become the first American League rookie to win the opener of a World Series. Now he was basking in even greater glory after his triumph in which he had also driven in the first run with a long single.

"What did you think of my hitting?" Shea was saying now to his teammates. "A few more feet and that would have been a homer, how's that? But we didn't need it. DiMaggio took care of the homer department. I had enough to do with the pitching."

The Yankee bats had made only five hits off four Brooklyn pitchers.

"I hit a fastball for that homer," DiMaggio said, "but I would have liked a couple others instead of those double-play grounders. But Shea made up for our hitting shortcomings. What a game he pitched! What a man!"

The Series returned to the Stadium where 74,065 fans, a Series record, packed the seats for the sixth game. The longest game in Series history was in the offing and it lasted 3 hours 19 minutes. The Yankees used 21 players (six pitchers), the Dodgers 17 (four pitchers).

With four runs in the sixth inning the Dodgers grabbed an 8–5 lead. Shotton revised his lineup to inject more defensive strength into the outfield. Al Gionfriddo, a five-foot-six-inch flashy outfielder who had been tossed in as an extra in the Dodgers' $300,000 deal with Pittsburgh in May that sent Kirby Higbe, an ace right-hander, to the Pirates, was sent to left field. Gionfriddo replaced Eddie Miksis, usually a reserve infielder, who had been in the outfield for one inning and had lost a ball in the sun for an error.

Two men were on base and two were out when DiMaggio went to the plate in the sixth. He drove a tremendous 415-foot drive off Joe Hatten toward the left-field bull pen. Running almost blindly to the bull pen area where he thought the ball would land, Gionfriddo turned around at the last moment, leaned over the bull pen railing and caught the ball. It was a breath-taking catch and one of the most remarkable in a World Series.

DiMaggio thought he had connected for a score tying home run. As he rounded second base and saw that Gionfriddo had made the catch, he kicked the dirt in one of his few displays of anger on the field. Taking his position in center field for the start of the next inning, DiMaggio was still walking around in circles, unwilling to believe that his drive had been caught. In Ebbets Field, the ball would have cleared the left-field roof.

"It certainly would have gone into the bull pen alley for a home run if I hadn't got it," Gionfriddo said afterward. "The ball hit my glove, and a split second later I hit the gate. I knew I had it but I certainly couldn't have said I was going to get it—because how could any guy say he was on the ball all the way on one like that?"

The Dodgers held on and won the game, 8–6, forcing the Series to a seventh and deciding game. Shea started the finale, but lasted only 1 1/3 innings. Bevens got another chance to win a Series game as Shea's relief, but he lasted only 2 2/3 innings. The job was left to Joe Page. The superb left-hander allowed only one hit over five innings in a fitting climax to a remarkable season of relief hurling. The Yankees won, 5–2, and sealed another championship.

DiMaggio rarely lost his temper on the field. He was never thrown out of a game by an umpire for arguing a call. He was known never to have had a locker-room argument with his teammates.

"Joe had too much class for that," Tommy Henrich said years later.

Twice during his career, and each time in a World Series game, DiMaggio came close to losing his cool. His kicking the dirt on

Gionfriddo's catch was one. The other occurred also against the Dodgers, in the 1941 Series at Ebbets Field.

The Dodgers, trailing two games to one, were one strike away from a 4–3 victory in the fourth game and squaring the Series. Hugh Casey, the burly right-hander, struck out Tommy Henrich in the ninth inning, but Mickey Owen, the Dodger catcher, dropped the third strike, the ball rolling out of his grasp. Henrich alertly raced to first and beat Owen's throw. The misplay, scored as a passed ball, hounded Owen the rest of his career. It had given the Yankees a second chance. DiMaggio, Charlie Keller, and Joe Gordon promptly delivered three straight hits and the Yankees wound up with a four-run cluster. They went on to win, 7–4, and took a commanding 3–1 edge in the Series.

The following day, the Dodgers sent Whitlow Wyatt, their ace right-hander who had won 22 games, against the Yankees. Dodger tempers were short after their humiliating defeat the previous day. In the fifth inning Henrich clouted a home run off Wyatt. DiMaggio was the next batter. Wyatt, cautious lest he allow DiMaggio to repeat Henrich's feat, threw several pitches close to the slugger, a usual ploy for a pitcher especially after the preceding batter had hit a home run. Then DiMaggio lofted a long fly to Pete Reiser in center field. By the time Reiser caught the ball DiMaggio was rounding second base and was still angry over Wyatt's brushback pitches.

"Don't worry, the Series isn't over yet," DiMaggio said to Wyatt as he trotted toward the dugout, indicating he would try to even the score for the close shaves by getting a hit on his next turn at bat.

In the next instant, Wyatt suddenly charged at DiMaggio. Within seconds players from both benches and umpires stormed to the infield to prevent the two players from trading punches.

"You couldn't call that a fight," DiMaggio said later. "Whit and I never came within 20 feet of each other. He must have misunderstood me, but I guess I made a silly remark to the effect that the Series wasn't over yet. He did come charging at me, though. He was shaving me pretty close with his pitches. It wasn't unusual for a pitcher to treat a fellow that way after the preceding batter had tagged him for a long one. The players from both benches got between us before we even got close to each other. That was the nearest I ever came to having a fight on the field. As a matter of fact after the game, Wyatt came over to our dressing room and shook hands with me, Johnny Murphy, Joe

Gordon, Lefty Gomez, and a couple of the other slow dressers on the club. He congratulated us for winning the Series."

The Yankees had won the game, 3–1, and captured the Series.

DiMaggio finished the 1947 season a battered, worn out physical specimen. He had suffered through the pain of the bone-spur surgery in the winter and now he faced the prospect of another operation—this time on an ailing right elbow. Harris and Weiss had the title behind them for 1947—they had batted 1.000 on the bottom line. In baseball, as in every industry, last year's bottom line was only as valuable as yesterday's newspaper. Their eyes had already turned to the coming season with the last out of the Series.

If the Yankees were to successfully defend their title in 1948, they would have to take a long look at their inventory: their pitching was spotty; first base needed bolstering; Charlie Keller's return was uncertain (the Yankees had lost him on June 6 for the season after spinal disc surgery), and DiMaggio's elbow problem, coupled with his heel ailment, threatened his baseball future.

He checked in again at Johns Hopkins Hospital on November 9. Weiss had instituted a club policy requiring all Yankee players to have an annual physical examination. If they were found in need of repairs they were to have them done as soon as possible.

DiMaggio was convinced he needed an operation on the elbow, but he tried to minimize its seriousness.

"It looks like another operation," he said two weeks before he was scheduled for it. "But the way I feel, I'll have by best year since the war in 1948. The chip is nothing. I had it for a long time and it didn't bother me, but this year it moved and gave me so much trouble that I had only one good throw a day, that was all."

DiMaggio, whose throwing arm was respected by virtually every baserunner in the game, had felt twinges in the elbow for the first time about a year and a half before. In the middle of the 1947 season he was able to make only one hard throw a game. Other Yankee outfielders helped him cover up the weakness by moving over to assist whenever possible—and the opposition never got wise. He said that during the last part of the season and in the World Series, every time he threw he felt as if he was throwing his arm with the ball.

On November 17, Dr. Bennett, to whom DiMaggio had virtually entrusted his medical future, performed the operation.

"The bone has been resting on a nerve," Dr. Bennett said, "and it must have given him terrific pain every time he threw."

At the hospital, DiMaggio was visited by teammates and friends. He received thousands of letters and telegrams from fans. His early shyness, mistaken for conceit by teammates, was no longer a mask he found difficult to remove. Bucky Harris, a pleasant, amiable gentleman at ease in any company, helped bring him out of his shell. He confided in DiMaggio on baseball strategy and personnel. When Harris was planning to trade Joe Gordon to Cleveland to strengthen the pitching staff, he asked DiMaggio which pitcher they should go after.

"Allie Reynolds," DiMaggio replied without hesitation.

Sitting on the edge of his hospital bed, clad in blue pajamas, DiMaggio displayed his wrist-to-shoulder cast and joked about the souvenirs of his operation. He took a small bottle out of a bureau drawer and showed reporters two small bone particles, one about the size of a large pea.

"That's what the doc took out," he said. "He made two incisions, one on the side to remove the large chip and the other on the back of the elbow. The X rays showed both, and Dr. Bennett said he'd better remove the small one, too, or it would be as large as the other eventually, and then I'd be back here again."

One visitor, Tommy D'Alasandro Jr., the son of the mayor of Baltimore, came into the room carrying a big bunch of bananas. He placed them alongside a large stack of mail. Since he had developed ulcers DiMaggio guarded his diet vigorously. When he longed for a snack he favored pistachio nuts, pumpkin seeds, or bananas.

"It's hard to keep bananas around here," he joked. "I think the nurses eat them for breakfast every morning."

Despite his good humor, DiMaggio had a natural abhorrence for hospitals—he had been in and out of them for most of his career. On November 26, he abruptly left Johns Hopkins, ostensibly on an overnight pass. Hospital authorities said they had expected him to return the next morning to check out officially. He never showed up and the hospital listed him as officially "discharged," assuming he had returned to New York.

12

Pain Amid
a Torrid
Pennant Race

THE PENNANT AND World Series victories of 1947 were the trophies MacPhail personally had set out to win to prove his style could achieve success in baseball. He regarded the game as an attractive business in which to invest, provided it was marketed with flair and showmanship. As a strong-minded executive he had little patience with slower-paced approaches. He was innovative, but brash. He uprooted the Stadium, had large sections of it rebuilt, installed plush cocktail lounges, and the Yankees became the first club in baseball history to go over the 2 million mark in home attendance. It was inevitable that he and Topping and Webb would take divergent views on how to conduct Yankee business. Two days after the World Series had been won they bought out his share for $2 million. Topping took over as chief executive in name only.

The general manager's job now belonged to George Weiss and in that position his influence would broaden widely. Not only would he be able to develop the farm system, his pet project, and channel talent to New York, but he would also call the shots, in most cases, on salaries and in the selection of a new manager when the time came to replace Bucky Harris. Topping preferred to keep an eye on pro football.

Weiss had been thoroughly schooled in the minor-league system before he had moved up to the Yankees. In the Eastern League, at New Haven and other way stations, he already had a reputation as a shrewd appraiser and manipulator of player talent. Under Barrow he had learned what ingredients were essential for a winning team. He was not as conservative as Barrow, but neither was he as liberal as MacPhail. Weiss welcomed MacPhail's departure. It had been apparent for a long time that MacPhail's brash methods would give rise to internal bickering in the front office and that it would spill over to the players.

MacPhail had made public comments early in 1947 that DiMaggio had returned to action too soon. His suggestion that DiMaggio was not in proper condition when he returned and was hurting the team, angered the Yankee star.

"Who the hell does MacPhail think he is?" DiMaggio popped off to his friends.

It was almost a 180-degree turnabout in DiMaggio's opinion of MacPhail. Their first encounter had been cordial. MacPhail, then the new president, welcomed DiMaggio, just out of the service, and made his signing for $43,750 comfortable and easy. MacPhail's verbal pot-shots at DiMaggio had stemmed, of course, from his disappointment at not having won the 1946 pennant. He was laying the blame for that on DiMaggio's poor comeback season. In large measure, DiMaggio had absolved himself from that charge with his fine showing in 1947 when he won the Most Valuable Player award for the third time.

Now DiMaggio had one more bone to pick with MacPhail, who had bailed out of the Yankee picture and left DiMaggio holding an empty suitcase. For two seasons MacPhail had got DiMaggio to play for a salary he was earning before he entered the service. And he had left the team posthaste without fulfilling his promise of a $10,000 bonus to DiMaggio if he had a good season in 1947—which he certainly had. Topping and Webb were not part of the promise, but DiMaggio could remind them of it.

This, plus his statistics for the previous season, gave him some of the leverage he could use in trying to catch up with the salaries of other big stars in baseball who had outdistanced him in earnings. For the last three seasons—including his preservice year of 1942—he had received the same salary, $43,750. It paled against the $85,000 commanded by Bob Feller of the Cleveland Indians, the $75,000 earned by Ted Williams of the Boston Red Sox, and the $80,000 the Pittsburgh Pirates paid Hank Greenberg for one season. DiMaggio's objective was to join the top echelon and it didn't matter to him with whom he would have to do business now that MacPhail was gone.

The Yankees and DiMaggio agreed to conduct their 1948 negotiations in secret. He and Weiss met and talked after the New Year's holiday, which he spent in New York.

"It has been mutually agreed by DiMaggio and General Manager Weiss that no publicity will be given on any details . . . or mention of specific salary terms," a Yankee announcement said.

There were no prolonged, wrenching holdout threats by DiMaggio, no hold-the-line-at-any-cost stubbornness by Weiss as the representative of management. On January 6, the Yankees announced the signing of DiMaggio for $70,000. Only Babe Ruth, at $80,000, had received a fatter Yankee contract.

"I found Mr. Weiss the most pleasant man I've ever dealt with," DiMaggio said, obviously pleased with the outcome. "Mr. Weiss and I had only one other meeting prior to last night. That was last week and at that time we barely touched on salary. We talked mostly about my physical condition."

Weiss, of course, was concerned about DiMaggio's right elbow.

"The arm feels great and I could throw right now," DiMaggio said, indicating that he was fully recovered and that at 200 pounds he was only a few pounds over his playing weight. He was asked what he thought he would have to do during the season to merit the big raise.

"I think help the Yankees win another pennant, of course," he said, "and 35 home runs and 150 runs batted in for me."

The task for DiMaggio and the Yankees, even though they were world champions, would not be easy. Regardless of what he said about his physical condition, DiMaggio could not ignore the bone-spur operation on his left heel of a year earlier and the fact that he had to compensate for it throughout the season. His throwing arm had been vulnerable all season, too, because of his ailing elbow. In a way, DiMaggio had been lucky. An abundance of rain in the spring had not only dotted the early part of the schedule with postponements, but had helped to soften the playing fields.

"The outfields were soft and cushiony, perfect for my bad heel." DiMaggio said. "If the fields had been hard and sun-baked I doubt that I could have stood up under the strain. As it was I could continue to keep going, injured heel and all, while frequent postponements gave me extra and welcome rests."

DiMaggio's medical history wasn't the only one Harris and Weiss would have to be concerned about. Charlie Keller, who had not played since June, had undergone spinal-disc surgery and Spud Chandler, hoping to make a strong comeback after a 9–5 record in 1947 despite leading the league with a 2.46 earned-run average, had had bone chips removed from his pitching arm in the fall. The big right-hander had come back from military service in 1946 and posted 20 victories.

DiMaggio put worries aside after signing his contract and went off to Palm Beach, Florida, for a three-week vacation of deep-sea fishing and golf. He was confident that he could produce his best season in 1948 despite his chronic ailments.

At Griffith Stadium in Washington he opened the season against Mickey Haefner with a "terrific 450-foot swat that soared into the bleachers in dead center field" and then made a "beautiful throw" from center field that nailed Mickey Vernon, stretching a double, at third base for the third out that nipped a Washington rally. The Yankees lost, 6–3, but DiMaggio had satisfied himself that his timing was well-honed and that he could still throw the ball from the outfield with his old authority.

The home opener on April 23 marked the 25th anniversary of the opening of Yankee Stadium and nostalgia choked the fans. Their new pennant was hoisted high atop the rafters and DiMaggio was presented with the Landis Memorial Trophy, symbolic of the league's Most Valuable Player award. The Seventh Regiment Band, which had opened the Stadium in 1923 and had played at every subsequent home opener, paraded again to the center-field flagpole to play the national anthem. An ill and shrunken Babe Ruth, whose three-run homer 25 years before had beaten Boston, 4–1, sat behind the Yankee dugout. Joe McCarthy, who had managed Ruth, Gehrig, and DiMaggio and once was the invincible majordomo of the Bombers, now was piloting the Boston team. The Red Sox won, 4–0, and DiMaggio produced only a single and feebly popped up to the infield with the bases loaded for the third out in the fifth inning.

DiMaggio's bat was not to remain feeble for long. One of baseball's largest day-time crowds—78,431—watched him slug three home runs and a single in the opener of a double-header at Cleveland on May 23. It was the second time he had hit three homers in one game. He had done it in 1937 when he won the American League home-run title with 46.

This time he drove in all six runs in a 6–5 triumph. The feat was more notable in that he connected for two of the homers off Bob Feller, the $85,000-a-year right-hander whose 98-mile-an-hour fastball had made him the highest paid player in the major leagues. DiMaggio's third homer was hit off Bob Muncrief.

From June 20 to June 25 he cracked seven homers—better than one a day. He started the spree at St. Louis with three in a double-header. He hit his first in the ninth inning of the opener for a 4–2 victory. In the second game, he homered in the eighth and again in the ninth, with two men on, to power a 6–3 triumph. The next day at Cleveland, he hit another, No. 15 for the season. He belted No. 16 the following day, and against Feller on June 24 he hit the game-winner in the ninth. At Detroit on June 25, he connected again in the ninth inning, off the Tigers' ace left-hander, Hal Newhouser, but the Yankees lost, 4–2.

The American League pennant race was shaping up as the hottest in history. Cleveland took an early leap forward and was in first place for most of the first half of the season. Boston, 12 games off the pace at the start of June, surged to the top late in July. The Yankees, never in command, hovered within striking distance.

Sore heels and swollen knees put DiMaggio out of the Yankee lineup for one game just before the All-Star Game. It was the only game he would miss during the season, but he could have been out of many more with just cause. The race was so close that the Yankees could not afford to lose him.

Weary and worn, he welcomed the All-Star Game break. Because of his ailments he did not start in the July 13 classic at St. Louis, but he made a pinch-hitting appearance and drove in a run with a long fly in the American League's 5–2 victory. DiMaggio had good reason to limit his action with the All-Stars, but the fans and Harris, the American League manager, were rankled by the defection of Bob Feller, who refused to show up for the game and went hunting instead. Harris blamed Lou Boudreau, Cleveland's manager and the All-Star short-stop, for Feller's defection. Harris claimed Boudreau had encouraged Feller's boycott in order to keep him rested to pitch against Boston and New York the week following the game.

On the train to New York after the game, DiMaggio told John Corriden, a Yankee coach, that he was feeling better and wanted Corriden to ask Harris to start him in the Yankees' next series.

"I didn't know he was feeling that much improved," Harris said, "and I was resigned to get along a few more days without him. But he told Corriden on the train he felt sufficiently rested and would be ready for the Browns. It's amazing how old John finds these things out."

At Yankee Stadium on July 22 Feller and the Indians, now in first place 2½ games ahead of the Yankees, helped draw a crowd of 68,258. It was Feller's first appearance in New York since the All-Star Game and the fans booed him loudly and often. In the fifth inning, with the bases loaded, DiMaggio hit a fastball off Rapid Robert for a grand slam and a 6–5 triumph.

DiMaggio continued his hot pace with six hits in a double-header sweep from the White Sox, getting three singles in the opener and two homers and a double in the second game. Four times in the second game—in the second, fourth, fifth, and seventh innings—the game was held up for 10 minutes each time as youngsters ran out to center field to mob DiMaggio for autographs.

By August 14 he had hit 25 home runs and had driven in 102 runs. The goal he had set in the winter of a 35-homer, 150-runs-batted-in season did not seem out of reach, and the Yankees were still kicking in the pennant race.

The next day the Yankees lost valuable ground, losing twice by 5–3 scores to the A's and 72,468 fans saw the debacle. DiMaggio salvaged his 26th home run with a man aboard in the ninth inning of the first contest and sent it into extra innings. The A's got three runs in the 10th and DiMaggio, swinging from the heels to try to keep the Yankees alive, drove in a futile run with a triple.

The world and baseball were stunned and saddened on August 16 by the news of the death of Babe Ruth. St. Patrick's Cathedral in New York was overflowing with dignitaries and ordinary folk on August 19 for his funeral mass. DiMaggio was the only active player invited to serve as an honorary pallbearer. After the services he took a plane at La Guardia Airport and returned to Washington in time to rejoin the Yankees on the field in the third inning. As if in tribute to the Babe he opened the fourth inning with a single and the Yankees were off on a six-run uprising that produced an 8–1 romp.

An epidemic of pennant fever gripped Cleveland, Boston, and New York. The race grew hotter and fans and ballplayers seemed to tingle from the tension. In Cleveland the business in downtown movie houses dropped 25 percent and motorists had to wait for their gasoline while absentminded station attendants listened to one more play on the radio. A pair of tickets to a Red Sox game in Boston was being bought from scalpers for as much as $30. In New York, one fan reading the box scores on his way to work, tripped over a fire hydrant and banged his head hard enough to need stitches. The usually cool and relaxed DiMaggio was smoking up to a pack of Chesterfield cigarettes a day. On August 26, Boston was in first place, half a game ahead of Cleveland. The Yankees were third, half a game behind Cleveland.

Rumors cropped up that the Yankee household was divided and in turmoil. Weiss and Harris were feuding. Weiss, it was suggested, thought the Yankees by now should have been solidly in front, especially with DiMaggio slugging home runs at his best pace since 1937. Harris was getting flak from all directions from second-guessers who claimed he had mismanaged his front-line pitchers, most notably Spec Shea. After a sensational rookie year and an outstanding World Series in 1947, Shea reported to spring training grossly overweight and never rounded into top form. He made a few game-saving relief performances but failed as a starter with a 9–10 record. Harris was ticketed for dismissal, if not immediately, then as soon as the season ended whether the Yankees pulled out the title or not, the rumormongers insisted.

Weiss and Topping denied it all, but at the same time they did not go out of their way to give Harris a vote of confidence.

Early in September the Yankees put together an eight-game winning streak and Harris's position seemed a bit more fortified. DiMaggio's slugging just might have spared Harris from the guillotine.

Against the Senators in a double-header Joe hit three home runs and batted in seven runs in 6–2 and 5–2 victories. He hit homer No. 33 on September 5, driving the ball five rows of seats beyond the 344-foot marker in the Stadium's right field stand—the wrong field for a right-handed hitter.

Five days later, Boston was the hub for a dramatic showdown.

Boston fans, who revered Ted Williams, also had a special place in their hearts for Dom DiMaggio, Joe's younger brother, who was the Red Sox's reliable center fielder.

When the bespectacled Dom, who was known as the "Little Professor," went to bat during the season the Boston fans had devised a new chant to spur him on. It was a couplet sung to the tune of "Maryland, My Maryland" and went like this:

> He's better than his brother Joe—
> Dom-in-ic Di-Mag-gi-o!

It caught on and became very popular and now in the heat of the pennant race it was chanted when either of the DiMaggio brothers went to bat, intensifying the pressure on Joe, who generally thought the refrain was cute and who was happy for his brother's popularity.

Now with the score tied, 6–6, in the 10th inning Joe stepped to the plate against Earl Caldwell. There were two out and the bases were loaded. DiMaggio's clutch hitting throughout the season had been terrific.

A wag among the reporters sitting in the press box high atop Fenway Park said: "I'd rather be anybody in the world than Earl Caldwell right now. I'd rather be Henry Wallace."

Henry Wallace had been President Roosevelt's third-term Vice-President who was dropped for Harry Truman when F.D.R. ran and won a fourth term. Now in 1948 Wallace was running as an unpopular maverick minor party candidate against President Truman and Thomas E. Dewey for President of the United States.

DiMaggio settled himself in his wide stance and Caldwell threw.

DiMaggio drove a tremendous clout up into the netting near the left-field roof. It was foul by inches. Caldwell shrugged it off. On his next pitch, a fastball, DiMaggio again took a tremendous swing. The ball sailed deep to center field where Dom DiMaggio whirled and started running. Then he stopped. The ball traveled over the center-field bleachers more than 420 feet away. *The New York Times* described it as "one of the longest clouts ever seen in Fenway Park." The homer gave the Yankees an 11–6 victory and kept them in the race.

"My God! You don't hit two balls that hard in one day," DiMaggio said after the game. "Maybe you give it a little extra on big days. But you don't feel it. You must do it unconsciously. It's inside you and it does something to you. But you don't know it's there."

The grand slam was DiMaggio's second of the season and the Yankees' seventh. Still, they were 2½ games out of first place. On September 16, DiMaggio hit his 36th home run and No. 300 of his career. He was only the eighth man in baseball history to reach 300, joining Babe Ruth, Lou Gehrig, Mel Ott, Jimmie Foxx, Rogers Hornsby, Chuck Klein, and Hank Greenberg.

DiMaggio now was expending more energy than he could afford. At Detroit he was hit in the left hand by a pitch and suffered a contusion. He had also developed, in his left thigh, the worst charley horse he could recall. He wore a thick bandage over the thigh to support the strained muscles and a second bandage around his middle to hold up the first one.

"I feel like a mummy," he said.

In the final weeks of the season the tension mounted for everyone. It was compounded for DiMaggio when the press made disclosures he hadn't planned on.

The New York Daily Mirror revealed he was having trouble with his right heel and said it might be the cause for his painful charley horse. He was described as playing "on one leg." Speculation grew that he would need an operation on the heel at the end of the season. The report incensed DiMaggio.

"Such stories aren't going to do me or anybody any good," he said angrily. "Nor the club either at a time when we're all pulling together trying to win a pennant. I've been going to a hospital every fall for a checkup and if an operation is considered necessary maybe we'll have one. But I'm not worrying about that now."

The Mirror also disclosed that DiMaggio had gone out of his way to circulate reports that he would seek a $125,000 contract in 1949.

"I never have done anything like that in the past," he said, "and have no intention of doing it now. When the club sends me my contract in February we'll have our usual talks and if the owners want to make the terms public that's up to them. But I've never given anyone any figures before or after signing."

On September 19, with a game separating the three contenders, the Yankees split a double-header on a sweltering 96-degree day in St. Louis. DiMaggio hit his 37th and 38th home runs in his first two times at bat to salvage the split. Then he withdrew from the second game because of severe pain in his left thigh. The Yankees remained in third place, half a game behind Cleveland, with the Red Sox in the lead.

The next day, hobbling on virtually one leg, DiMaggio hit his 39th homer and singled, with the bases loaded, to keep the Yankees in contention. Two of the homers he had hit in those two days at Sportsman's Park went over the scoreboard behind the left-field bleachers. The distance from home plate to the base of the bleachers was 379 feet. Few hitters had ever put the ball over the scoreboard in that park.

With the scores all in that night, the Yankees, Red Sox, and Indians found themselves in a triple tie for the American League lead. Officials hurriedly called a meeting to decide what to do if the three teams remained deadlocked at the end of the season. They decided on a play-off game on October 4 between Cleveland and Boston, with the winner to face the Yankees October 5 in a one-game playoff for the title.

On September 28, the Yankees lost to the A's in Philadelphia and their chances of survival seemed slim. The physical strain on DiMaggio became visible to everyone. In the first inning, Eddie Joost hit a fly ball to deep center field. DiMaggio, limping painfully, could not reach it. A New York writer wrote: "It was only a question of time when DiMaggio's inability to cover a reasonable amount of ground with only one good leg would catch up with the Yankees. A two-legged DiMaggio not only would have caught Joost's lofty shot in the first inning, he would have been under the ball waiting for it to come down."

The next day, Hank Bauer, a rookie, hit a three-run homer to send the Yankees into a 4–2 lead. In the bottom of the ninth, Carl Scheib of the A's hit a harmless fly to short center field behind second base.

DiMaggio, limping in, got under the ball in plenty of time and appeared to have caught it. But the ball popped out of his glove as he was in the motion of throwing the ball into the infield. Bob Porterfield, the Yankee pitcher, was stunned. He got Joost for the first out, then yielded a double to Barney McCosky, putting runners on second and third. Joe Page relieved Porterfield and walked Ferris Fain to fill the bases. Then Allie Reynolds went in for Page and got Hank Majeski to hit into a double play. DiMaggio was off the hook.

The Yankees, who finished in third place, were eliminated on the next-to-last day of the season. In the last game, at Boston, DiMaggio made four straight hits before he was taken out.

As he limped to the dugout, the Boston fans gave him one of the biggest ovations a visiting player had ever received at Fenway Park.

When the 154-game regular season ended, Cleveland and Boston were deadlocked for the championship. The Indians won the one-game playoff, the first ever in the American League, and went on to their first World Series since 1920. They would face the Boston Braves, who had not been in a World Series since 1914.

DiMaggio completed the season with 39 home runs and 155 runs batted in, the best figures in those categories in the league. His batting average was .320 and he was the leader in total bases with 355. They were impressive statistics, but they had been achieved at an enormous cost of pain and endurance.

13

Not for Sale at Any Price

THE RUMORS OF Harris's impending dismissal were no longer rumors. On October 4 he was released as manager of the Yankees. Over the last six weeks of the 1948 season the rift between him and Weiss had widened and the Yankees' failure to overtake Boston and Cleveland in the final days did not help him. Even DiMaggio's brilliant efforts could not help.

Actually, Harris's eventual demise seemed inevitable after the departure of Larry MacPhail as a Yankee executive. MacPhail had brought Harris up from Buffalo where he had managed the International League franchise in 1946. Two days after he had accepted the Yankees' managerial post, Harris was offered the job of general manager with the Detroit Tigers. He had stayed with the Yankees out of loyalty to MacPhail, who had brought him back to the majors from the obscurity of Buffalo. His loyalty to MacPhail, however, helped build the friction that ensued between himself and Weiss. When he left New York, he would not demean the Yankees and kept intact his reputation for being a gentleman.

"I am leaving on friendly terms and have no further comment," he said.

Harris had managed four major league teams and the Yankee job would not be his last.

Weiss now had his long-awaited chance to demonstrate how good an executive he was by selecting a proper Yankee manager. It would be his first big move in reshaping a new Yankee dynasty.

For public consumption he told reporters that a new manager "would be announced at some future date" and that "several candidates, not including any player active with the Yankees in 1948" were being considered. That ended all speculation that had arisen as soon as Harris was dismissed, about the chances of Tommy Henrich or DiMaggio succeeding Harris. In its imaginative way, the press had drawn conclusions about Henrich and DiMaggio that were not necessarily applicable to the situation. However, where there is smoke, there is fire, and in their footwork to dig up stories the reporters had distilled enough information to conclude that neither player would have turned down such an opportunity.

For DiMaggio's part, however, even if he had been offered the job, it seemed more likely that he would have declined it at that stage of his career. His prime objective was still to seek the big money and he could only do that if he remained a standout player and a drawing card.

Weiss made his first broad stroke on the Yankee canvas of the future on Columbus Day when he introduced Casey Stengel at the "21" Club in New York as the team's new manager. At the World Series in Boston and Cleveland, the talk among the baseball gentry was that Stengel was in line for the job after he had guided the Oakland Acorns to the Pacific Coast League title and play-off championship. Weiss had given Stengel a taste of the Yankee organization in 1945 by naming him manager at Kansas City in the American Association. The next season, however, Stengel moved to Oakland, where he made his home, and worked for Clarence "Brick" Laws, the president of the independent club. Laws, who was present at the "21" Club signing ceremonies, had released Stengel from his contract so he could accept the post with the Yankees.

The 57-year-old Stengel had been a much-traveled player and manager in a career that went back to 1912, when he first broke into professional baseball at Kankakee, Illinois. He was a garrulous, argumentative, humorous, aggressive performer who played for John McGraw's New York Giants, the Brooklyn Dodgers, Philadelphia Phillies, Pittsburgh Pirates, and Boston Braves and more often than not provided abundant bons mots—humorous, controversial, or otherwise—for sportswriters in whatever town he happened to be. Born on July 30, 1890, Charles Dillon Stengel had taken the nickname Casey from the first initials of his hometown, Kansas City, Missouri.

Stengel was a dependable slugger and compiled a .284 career batting average. Weiss had picked a silver anniversary day to name him to baseball's most coveted job. Twenty-five years before to the day Stengel had hit a home run off the Yankees' Sad Sam Jones in the seventh inning to provide McGraw's Giants with their only run in a 1–0 World Series triumph. Two days before that he had hit a homer to beat the Yankees, 5–4. The Yankees won the Series, four games to two, but Stengel had single-handedly beaten them twice.

"There'll likely be some changes," Stengel said to the gathering at the "21" Club about his plans for the Yankees, "but it's a good club and I think we'll do all right. We'll go slow because you can tear a club down a lot quicker than you can build it up."

The Yankees of 1948 had been considered badly outmatched, even though they stayed in the thick of the pennant chase down to the wire. They were considered weak at several key positions by comparison with the Indians and Red Sox and their pitching was erratic. Many wondered whether Stengel was making a wise choice in taking over a team that was not in the best of shape and that had dropped its manager without giving a proper rationale for the dismissal. After all, Harris had won in 1947 and had missed by a hair in 1948.

Stengel was no pushover in the managerial wars. He had made the rounds of small and big towns like a traveling medicine man shrewdly hawking his wares, waiting for the main chance. When it came, Stengel was eminently prepared.

After he had ended his playing career in 1925, he hooked on as manager of the Worcester club in the Eastern League. He made the acquaintance of Weiss, who was running the New Haven franchise. He moved on to Toledo, where he was player-manager of the Mud Hens of the Triple A American Association. In 1932 he was in the major leagues at Brooklyn as a coach under Manager Max Carey. Two years later he took over the top job after Carey was dismissed, then managed the Boston Braves from 1938 to 1943. All this time he had failed to produce a winner in the majors, was shuffled off to the American Association again, and took over from Bill Veeck, Sr. as pilot at Milwaukee.

Wherever he went Stengel brought with him a reputation of not always accepting the rulings of umpires as gospel. But he gave it more than bombast and hard-headedness. He was the master of comic relief. Rather than alienating the umpires, he won them over with princely clowning. His most famous incident occurred, of course, when he walked out to the plate, bowed to the umpire and doffed his cap—from which a sparrow flew out.

DiMaggio was at the "21" Club to meet the new manager. Reporters followed up on their earlier thesis and wondered whether he was disappointed that he had not been offered the job as Yankee manager.

"You know me, boys," he said, "I'm just a ballplayer with only one ambition, and that is to give all I've got to help my ball club win. I've never played any other way."

It was a curt response and seemed to obfuscate the question, as if DiMaggio was indeed disappointed at not being asked to take the job. In later years he would confide to friends that he was never approached about it and that he thought it would be bad form for him openly to have sought the position.

Then, as television and newsreel cameras whirred, he and Stengel shook hands and he wished his new chief the best of luck. The occasion also served to circulate the rumor that he and Dan Topping, the Yankee president, had already come to terms on his 1949 contract, but he denied it.

"I spent several days with Mr. Topping during the World Series," he said, "but we never even discussed my salary for next year."

He spent the next two weeks on a vacation, hunting and fishing in South Dakota, then returned east. On November 11 he checked into a familiar haunt—the Johns Hopkins Hospital in Baltimore. For the first time he disclosed publicly that his right heel had been ailing since the summer of 1947 and that his thigh and leg problems during 1948 had worsened because he was favoring the heel when he ran.

A week later Dr. George Bennett removed bone spurs from the heel and he was discharged from the hospital on November 24, hobbling on crutches and wearing a cast on his right foot.

Early in December Weiss and Stengel prepared to attend the winter baseball meetings in Minneapolis. Weiss had made plans to get there earlier than usual because he wanted to explore the trading market. Several teams had put out feelers and were interested in some of the Yankees. Some owners, however, Clark Griffith of the Washington Senators in particular, would have nothing to do with the New York club. Griffith felt he had been rubbed the wrong way by MacPhail in earlier dealings and even though there was evidence to the contrary he felt Weiss's policies were, or would be, a carryover from MacPhail's.

Before he left for Minneapolis, Weiss gave the Yankee regulars something to think about over the winter months. He said that every Yankee was expendable except DiMaggio and Henrich. Those two, he said, were not available "at any price."

"By this I don't mean to give anyone the impression," Weiss said, "the Yankees are going out to the meetings with the idea of tossing our players around to the four winds."

Stengel had implied when he took over that he would proceed slowly and carefully in making changes. He had said it was easier to tear down than to build a team. There were personnel on the club whom Stengel could preserve and some who were expendable, but if a few deals could be made that might provide some tried and true veterans, he might eventually have the kind of team he wanted. Under Weiss, the farm system might send up a rookie or two who might blend in and put the Yankees back at the top.

Weiss kept these factors in mind and made the appropriate statement.

"We still feel as we did at the close of the season," he said, "that the Yankees basically are still a strong club and will be able to do all right next season even if we make no deals at all. However, there has been a lot of talk by other clubs of their willingness to trade, so we're just setting everyone straight on where we stand. With the exception of DiMaggio and Henrich, we are ready to make a deal for any player on our club, provided Stengel believes it will help us. But we won't be giving anything away for nothing."

14

A $100,000 Comeback
but the
Bone Spurs Hurt

$\mathcal{D}$ IMAGGIO HAD NOT **actually undergone** a metamorphosis from his early reserve, but it seemed that by age 34 he had acquired a demeanor that was synonomous with "class." If his playing ability was a natural gift, his new personal style was an acquired gift naturally come by. As an athlete, he took his calling seriously and gave it top priority, even in the face of adversity, in order to assure the fans his best.

On Broadway in the spring of 1949, *South Pacific* would open at the Majestic Theater and would sweep the nation off its emotional feet. In the song "Bloody Mary," Hammerstein's lyric, "Her skin is as tender as DiMaggio's glove . . ." would be a reminder once again of the Yankee Clipper's graceful style.

Until 1948 when the Yankees paid him $70,000, DiMaggio had felt he was not always appreciated by the team's management. Other stars had been paid much more than that on losing teams.

The 1948 season had proved his toughness and durability against long odds and solidified his popularity with the fans. The members of the press, who had been his severest critics, had been won over, too. His quest for even bigger money, void of holdout threats, took on a more sophisticated manner, one in keeping with the public's perception of him. It was the time now to seek the gold ring he had set out to get as a teenager mulling his future in North Beach.

One snowy night in January 1949, DiMaggio and Tom Meany, a sportswriter for the *New York Star* who was DiMaggio's ghost writer in 1946 on a book about his life, *Lucky to Be a Yankee,* were walking past Radio City on 52nd Street.

"You know, Tom, this year I'm going to ask for $100,000," DiMaggio said casually. "I think I can get it."

"Joe," Meany said, "you've got the fans on your side and I think Topping, Webb, and Weiss know that. If anybody can get it, you're the guy. Good luck."

Meany's advice didn't convince DiMaggio on the spot, but it encouraged him to talk it over some more with other friends. Meany thought he had an exclusive story and that he would be able to write it for the *Star* the next day. Ironically, while Meany was listening to talk about a six-figure salary and offering encouragement, the paper he worked for was going out of business. The next day the *New York Star* folded and Meany found himself among the unemployed.

Toots Shor, the New York restaurateur, was a friend and confidant of DiMaggio. His midtown Manhattan eatery had become a mecca for popular personalities in sports, show business, politics, and industry. He was a diehard Yankee fan and he considered DiMaggio the greatest ballplayer alive. He would play a large role in DiMaggio's 1949 salary negotiations.

When contract negotiations began, Dan Topping and Del Webb, in consultation with George Weiss, came up with a plan to offer DiMaggio $90,000. There would also be a clause in the contract calling for a percentage of the gate. If the Yankees had a good season and drew good crowds, it could easily put DiMaggio in the $100,000-a-year class.

DiMaggio was still keen on the straight $100,000 contract and the new offer presented him with a dilemma.

One night at Shor's restaurant he discussed the proposal.

"I don't know what to do, Toots," DiMaggio said. "I'd like to go for $100,000, but if the Yankees have a very good year, the bonus clause might turn into a bonanza."

"If I were you, Joe," Shor said, "I'd go for the $100,000. You'd be the first player in history to get that much. Think of it, not even the Babe got $100,000."

"You might be right," DiMaggio said.

"Sure, I'm right," Shor answered. "The first player ever to get a $100,000 contract. Nobody will be able to take that away from you."

On February 7 at the Yankees' Fifth Avenue offices, DiMaggio became the first baseball player to sign for $100,000. If he thought he was underpaid in previous seasons, now DiMaggio could feel he had been reimbursed for past performances. Besides leading the league in homers, runs batted in, and total bases in 1948, he had made 190 hits, 26 doubles, and 11 triples. He would have finished with 40 homers, but he lost one he hit in the first inning of a rained-out game on May 12. Ironically, he had won the 1947 Most Valuable Player award with far less imposing credentials. In 1948 he placed second to Lou Boudreau of the Indians. Had the Yankees won the pennant, most sportswriters agreed, DiMaggio most likely would have won the most valuable award for an unprecedented fourth time.

Thus 1949 became a pivotal season in the careers of Stengel and DiMaggio. For Stengel, it would be a touchstone that would take him to undreamed of success. For DiMaggio, it would test his leadership qualities and his ability to overcome injury and defeat.

At 34, DiMaggio was aging as ballplayers go. He had undergone three operations in the two previous years for bone spurs in both heels and bone chips in his right elbow. He was a museum piece and fans wondered how long he would last. Stengel, too, must have wondered. His success as a first-year manager of the Yankees hinged on DiMaggio's availability and effectiveness.

DiMaggio reported to spring training on March 1 without fanfare, one of the few times he was present at the start. He hoped to be 100 percent fit after his surgery, capable of playing 150 games. Stengel had called for two-a-day workouts immediately and had made it plain he would conduct a rigorous camp and tolerate no slack from anyone.

Training camp wasn't a day old when concern hit the Yankee front office. DiMaggio worked out hard the first day, but overnight his right heel flared up. A hurried phone call went out to the team's orthopedist, Dr. Sidney Gaynor, who immediately recommended that DiMaggio be flown to Johns Hopkins in Baltimore. Once again DiMaggio was entrusted to the care of Dr. George Bennett, who had performed the bone chip operation on his elbow and the bone spur surgery on his heels.

Dr. Bennett's diagnosis indicated that DiMaggio had pulled some adhesions in the right ankle, possibly because of the strenuous workout the first day of training. X rays showed no immediate need for surgery. DiMaggio returned to camp. He underwent whirlpool baths and limited his conditioning pace. He knew the operation in November had not offered a guarantee of a permanent cure. On March 3 he was still limping and in pain. He grew disconsolate.

"I suppose I look on the dark side of things," he said, "but I think that's wise. Maybe the pain will disappear. But if it is going to act up again, I believe now is the time to take the matter in hand. The pain Tuesday [March 1] didn't come from too much work the first day. It was just there and it became more intense after the workout, even though I wore sponge in my shoes.

"Last season [1948] the pain was so intense it affected both my legs. The calf of my right leg stiffened because in favoring the heel, I was using an unnatural stride. Both thighs pained me. That's what I want to try to avoid this year. Maybe it will clear up. I hope so."

The doctors in Baltimore developed special sponge-rubber inner soles with depressed sections in the heels to help him relieve the pressure and pain when he ran. Near the end of the first week of training, during a short drill, DiMaggio developed three painful blisters—two on the middle toe of his right foot and the other on the second toe of his left foot. Again the Yankees were alarmed. They ordered spiked shoes half a size larger than DiMaggio's regular size.

Other Yankees were injured, too. Charlie Keller and Hank Bauer had injured ankles, Phil Rizzuto was underweight, and Yogi Berra drove his car into a tree on the way from his beach home and hurt his right knee. Besides the injuries, disciplinary problems took hold on the squad and Stengel began to wonder whether his reputation for clowning might have preceded him. He discovered the players were violating his training rules. An atmosphere of uncertainty pervaded the camp. The local dog-racing track, a betting haven the players liked to patronize, had been declared off limits to the players except on Thursday nights. Stengel learned that they were there every night and that DiMaggio was one of the violators, if not the ringleader.

"I will handle this situation in my own way," Stengel said, "if I have to go out to the track myself. DiMaggio admits he feels badly about it."

Stengel's mention of DiMaggio confirmed his involvement in the escapade, but he would not admit it. No fines were issued, but Stengel threatened to take away several privileges the players enjoyed. He banned the players from living away from the team's hotel and imposed a midnight curfew and a 7:30 morning call. The bowlegged Dutchman was determined to run the team his way, and he had Weiss's whole-hearted support.

In an exhibition game against the St. Louis Cardinals on March 12, DiMaggio limped to the batter's box to pinch hit and delivered a single in the fourth inning. The next day an ominous cloud came over Miller Huggins Field. Jackie Collum, a rookie with St. Joseph's of the Class C Western Association, struck out the pinch-hitting DiMaggio on a 3–2 count with the bases loaded. Among the diehards in the Florida crowd of 3,383 many were saying, "DiMaggio will never finish the season."

Still, the Yankees refused to count out the Big Fellow for the season opener. Weiss announced boldly, after consultation with Dr. Bennett and Dr. Gaynor: "Both doctors are optimistic that the Yankees' center fielder on opening day at Yankee Stadium will be Joe DiMaggio."

No one, of course, could be certain that the Yankee lineup for the April 19 opener would show No. 5, DiMaggio, cf, batting in the No. 4 slot. Weiss's pronouncement that it was a virtual certainty sounded to members of the press corps more like whistling in the cemetery.

Reality dawned on Weiss and Stengel on a Saturday afternoon in Beaumont, Texas. The Yankees had pulled up stakes in Florida and were swinging through the Southwest en route to New York. After playing seven innings at Beaumont, DiMaggio limped off the field and told Stengel: "I'm sorry, Casey, but this heel is no better now than at any time since I started training."

If the Yankees were deceiving themselves about DiMaggio's condition, they could no longer afford the luxury. Dr. Bennett was called again in Baltimore and he recommended an examination in Dallas by Dr. T. M. Girard, a well-known orthopedic specialist.

A four-hour examination by Dr. Girard disclosed that DiMaggio had a "hot" condition in the right heel, unrelated to the previous surgery. He would have to be hospitalized. Dr. Girard gave no indication how long the treatments, consisting of X rays and injections of Novocain, would take. They were aimed, he said, at easing the pain and allowing the ailment to run its course.

The news frustrated DiMaggio. For the eighth time in 11 seasons he would miss the Yankee opener. This time he would be sidelined indefinitely. Now he saw himself as an overpriced player whose career was in jeopardy of being cut down before its time.

He left Dallas Airport late in the day and arrived at Johns Hopkins Hospital at 2 A.M. on April 13 after a stormy and uncomfortable flight.

"It was a terrible day to fly," he said. "There was a storm all over the South. We were traveling through rain and fog banks, and everybody on the plane got airsick, including me."

En route to Baltimore, when the plane touched down at several airports, DiMaggio was besieged by local newspapermen and photographers asking questions about his chances for recovery and whether he planned to retire from baseball.

"I had seen myself in the washroom mirror," he said, "and I knew how I looked. My face was white, my eyes were hollow, and I even needed a haircut." His mood was one of frustration and pique.

Later in the day, after he was admitted to the hospital, doctors issued a bulletin on his condition. "DiMaggio has immature calcium deposits in tissues adjacent to the heel bone," it read. "It is expected he will be discharged on April 14 but will continue treatment as an outpatient. The length of the disability will be determined by the results of the treatment."

DiMaggio's heel had become the most famous since Achilles'. It was described by writers of high and low station, in sports and elsewhere, in their Iliads on baseball lore.

Although DiMaggio's hospital stay was brief, he endured a great deal of mental anguish. He became edgy, nervous, and irritable. He had requested that a DO NOT DISTURB sign be posted on the door of his room so he could rest, but the sign went unheeded. The news of his whereabouts spread quickly. Hospital patients got word of his being there on the radio. They badgered his nurse to get them his autograph. Others offered sure cures for what ailed him. Strangers, with or without hospital passes, tried to get into his room to see him. Once, after waking from a nap, he saw a man and woman staring at him. When he was fully awake and had opened his eyes, they walked out without saying a word.

"I began to feel like a freak," he said. "I thought, 'Why can't a man have a little peace?'"

The culmination of his despondency came the next day when he was discharged. Hobbling through the hospital lobby on crutches, he was confronted by a battery of reporters and photographers again. He had tried to keep the time of his discharge a secret, so he could get away unnoticed. He was angry that his privacy once again had been invaded. He knew, of course, that as a public figure he could not afford such a luxury, but he had hoped he would be given enough latitude to be left alone.

The trauma made him lose control, and he scowled and shouted at the press: "Don't you think you've gone far enough? You guys are driving me batty! Can't you leave me alone? This affects me mentally, too, you know. I got to think of myself, too. This is tough on me."

Then he stormed out of the lobby to be driven to a hotel, the location of which he had managed to keep a secret.

The incident was uncharacteristic of DiMaggio, who had worked hard over the years to develop a genial, pleasantly quiet relationship with reporters. Later he regretted the quarrel, but his remarks had already received full-scale coverage in the media.

"I've regretted it," he said later, "but under the circumstances I don't see how I could have avoided it."

On opening day, DiMaggio sat on the bench in the Yankee dugout dressed in a blue suit and camel-hair overcoat instead of the pinstripes bearing No. 5. It was small comfort to him that the Yankees won, 3–2, and that 40,075 fans were in the stands enjoying this rite of spring along with Secretary General Trygve Lie of the United Nations.

For the last day of their first home stand on May 2, the Yankees drew 54,328 customers. Ted Williams hit a grand slam off Spec Shea and the Bombers lost, 11–2, to the Red Sox. DiMaggio, still undergoing treatments, was left at home for their first road trip. He remained confined to the quiet elegance of his hotel suite at the Hotel Elysée in Manhattan. He was not far from the theatrical district and spent his time resting and seeing some of his favorite musical comedies—*High Button Shoes, Show Boat* and *Annie Get Your Gun.*

The Yankees continued to issue bulletins on his condition. Weiss said he was improving and the club expected him back in uniform when the team returned home on May 17. The club never failed to mention a precise date for his return, although no one, not even DiMaggio, knew when he would return, if at all.

Two days after the Yankees left for the West, Joe received word that his father had died in San Francisco of a coronary occlusion. DiMaggio left immediately for his home on the West Coast for the funeral. The treatments for his heel, and his recovery, were delayed for at least 10 days.

Still harboring a touch of Barnum in their public-relations hearts, the Yankees announced that DiMaggio would be in uniform for a night game at the Stadium against the St. Louis Browns on May 23. The Browns, of course, were the perennially last-place team in the American League, although they had won their only pennant in 1944, a wartime year. Now they were last again, 12 games off the pace already. The Yankees added no frills and raised no hopes—DiMaggio would not play, he would simply take a few swings during batting practice and shag a few fly balls in the outfield. This strategem brought out a windfall of 37,376 paying customers, and fickle as they might have been, they feasted on the sight of the $100,000 athlete doing what had been advertised. DiMaggio took a few swings, developing blisters on his hands in the process, and shagged a few flies. His appearance brought a thunderous ovation. Yankees fans had been assured that their idol was alive and well, and that by hook or crook, someday soon he would be back in the lineup.

But the pain would not vanish and DiMaggio spent long hours in his hotel suite brooding.

Out-of-town visitors, New York cronies, and newspapermen, seeking an update on his condition, spent some time with him. He could not relax. On occasion, his 8-year-old son visited him and they passed the time playing with a miniature railroad train. The one thing he guarded was his sleep, managing to get at least eight hours a night. He refused numerous invitations to dinners and social events. The ordeal made him dour, somber and impatient; he became a virtual recluse. Good and bad advice poured in from his friends. Toots Shor brought him messages from acquaintances who stopped at the restaurant, and Shor brought his own brand of get-well humor. He carried a message from Rogers Hornsby, who like DiMaggio had suffered from heel spurs late in his career. The injury played a major role in Hornsby's decision to retire.

"Roger told me to tell you, Joe," Shor said, "just to be patient, that the only thing that can help one of those things is rest." That advice came late in May and by that time DiMaggio's patience was wearing thin.

DiMaggio had told some of his friends, including Topping and Webb, that he did not expect to be back in the lineup until July 14, two days after the All-Star Game scheduled for Brooklyn. The All-Star Game break was the juncture at which baseball traditionally marked the end of the first half of the season. DiMaggio thought if he could be ready by then, he could at least help the club in its second-half drive.

One morning in mid-June he stepped out of bed, expecting pain to shoot through his heel and leg as usual.

"Nothing happened," he said. "I felt the heel and leg with my hand; it was no longer hot. It had completely cooled down and I could step around the hotel room without feeling any pain. I was elated. The team was still in the West on a road trip. When they got back I surprised them by going to the clubhouse and putting on a uniform. I figured I could give it a try."

While DiMaggio naturally was eager to return to action, in the back of his mind he was thinking about the All-Star Game. He had been selected to the team every season since he was a rookie, with the exception of the three years he was in military service. He regarded selection to the team as the quintessential honor for a star player, and he feared he would be left off for the first time because he had not played an inning.

Every day he drilled for 15 minutes in the infield, scooping grounders and throwing to the bases to improve his timing. He worked five additional minutes in the outfield, taking fly balls and grounders. He went through a full stint in the batting cage.

Lou Boudreau, the manager of the Cleveland Indians, would be the skipper of the American League All-Stars. The voting deadline for the fans to choose their stars was only a few weeks away.

The Indians were in New York for a three-game series. On the Stadium field before the first game, Boudreau and DiMaggio had a short conversation.

"Joe, how do you feel about the game? I'd kind of like to have you, you know," Boudreau said.

"You know how I feel about it," DiMaggio said, "but I'm not even in the running."

"I think it can be arranged," Boudreau said, "but keep it under your hat until the teams are announced."

Later DiMaggio said, "I wanted to shake his hand, but that wouldn't have looked very good on the playing field. So I just said, 'Thanks, maybe by that time I'll be in shape to pinch hit for you, if you need me.'"

Then, in the last week of June, the Yankees had another opportunity to lure the fans with DiMaggio's invisible magic wand. The buildup this time was for the Mayor's Trophy Game against the New York Giants'—an intracity rivalry played for the benefit of sandlot baseball, and in some minds for the championship of New York City. The Yankees announced that DiMaggio would take part in a home-run-hitting contest before the game, no more, no less.

On the night of the game, June 27, a Monday and an off day on the regular schedule, DiMaggio decided he would play and test his heel. His training pace was progressing rapidly and he felt confident.

Stengel had always said, "When he's ready, he'll tell me."

In the home-run-hitting contest DiMaggio poled one into the left-field stand and the crowd of 37,637 broke into pandemonium. When his name was announced in the starting lineup, they roared again—DiMaggio was throwing in a bonus for them.

The Giants held him hitless in four appearances, but in the field he caught two flies and handled flawlessly the four singles that were hit to him. Most importantly, he had lasted nine innings. It was his first full game since he was sidelined on April 11.

Having missed the first 65 games of the regular season, DiMaggio was itching for action. He decided the time had come to give his heel a true test. He joined the team the next day for the flight to Boston, where the Yankees and Red Sox would open a three-game series that night.

"I think I'm ready," he told Stengel.

For more than two months, almost half the season, DiMaggio had unwillingly denied New York's fans the opportunity of watching him perform and now he grudgingly offered a crowd of 36,233 in Fenway Park the chance to sit in judgment not only on his fitness to play but on whether he could play like the DiMaggio of old.

The crowd was the biggest of the year at Boston and a record for a night game at Fenway Park. The Yankees were in first place, where they had been since opening day despite the loss of DiMaggio. They were risking a two-game lead against the Red Sox, who were riding a four-game winning streak and had won 10 of their last 11 games. A Boston sweep of the series would lift them to the top rung and perhaps send the Yankees into the downward plunge most sportswriters had predicted for them at the start of the season.

DiMaggio said he felt as if he were on the edge of a cliff—he saw his baseball future plummeting into an abyss if his tools and skills betrayed him.

For the opening game DiMaggio wore a special shoe that had no spikes on the heel of the right foot. He was still 15 pounds underweight. Maurice McDermott, a strong, promising 20-year-old rookie left-hander with a good fastball and strikeout record, was the Boston starter.

In his first appearance against McDermott in the second inning, DiMaggio lined a solid single to left-center field. With two out, Johnny Lindell walked and then Hank Bauer drove a towering home run for a 3–0 lead, DiMaggio scoring his first run of the season.

In the third inning, Phil Rizzuto singled. Then DiMaggio slashed one of McDermott's fastballs into the screen high above the left-field wall for his first homer and the Yankees led, 5–0. The Boston fans, who had always treated DiMaggio with admiration, gave him a standing ovation—the enemy applauded in an enemy's park.

On his next time at bat DiMaggio grounded to the pitcher, who threw him out at first. He drew a walk in the eighth inning, but his day's work was not yet complete. Yogi Berra followed his walk with a grounder to Bobby Doerr at second base. It seemed like a certain double-play ball. DiMaggio, more like an eager rookie than a wounded veteran, went into second with a take-out slide that prevented the shortstop, Vern Stephens, who had taken the throw from Doerr, from making the relay to first and doubling up Berra.

"DiMaggio's out of his mind," said one of the Boston writers in the press box.

Boston's hard-bitten writers might admire DiMaggio's gameness and smart base-running on the play, but was he dotty attempting a slide with his delicate and imperfect heel? (After the game, DiMaggio explained why he did it. "With my sore heel it was better for me to slide so I'd get off my feet than to go straight in and let my heel take a pounding.")

If the fans thought they had seen enough, DiMaggio was to give them one more example of his grace under pressure. In the bottom of the ninth, with the score, 5–3, Matt Batts tripled for Boston and Birdie Tebbetts drove him home with a pinch single. Lou Stringer went in to run for Tebbetts and the next batter was Ted Williams, who had won his fourth batting title in 1948 with .369. A hit would tie the score and with Williams at bat a winning home run was no wild dream.

Joe Page had gone in as a reliever for the Yankees. He threw a fastball to Williams, who sent it screaming more than 400 feet to deep center field. DiMaggio drifted back in his loping style, having drawn a bead on the ball at the crack of the bat, and made the catch, making it look easy all the way.

It had been a day to remember. DiMaggio had caught six fly balls in the outfield and had cleanly retrieved three singles hit into his territory. He had played a part in the Yankee scoring, assuring a 5–4 victory with his home run and his fielding.

The next day, a lazy summer Wednesday afternoon, the Red Sox selected Ellis Kinder, their strongest right-hander, as their starter. Before the game was four innings old they had staked him to a 7–1 lead with a barrage against Tommy Byrne and Cuddles Marshall. In the fifth, Kinder issued walks to Rizzuto and Tommy Henrich. Then with two out, DiMaggio hopped on Kinder's fastball and drove it into the net in left-center field for a three-run homer, cutting Boston's lead to 7–4.

Kinder left the game and Tex Hughson took over. In the seventh inning Gene Woodling crashed a double off Hughson with the bases loaded and the Yankees were all even at 7–7.

Earl Johnson, a left-hander, replaced Hughson and prepared to face DiMaggio in his next time at bat in the eighth. DiMaggio went to the plate again with two out. Johnson's fastball came in letter-high and DiMaggio sent it sailing high over the 20-foot netting atop the 40-foot wall in left-center field and into the street.

"It was a ball marked home run from the instant of contact," wrote Louis Effrat of *The New York Times.*

Cheers from the crowd of 29,563 fans greeted DiMaggio as he crossed the plate. They did not seem to care that he had sent their team to a 9–7 defeat.

On Thursday afternoon, DiMaggio, now the subject of newspaper editorials everywhere, continued his rampage. The next pitcher he faced was Mel Parnell, another left-hander and the ace of the Boston staff. With the Yankees leading, 3–2, in the seventh inning, Snuffy Stirnweiss and Henrich singled. DiMaggio worked Parnell to a 3–2 count and then ripped into another fastball for his most lethal blow of his three-day, one-man attack. The ball cleared the net in left field, rammed a light tower, bounced back onto the field and rolled dead near second base. It gave the Yankees a 6–3 victory and a sweep of the series. In three games and 11 trips to the plate, after missing 65 games, DiMaggio had crashed four home runs and a single and driven in nine runs. In the field he had gathered in 13 putouts.

Suddenly, DiMaggio had become the architect of a heart-warming comeback. *Life* magazine put his picture on its cover and from one end of the country to the other his fantastic outburst at Boston had become a topic of conversation, even among people who had never seen a game. It had happened to him before—in 1941 when he fashioned his record of hitting safely in 56 consecutive games.

Robert Ruark, the Broadway columnist, wrote: "DiMaggio is the first real sports colossus since the Dempsey-Jones-Ruth era."

He had beaten his own timetable for his return by almost two weeks and had helped the Yankees widen their hold on first place. He had disspelled whatever misgivings he had had about being a nonproductive, $100,000-a-year player and of his career going into limbo. He need not have worried so much about that. The Yankee owners, Dan Topping and Del Webb, were businessmen as well as sportsmen and DiMaggio was their showcase property. They had enjoyed his company many times and they knew he helped pay dividends by creating a public image of a beneficent player-owner relationship. All along, DiMaggio had told them he didn't think he'd be ready until about July 14.

"Here it was still June," DiMaggio said later, "and I was back in action and getting some hits. After the second game of the Boston series I received a telegram from Webb. It read: YOU CROSSED ME UP. HOW AM I GOING TO EXPLAIN THIS TO MY FRIENDS? It was the thing I needed. I let out a roar and one of the players said, 'Joe, that's the first time I've seen you laugh all year.'"

On July 2, the fans' 4,637,000 All-Star Game votes were counted. The American League outfield would have Williams in left field, Dom DiMaggio in center field and Henrich in right field. Joe of course, could only make the team by special appointment. As manager, Boudreau had the prerogative to pick eight nonpitching players to round out the roster.

True to his earlier commitment to DiMaggio, Boudreau named him officially to the squad.

"Joe DiMaggio said he would like to be on the All-Star squad," Boudreau said. "I felt he belonged on it even though he had not played because of injury and I wanted him on the team I'm to manage. He's a great star who deserved to be named this year as he deserved to be named 10 previous times."

The announcement was academic. No dyed-in-the-wool baseball fan would have denied the slugger a place on the team, even by special appointment, after his heroic exploits a week earlier.

Stengel, never at a loss for hyperbole, commented on Boudreau's move to place DiMaggio on the team.

"With Joe DiMaggio in action," Stengel said, "the American League will be 50 percent better."

If there were critics who had wanted to protest DiMaggio's All-Star appointment, even they might have been assuaged after his performance at Ebbets Field in Brooklyn. When he replaced his brother Dom in center field, the crowd of 37,577 stood and applauded the Yankee Clipper. He batted in three runs with a single and double and helped assure Boudreau's team an 11–7 victory.

Even before Boudreau's gesture, however, baseball officialdom, always mindful of displaying its crowd-pleasing merchandise at strategic places, had decided to make DiMaggio a part of the all-star cast. Commissioner A. B. "Happy" Chandler had suggested to Will Harridge, president of the American League, that if DiMaggio was not named as a player he would be invited as a guest of honor. It was a role that DiMaggio, long after he had retired as a player, was called upon to play many times. He always felt obliged to accept, not so much because he was asked by baseball's moguls or by the Yankees and other teams, but because he loved the spectacle of the game as well as the adulation of the fans. It became a way to keep himself visible to generations of fans, many of whom had never seen him play.

For DiMaggio the season had taken so many twists and turns, he felt he was caught in a labyrinth. A weird incident that plagued him for many weeks during his isolation in his hotel room was revealed in the press on August 1. He had been receiving mash notes from a woman he did not know. At the same time Broadway's gossip columnists, some of them among DiMaggio's friends, had been receiving notes from a woman linking herself romantically with DiMaggio. The notes to the columnists were written on stationery and in handwriting remarkably similar to those sent to DiMaggio.

The notes the columnists received were signed, "Junior Standish." Some of the columnists exploited the DiMaggio-Standish romantic angle. She was an attractive blonde, blue-eyed Broadway dancer. Friends of both DiMaggio and Miss Standish said the two knew each other but had never been involved romantically. Miss Standish issued a statement denying she had ever written any notes, either to the press or to DiMaggio. She and DiMaggio, in a joint statement, denied any romantic entanglement between them.

Meanwhile, the episode grew more serious for DiMaggio. The woman's notes continued to arrive at his hotel and now included threats to take her life if she were spurned by the ballplayer. The woman had tried to visit DiMaggio at the hotel.

The Yankees, who had hoped the incident would fizzle out from its own steam, assigned a bodyguard to watch DiMaggio around the clock. Arthur Patterson, the Yankees' public relations man who had been living with the problem for as long as DiMaggio had, finally sought help from the police, who opened an investigation late in July.

After a week of investigation and another note to DiMaggio in which the woman again threatened suicide, both the police and the Yankees figured a little publicity in the press might help trace the woman. It worked, and finally a petite, 30-year-old brunette was brought into police custody and questioned by Assistant District Attorney O'Brien in the Manhattan office. While she was being questioned, the woman became hysterical, screaming that she would kill herself. She was taken to Morrisania Hospital in the Bronx for psychiatric examination. The hospital agreed to release her in custody of her father on the promise that she would obtain psychiatric treatment and that DiMaggio would be left alone. The woman had never met DiMaggio and her identity was not disclosed by the police.

The police theorized that the woman had been influenced by reading accounts earlier in the season of the shooting of another ballplayer, Eddie Waitkus of the Philadelphia Phillies. Waitkus had received a mysteriously worded note that lured him to a hotel room in Chicago. On his arrival he was shot by 19-year-old Ruth Ann Steinhagen, who claimed Waitkus had spurned her. Waitkus missed the rest of the season after having played in only 54 games.

By this time, the Yankees did not need so many distractions in their struggle to hold the league lead. Stengel had had to resort to patching his lineup like a master quiltmaker. In all, the Yankees had suffered 70 injuries and other ailments during the campaign. Stengel got the most out of his personnel by using a platoon system, virtually improvising his lineup from day to day. The three sluggers he had hoped to rely on steadily—DiMaggio, Henrich, and Berra—appeared in the same lineup only 12 times during the first 148 games. Stengel's magicianship in juggling his players and getting the most out of their talents was to win him a unique place as a baseball strategist and an eventual niche in the Hall of Fame.

DiMaggio's health and his knack for getting decisive clutch hits kept him in the headlines. Sometimes an offhand remark also focused attention on him. He had become a central character in a season-long odyssey of baseball writers in search of a story.

On August 13, the Boston sportswriters, who had always been overly critical of Ted Williams, wrote that DiMaggio and Williams were feuding and engaging in name-calling unbecoming the two highest paid players in the game.

The Yankees had completed a series in Boston on a Wednesday night with a 3–2 victory. With the score, 3–2, Williams sent a hard hit deep to right-center field, DiMaggio's territory, and wound up at second base with a double. Some reporters and particularly Williams's critics in the Boston corps, thought he could have made a triple out of it if he had shown more hustle. It was possible, they wrote, that he could have put himself in position to score from third on a long fly ball. In theory at least, they reasoned, he might have helped tie the game.

DiMaggio was quoted in the Boston papers as having said: "When I picked up that ball [that Williams hit] and then looked up and saw

Williams standing on second I was stunned. I thought sure he'd be resting on third."

Williams retaliated by saying: "Nobody said anything when Joe DiMaggio failed to reach second base when he hit the top of the left-field wall Tuesday night."

On that hit DiMaggio apparently was satisfied with a single, but Williams's remark piqued him and prompted him to pursue the colloquy and fan the fire a little more. DiMaggio was quoted again, this time as having said Williams was a "crybaby."

A day later in Philadelphia, DiMaggio admitted to The Associated Press that he might have called Williams a "crybaby" in an "offhand remark" but added quickly that he "did not emphasize it by saying 'certainly he's a crybaby,'" as the Boston newspapers reported it. In an almost apologetic reaction DiMaggio tried to clear the air.

"Listen, I wasn't giving Williams any thought at the time," he said. "I had all I could do to catch up with the ball. It looks like somebody is trying to build up a situation that doesn't exist. I don't want to make any more comments because the thing might get snarled up. These things can get awfully mixed up if they are strung out."

He said he wanted it understood that there was no animosity between himself and Williams. What Tony Lazzeri and Frank Crosetti had tried to teach him 13 years earlier apparently had sunk in.

There was still a grueling month and a half to go in the stretch drive. DiMaggio's return had helped the Yankees stride 5½ games ahead of the second-place Indians. Late in August, Joe was sidelined again for a week with a sprained left shoulder. On August 24 the Yankees dropped a 13–2 decision to Red Rolfe's Detroit Tigers and their lead had dwindled to two games, with the Red Sox now their closest pursuers.

In Chicago, on August 28, they lost Henrich when their All-Star right fielder crashed into the right-field wall in the first inning of the first game of a double-header and fractured the second and third lumbar vertebrae in his back. A strong DiMaggio, or one who could function at least at 75 percent proficiency, was a necessity. He was back in the lineup for the double-header, cracking four hits, including a homer, and sparking 8–7 and 7–5 triumphs. On September 5 he blasted a grand slam and drove in five runs against the A's in a 13–4 romp. But after an inning and a half of the second game he was out again—this time with leg cramps.

DiMaggio's physical problems were destined to last to the very end of the season. After taking batting practice at the Stadium on September 18, he complained of not feeling well. He was sent to the locker room and was examined by the team physician, Dr. Jacques Fischl. He was running a 102-degree fever and was ordered to bed. Dr. Fischl estimated he would be out a week. The week passed and DiMaggio was still ailing. The doctor revised his diagnosis. Now, he said, DiMaggio was suffering from "pneumonitis," a mild form of pneumonia, and he would not predict how long it would take him to recover.

The Yankees needed victories over the Indians in a two-game series to stay in the lead. Stengel again juggled his lineup, sending Cliff Mapes to center field to replace DiMaggio, and Hank Bauer, who had been out with an injury, to right field, with Charlie Keller in left for a Sunday game. The crowd was 64,549 and lifted the Yankees' home attendance over the 2 million mark. Bauer filled the breech with a single, a double, a triple, and three runs batted in as the Yankees won, 7–3.

The next day Henrich returned to the lineup at first base after a three-week absence. He drove in two runs in support of Eddie Lopat's five-hit, 5–0 shutout. It was the final game of the season between Cleveland and New York and the Monday crowd of 27,839 pushed the attendance for the 22 games these teams had played during the season in both cities to 1,017,553—an incredible average of 46,251 a game.

On September 26, the Yankees, still without DiMaggio, lost to the Red Sox and fell from first place for the first time. Only five games remained, three against Philadelphia, and two with the Red Sox in New York on the last two days of the season.

The Yankees designated Saturday, October 1, as Joe DiMaggio Day, a fan appreciation event for the star, and indicated that he had received a medical green light to play. For a baseball fan the weekend attraction, already sold out weeks in advance, was an event not to be missed—two games that would decide the pennant and a tribute to the comeback player of the year. One couldn't ask for more.

A crowd of 69,551 had turned out at the Stadium to shower their affection on DiMaggio, still weak from his infirmities and 15 pounds underweight. DiMaggio listened as he was extolled for a solid hour as Mel Allen, the broadcasting voice of the Yankees, introduced the speakers. Ethel Merman sang some of her show tunes and Phil Brito sang the national anthem. At the plate DiMaggio was surrounded by a veritable trainload of gifts, ranging from 300 quarts of ice cream to a super special speedboat. His mother, who made the trip from San

Francisco with his brother Tom, received an automobile and flowers, and Joe's son, Joe Jr., received a bicycle and an electric train. Mayor William O'Dwyer of New York explained that at DiMaggio's insistence all the cash gifts he received that day would be donated to the New York Heart Fund and the Damon Runyon Memorial Cancer Fund. In DiMaggio's name a four-year scholarship to any New York university for a deserving youth was donated. The New York, New Haven and Hartford Railroad arranged a special nine-car train, designated "The Joe DiMaggio Special," to transport 1,000 fans from New Haven. The press came from everywhere, including a special correspondent from Japan.

DiMaggio made a short acceptance speech.

"When I was in San Francisco, Lefty O'Doul told me: 'Joe, don't let the big city scare you. New York is the friendliest town in the world.' This day proves it. I want to thank the fans; my friends; my manager, Casey Stengel; and my teammates, the gamest, fightingest bunch that ever lived; and I want to thank the good Lord for making me a Yankee."

The Red Sox had presented DiMaggio with a surprise gift, a plaque autographed by all the Boston players and Joe McCarthy, his old manager. DiMaggio was especially pleased by the gesture and said, "They're a grand bunch, too, and if we don't win the pennant I'm happy that they will."

His first appearance at bat in the first inning was described in *The New York Times*: "Then DiMaggio stepped to the plate and the cheers that greeted the Clipper earlier during the Fan Day ceremonies were as nothing compared with the thunderous welcome that attended his official return to action."

Mel Parnell struck out DiMaggio. But in the fourth inning, he lashed a liner for a one-hop ground-rule double into the right-field seats, driving in the first Yankee run. Later he kept a rally alive with a single off Joe Dobson as the Yankees scored twice and tied the score, 4–4. Johnny Lindell hit a long homer in the eighth and the Bombers held on to win, 5–4.

The lead paragraph in the game story of *The New York Times* read: "And so it develops, those battered Bombers with their countless aches and bruises, weren't ready to be rolled into a boneyard after all."

If the Yankees were to be rolled into a boneyard, it would have to happen the next day, Sunday, October 2.

Vic Raschi was the Yankee pitcher, going for his 21st victory. Ellis Kinder, seeking No. 24, was Boston's choice. The crowd numbered 68,055. Kinder yielded a run in the third and then he and Raschi hooked up in a tight pitching duel until the eighth inning. Henrich connected for a home run and Jerry Coleman cleared the bases for three more runs with a double for a 5–0 Yankee lead. The pennant appeared to be only one inning from New York's grasp.

The Red Sox struck back in the ninth. Vern Stephens singled and Raschi issued a walk. Bobby Doerr drove a long ball over DiMaggio's head. DiMaggio made the pursuit on shaky legs. The ball went for a triple and two runs scored, cutting the Yankee lead to 5–2.

Then in a dramatic moment that brought a hush from the crowd, DiMaggio called time out. He waved to one of the umpires and trotted into the infield, then jogged into the dugout. He had taken himself out of the game.

"He received an ovation as he jogged to the Yankee dugout. The fans understood well enough why he was leaving," the *Times* reported.

DiMaggio felt he should have been able to catch Doerr's drive that went for a triple. In his judgment, he knew he had been unable to do his job. Raschi allowed one more run and the Yankees captured another championship.

In a quiet moment after the victory celebration in the dressing room, DiMaggio summed up what he had done.

"I should have removed myself on Vern Stephens's single in the ninth," he said. "I had terrible pains in my shinbones. And when I didn't catch Bobby Doerr's triple, which was catchable, I didn't hesitate any longer and walked off. Gosh, we had only a three-run lead and I didn't want to hurt the club by falling on my face if another fly had been hit to me."

15

*The Slump
to End
All Slumps*

*W*HEN JOE DIMAGGIO got his 2,000th hit, in a night game at Cleveland on June 20, 1950, some Broadway columnists and sportswriters were sitting at a table in Toots Shor's restaurant in New York talking about his career. Between drinks the conversation drifted to a discussion of the invasions of privacy DiMaggio had endured over the years as a sports hero in the great metropolis.

"Name me one other guy who's lived in New York so many years as DiMaggio has and never took a ride on a subway?" one of the columnists asked.

"If DiMaggio took a ride on a subway, it would cause a riot," another columnist said.

"He can't even eat a meal in a public place in peace, unless it's in this joint," one of the sportswriters chimed in. "At least Toots sees to it that he's able to eat without anybody pestering him, sticking a piece of paper or a pen under his nose. Most places a guy can leave a tip of a quarter or a half a buck, but he's always expected to leave a buck or two on the waiter's tray because he's supposed to be in the big chips."

"That subway thing," another sportswriter said, "he can't even take a bus. It's got to be a cab to get from one corner to the next and those fares can mount up. The guy's lucky if he can hang onto the dough he's making."

"He can't even sit at a table with some dolls without being linked romantically with one of them. He can't take a walk in a park or up a street to window shop. He can't go to a movie alone. Waiting in line for a ticket he'd cause a traffic jam."

The writers went on in the same vein, talking about DiMaggio for half an hour.

"It's an unnatural existence," one of them said. "The guy lives in a glass house. He can't go where he wants without attracting a crowd. He can't even stop for a beer at a local bar without somebody thinking he's a lush."

"If it wasn't New York, it would be different," the first columnist said, "but then he wouldn't be DiMaggio."

New York, of course, did the same thing to all its popular celebrities. It went with the territory. DiMaggio was well aware of that—and he had also heard how fickle and fleeting fame could be. Early in January the Yankees were thinking of revising his contract. They invited him East to talk about it. Under baseball law, a player's contract could be cut 25 percent of his salary. Rumors were afloat that this was what the

Yankees intended for DiMaggio. Actually, he did receive a tenuous proposal of a flat $75,000 contract, with a bonus clause attached, based on attendance. Conceivably, DiMaggio could make as much as $125,000 under this proposal. He held fast to his pragmatic bird-in-hand philosophy, however, and on January 24, after a short conference with Weiss, he took his second $100,000-a-year contract straight.

He said he thought he could play for at least two more Yankee pennant-winners.

"I am very happy about it all," he said, "and I feel better right now than at any time since the war. I've been playing golf regularly, getting in a lot of walking. It gives me an appetite. I want to put on about eight pounds so I can go to training camp around 210. That will give me a little to work off to get to my playing weight of about 202."

After his bout with pneumonitis he had played the last two games of the 1949 season at 179 pounds. He had only played in 76 games, but he wound up with a .346 batting average with 14 homers and 67 runs batted in, and was voted the comeback player of the year by The Associated Press. He had spent the winter at his mother's home in San Francisco, enjoying the outdoors and stoking up on her Italian cooking.

In Florida, DiMaggio was impressing Stengel with his hitting and fielding. Worn out after the 1949 season, DiMaggio was allowed to set his own spring training pace. He pulled himself out of the lineup whenever he felt sore or achy or pulled up lame with a charley horse or developed blisters on his feet. Stengel was taking no chances with his star and he was making predictions that the team would easily retain its title.

"I would say we are going north this spring with a good club," Stengel said, "better set and faster than it was a year ago and one that looks to me to have an excellent chance of winning the pennant again. A year ago when I first took over this job, I had no idea what I had. Joe DiMaggio was a doubtful starter and the depth of the club was something I wasn't to learn about until later. But I've got a lot of players in the infield spots, and in the outfield I've got a great bunch of ball hawks."

At Memphis on April 9 the Yankees met the Chicks in an exhibition game. A crowd of 16,138 hoped to get a glimpse of DiMaggio in action. He had pulled a muscle in his left calf a few days earlier and the decision on whether he would play was made only a few minutes before game time, after he and Stengel had discussed his condition. DiMaggio played and hit a home run.

"I know there's a lot of pressure on to have DiMaggio play, especially with a big crowd as we had today," Stengel said, "but what I'm more concerned about is the shape he'll be in on opening day. I don't care how many of these games he misses, but I do want him in there when we open in Boston. However, he's still training himself and if he says he's sound enough to play that's O.K. with me."

DiMaggio was more than sound for the opener at Boston. He hit a triple, a double, and a single and made two spectacular fielding plays, reminding the crowd of 31,822 of his great comeback effort in June of the previous season. This time DiMaggio had helped whittle away a 9–0 Boston lead, and with nine runs in the eighth the Yankees won, 15–10.

Arthur Daley of *The New York Times* wrote: "How good and how well is DiMaggio? The Jolter was Frank Merriwell on spikes. In his first time at bat he tripled to center over the head of his brother Dom. He later singled to left and doubled to center. He threw a runner out at third with a rifle peg. He raced up against the center-field bull-pen fence and made a miraculous catch in the fingertips of his glove."

With his 2,000th hit DiMaggio reached a plateau that only 88 others had attained since 1876. The prospect of his reaching 3,000 hits, he knew, was virtually impossible. He had lost three years to the Air Force and with his aching body at 35 years old he thought he would be lucky to last two more seasons.

He had made two hits in the game at Cleveland to reach 2,000 and he lingered nostalgically on the moment. His first hit had come off Bob Lemon in the third inning and had driven in two runs. In the seventh he singled to left field off Marino (Chico) Pieretti with two out for No. 2,000. Dale Mitchell, the Cleveland left fielder, threw the ball in to Pieretti, who took it to DiMaggio. He gave it to Bill Dickey, coaching at first base, to save for him. He wanted the ball as a keepsake—it had taken him 1,537 games and 6,050 turns at bat to earn it.

In the clubhouse, he sat calmly drinking a beer and recalling the first hit he made as a major-league rookie in 1936—off Elon Hogsett on May 3, against the Browns at the Stadium.

"I'd missed the first 17 games because of that burnt foot," DiMaggio said, "and the day before they had announced through the megaphone they used then that I'd make my debut the next day. I got two more hits that day, a triple and another single, but I can almost feel the thrill of that first one now.

"But this was as much a thrill as any. Maybe you appreciate them more as you get older. What gives me such a bang is that it was in the same park and against the same Indians who stopped my hitting streak in 1941. This sort of evened things up for that one. Funny thing, it was a night game, too. Al Smith and Jim Bagby were the Indians' pitchers that night and Ken Keltner was at third. He was the guy who hurt me most with those great stops of his."

Bobby Brown, the Yankees' third baseman, went over to sit at the next locker. Brown, who was in a batting slump and was hitting .208, was in an unhappy mood.

DiMaggio paused from his reminiscences.

"Stop worrying about it, kid," he said to Brown. "I know how you feel. I've had a lot of nights like it this season myself. But you'll come out of it if you just keep swinging. We all do."

Before the season ended DiMaggio would have to take the advice he had given Brown—"just keep swinging"—and use it personally to lift himself out of the worst slump of his career.

He had hit a home run on July 2 in Boston when Stengel announced that he was taking DiMaggio out of center field and starting him at first base the next day in Washington. Not since he played in the sandlots of San Francisco had DiMaggio played that position. At the beginning of his career, with the Seals in 1932, he played three games at shortstop and from then on he was always in the outfield. Only briefly had he played anywhere but center field, a position he had mastered so well that experts ranked him the equal, if not the superior, of the great Tris Speaker in covering that territory. In 1936 he had broken in as the left fielder for the Yankees and had played there for half a season. For the 1936 All-Star Game he was in right field. At all other times, center field was his province.

Stengel's decision was considered rash and raised many eyebrows. The move was called the most revolutionary any Yankee manager had ever undertaken. He justified it on the ground that he had problems at first base and wanted to end the two-platoon system he had installed with his outfielders. Tommy Henrich, who had been shifted from right field to first, had a buckled left knee and was out indefinitely. Johnny Mize, a veteran first baseman acquired at the end of 1949 from the New York Giants, had an ailing throwing arm, and Joe Collins, a rookie up from Newark, had an anemic bat. Stengel was eager to give Hank Bauer a regular job in right field. By positioning DiMaggio at first, he could use all his options, with Cliff Mapes in center, Gene Woodling in left, and Bauer in right. Jackie Jensen, a sensational bonus rookie, would be an alternate in the outfield.

"This is strictly my idea," Stengel said about shifting DiMaggio to first base, "and DiMaggio is going to give it a try because he is that type of player. When I asked him whether he'd try playing the bag, he replied, 'Certainly. I'll play anywhere you want if you think it will help the club.' "

Stengel was also thinking about dropping DiMaggio from the clean-up spot in the batting order—a move he eventually adopted briefly. His rationale made good baseball sense.

"Left-handers have been pitching too cautiously to him, not minding even walking him with the left-handed Berra behind him," Stengel said. "With somebody else, say Berra, in the number four spot, DiMaggio batting fifth and Bill Johnson sixth, opposing managers will have to change their strategy."

On the Fourth of July in Washington, DiMaggio played first base for the Yankees. He handled 13 putouts without error and looked comfortable around the base. Later he said he had put stress on seldom-used muscles and had aggravated some that were already sore. Ironically, Bauer injured his right ankle in the game and was declared out of the lineup indefinitely. Like the best laid plans, Stengel's experiment went awry for the time being and DiMaggio was in his customary position the next day. Mize, sore arm and all, took over at first where he belonged, and DiMaggio, safe in the No. 4 hitting slot, unloaded a bases-filled triple to spark a 16-9 triumph.

Stengel, of course, was no fool although he often couched himself in the words and antics of a clown. He had been in baseball so long he could tell when a player had lost a step or had developed a split-second hitch in his swing that cost him hits. Maybe he knew something about DiMaggio that the slugger didn't know about himself.

DiMaggio went into a horrendous slump. Early in May his batting average had dropped to .220; in late June it was at .253. Although he had hit 14 homers and had driven in 54 runs—the most in those departments among the Yankees—sportswriters were beginning to write his obituary as the leader of the Yankees.

On August 11, he was benched for the first time in his career other than for a specific injury or illness. He had made only four hits in his last 38 times at bat—an average of .103. The Yankees were still in contention, hoping to launch a drive for the top, but DiMaggio's silent bat was more a liability than an asset. The writers had him ready for embalming if not for burying.

Throughout the siege, DiMaggio was moodily silent, sensitively aware of what was being written about him. He could not deny he was in a slump and he didn't want to talk about it.

"I don't like to talk about slumps," he said. "It can be caused by almost anything, pressing too hard, hot weather . . . "

He had been in the lineup for every game, playing with shaky legs, sore muscles, and a virus that plagued him all through June. He welcomed the rest Stengel had given him.

Stengel put him back in on August 18 at Philadelphia. He grounded out his first three times at bat, then in the ninth he hit a home run, his 100th hit of the season.

He was off on a month-long spree of the most sustained hitting in his 12-year career. By September 1 he had raised his batting average to .285, with 23 homers and 92 runs batted in. The next day he hit No. 24. The Yankees had won their sixth game in a row and the 15th in their last 17 and were challenging the leaders again. On September 10, he became the first player to hit three home runs in a game at Griffith Stadium in Washington. All three traveled over 400 feet in a park regarded as the ultimate test for power hitters, and especially right-handers, with its prohibitively long dimensions to all fields. The left-field foul line carried 405 feet to the bleachers; the flagpole in left center was 409 feet away, and straight-away center was 420 feet. The right-field fence was 328 feet out, at the foul line.

He added a double and had a total of four runs batted in, putting him over 100 for the ninth season. On September 14 the Yankees took first place; DiMaggio had hit safely in 19 straight games. In all, from August 18 to September 30, DiMaggio had batted at a .376 clip. It restored him to the class of .300 hitters. He completed the season at .301, with 32 homers and 122 runs batted in.

DiMaggio's batting affliction was so spectacular it magnified him in the sports pages as much as his bone-spur affliction had in 1949. Invariably, the fans had faith in him. In a double-header against Cleveland, he went to bat eight times and couldn't produce a hit. The fans applauded him with "more vigor and greater warmth the last time he took his turn than he had been the first" one writer wrote.

The slump gnawed at DiMaggio and its symptoms were "manifested by an almost monastic silence. . . . He maintained an air of stricken quiet and took on the sorrowful dignity of a flawed masterpiece," wrote Gilbert Millstein of *The New York Times.*

Whether DiMaggio saw his future as a ballplayer coming to an end, and refused to acknowledge it, or whether he intuitively believed he could last several more seasons, only time and his performance could answer. He worried constantly about it. He was always one of the last players to leave the dressing room after a game whether he was hitting or not. He went through a precise ritual of drying out. He showered and dressed, usually with a beer or a half cup of coffee and a cigarette close by, as if they were pacifiers to ease his tension. Often he consumed a pack of Chesterfields a day, sometimes two packs. If he wasn't hitting, he was the last one out of the dressing room. Once after a long, hard night game, he didn't leave until 2:30 in the morning, moody and down on himself.

"Base hits are my job," he said. "When I'm not getting them, I worry, same as any businessman who's not doing much business."

Joe Page, DiMaggio's roommate, recalled that he awoke one night to find the bedroom lights blazing and nobody in DiMaggio's bed. DiMaggio was standing instead in front of a mirror in his pajamas, taking swings with an imaginary bat. "Joe is the kind of guy he's got to be—that's all—he's just got to be that way!"

All ballplayers have slumps. No matter what psychological approaches they adopt to overcome them, they cannot be simply wished away. DiMaggio kept regular training hours, but he also enjoyed his free time. Night life and nightclub-hopping were part of his style.

"I know a lot of players who get to bed every night at 10 and don't get to hit just the same," he said.

Tommy Henrich had been sidelined most of the season with a bad knee. He had been a victim of batting slumps, too, and he thought he had a remedy for combatting them.

"The idea is to go out and relax," Henrich said. "Forget the game. I don't mean get tight. Just go away from it, like a businessman does at the end of the day. Joe's a very serious guy. He has a bad day and he gets mad at himself. I think a slump hurts him more than it does most guys."

Despite his constant worry, DiMaggio believed he would come out of his slump naturally, as he eventually did.

"Hitting's all timing," he said. "Your timing goes off and before you know it you're in a slump. Nobody likes to be in one, but it's got to come out naturally. You start pressing and you get in a rut. You lose your snap, your whip. So you get up to the ball park earlier and take more times at batting practice. Nothing works. And then you come out of it without knowing it. You think you're doing the same things wrong and suddenly you're hitting. A man is never satisfied. You go up there and get four hits and you want five so bad you can taste it."

DiMaggio's talents were gifts. He could do things instinctively, while less gifted players, even very good ones, had to go through drudgery to learn them. He gave the semblance of ease, but he complemented his natural talent with what he studied and learned. Over the years he had reinforced his gifts by keeping a book on his opponents. He could figure out where his rival batters were likely to hit a ball. For example, a right-handed power hitter would ordinarily pull the ball to left field. DiMaggio also considered other factors—the dimensions and wind patterns of the ball parks, for instance. He had figured out the tendencies of the hitters and applied them to the prevailing conditions. For a high fly or a low line drive to the same spot on the field, he would not necessarily set out in the same direction. Each had to be measured under the existing wind, or lack of it, and so forth. This was the edge he often spoke about, his "little trick" of getting a jump on the ball and heading in the right direction at the crack of the bat. It was the advantage he created that made his great fielding seem all too easy. He was not a player to be overmanaged or second-guessed and even opposing managers knew that.

One opposing manager who learned it first hand was Oscar Vitt, who guided Cleveland in 1938, 1939, and 1940. Vitt, who had been a guest at DiMaggio's wedding in 1939, was part of a group called the Yankee Alumni Club made up of Bay Area residents who had served time in the Yankee organization. The group was founded by Joe Devine, a Yankee scout. Vitt had become a member of the club because he had managed the Yankee farm club at Newark, New Jersey, before going to Cleveland. He had helped develop some of the outstanding stars who moved from the Newark Bears to Yankee Stadium.

DiMaggio had been particularly effective against some of the Indians' best pitchers, among them Bob Feller, Mel Harder (whom

DiMaggio considered the toughest pitcher he had faced), and Al Milnar. Vitt had gained respect for DiMaggio's fielding and hitting and he was one of his biggest boosters at Alumni Club gatherings.

"Everybody talks about Joe DiMaggio's hitting," Vitt said. "But Joe won more games with his glove and arm than with his bat. When I was managing the Indians we were playing the Yankees one day in that big Municipal Stadium in Cleveland. We had the bases loaded with two out and Hal Trosky, our first baseman, cow-tailed one out of sight. I waved our runners around. 'DiMaggio,' I said, 'get that one!'

"He did! He went back to the wall, over 400 feet away, and speared it one-handed. So O.K., I figured, DiMaggio can play deep. The next time up Trosky took his usual toe-hold and DiMaggio was in deep center. But Hal hit the ball on his fists for a blooper behind short. 'O.K.' I muttered, 'get that one, DiMaggio.' He did—raced in and took it off his shoetops. After that I was through challenging DiMaggio. I never did it again."

During the slump Stengel was watching DiMaggio at batting practice one morning.

"He tends to business," Stengel told a reporter. "He knows where the ball park is and he knows when to get there. You never see him gassing. There isn't a point he is lacking in and he does everything easy. He makes big league baseball look simple. It isn't that simple. He would make any manager look good. That's about the best thing you can say about any ballplayer."

These platitudes from Stengel, a man from whom it was not easy to extract raves, described a 35-year-old player whose hair was already flecked with gray and whose body had been racked with so many infirmities he would make a good case history in a medical journal. In his 12 years in the majors, DiMaggio's ailments had run the gamut— ulcers, a burned ankle, tooth, tonsil and adenoid trouble, charley-horses, blisters, infections, a trick right shoulder, pulled back muscles, a swollen neck, and of course, bone chips in his right elbow and bone spurs in both heels, virus pneumonia, and colds. And there were enough aches and pains to put any working man on sick call for days on end.

If DiMaggio had been an enigma to his early critics, his friends saw nothing puzzling about him. They showered him with adulation and loyalty, even protection; he could do nothing that could diminish their affection for him.

When he was in New York, he roomed in a midtown Manhattan hotel suite with George Solotaire, a ticket broker and devoted Yankee fan who had become one of DiMaggio's closest friends. Solotaire willingly ran errands for DiMaggio, who often had to dodge the public to get even the simplest of personal necessities—tooth paste and aspirin at a drugstore, shoes shined, clothes cleaned and pressed. Their friendship stemmed from a common interest in many diversions besides sports and it lasted until Solotaire died in 1965.

"We appreciate the same things," Solotaire told an interviewer about his friendship with the ballplayer. "We get the same kicks out of the same situations. We get a lot of laughs together. What more can you ask?"

Solotaire suffered with DiMaggio when the ballplayer failed and he celebrated when he produced fabulously. Together they made the rounds of New York's more fashionable night spots—El Morocco, the Barberry Room, Bruno's Patio—and restaurants, Le Pavillon and The Colony.

One night, after DiMaggio had had a brilliant game at the Stadium, Solotaire thought the slugger might enjoy a snack when he got home to their suite. Solotaire, of course, had been to the game, but on his way home he stopped at Le Pavillon and ordered a ham-and-cheese sandwich to go out. The sandwich was daintily wrapped and placed in a wicker basket. It cost Solotaire $12.

When DiMaggio got back to the hotel, he said he wasn't hungry.

"Hey, Joe," Solotaire said, "c'mon, this sandwich cost me 12 bucks."

"Then you better eat it yourself," DiMaggio said.

Solotaire took his advice. "It tastes like gold," he said.

Solotaire had come to the New York scene after he left an orphanage at the age of 14, hoping to become a song writer, take Tin Pan Alley by storm, and win acclaim as another Irving Berlin. He never wrote a successful song, but he fell in love with New York City. DiMaggio, even years after Solotaire died, liked to recall his love affair with the city.

"Whenever he had to leave town," DiMaggio said later, "he would tell me. 'I've got to go camping for a few days,' and when he returned he would say, 'It's so good to be back in America.'"

When song writing didn't pan out, Solotaire stayed on the fringes of show business by plugging away instead as a ticket broker. He established the Adelphi Theater Ticket Service in a small shop on Times

Square and hawked pasteboards with such abandon that he eventually won the sobriquet "millionaire ticket broker."

The Broadway scene was the ballpark Solotaire wanted most to play in, and he had found a way to do it. By catering to producers, directors, actors, and other celebrities, many of whom he knew casually at least, he attained a sense of legitimacy and belonging. It was the objective of all Broadway aficionados regardless of their occupation or talent.

His ticket office was patronized by the well-to-do, among them the Astors, the Vanderbilts, the Whitneys. Solotaire could get you the hottest ticket in town on short notice provided you had the right price (in 1927 he was fined $100 for selling World Series tickets at a 200 percent markup over the retail price). He once supplied J. P. Morgan, the financier, with tickets to the same show for seven successive Saturday night performances, explaining that the banker "must have an eye for one of the dames in the show."

Through his desire to write song lyrics and his show business connections, he landed an honorarium that nudged him by name and reputation into the "literati" circle of Broadway newspaper critics. For many years, for no fee, he wrote two-line couplets for the *Hollywood Reporter,* a trade paper. His piece appeared at the end of the column written by the paper's drama critic. For example, his couplet for a poorly reviewed Ethel Merman musical went; "The show isn't firm, / But it's still got the Merm." For "Fiddler on the Roof" he wrote: "Have no fear about Fiddler; / This is a triple A honest diddler." He was an innocent in the arts, but with limited talent he had found a milieu and wealth.

Another of DiMaggio's close friends was *Times* photographer Ernie Sisto, who was born in the Hell's Kitchen section of Manhattan and who came from a large Italian-American family. The two had become chums during DiMaggio's first season with the Yankees.

"I was Ernie to him and he was Joe to me," Sisto recalls. "We just hit it off at the start. Joe was a very shy guy even then. Even with all that publicity when he came up, to me he was just another ballplayer. I took to him not because I thought he was going to be a great ballplayer, but I just took to him and he took to me. It wasn't that I was going to take advantage of being a friend of his. I was just a photographer, a jerk photographer, but Joe never made me feel that way. He was famous in his first season—he looked so terrific out there, he just took off. And when everybody, especially guys like Lou Gehrig started talking about him, it made me say to myself, 'Geez, this guy is better than I thought.'"

Sisto and DiMaggio ribbed each other a lot, especially about their long, aquiline noses (when Jimmy Durante met Sisto, the comedian warned, "One of us'll hafta get out of town," and a writer once compared DiMaggio with Cyrano de Bergerac. The player took umbrage, however, when *Esquire* magazine once illustrated a story about him with an exaggerated caricature of his nose).

Sisto took thousands of pictures of the star for publication, for fans, and for his private collection. They were a Mutt and Jeff picture themselves whenever they were together—the five-foot-five-inch photographer alongside the six-foot-two-inch ballplayer.

"Once kidding around with me he said, 'Ah, you guinea bastard,' We were kidding around, I forget what it was really, but that was the first time I had heard him say anything off color. He never liked to use coarse language. He drew a lot of Italians into the Stadium, you know. They used to wave Italian flags out there. I saw all those kids waving flags, but it didn't bother him. Even if he didn't like it, he liked the adulation. He still does. When he arrives at the Americana Hotel [now the Sheraton Centre] where he stays now when he's in New York, people start rushing over to him. He says he hates it, but I know he still likes it. It makes him feel good that they still remember him.

"I've had a lot of laughs and good times with Joe over the years. He always helped me out when I was in a jam. I was sent to Florida one spring training on a last-minute assignment. The paper wanted me to do a pictorial feature on the Yankees.

"So I get down there and go to a hotel called the Yankee Clipper. I don't know if it was named after Joe or what. I go to the desk to check on my reservation and find out the *Times* didn't make an advance reservation for me. Geez, that's fine. The bastards, I say to myself. It's already midnight and I'm wondering where the hell I'm going to stay. Try and find a hotel at that hour.

"So I said to the clerk, 'Is Joe DiMaggio registered here?'

"He says, 'Yes, he is.'

"So I get on the phone and call Joe.

"'C'mon up here. We got plenty of room,' Joe says. I got up and you know who's staying with him? It's George Solotaire.

"Joe depended on that guy for everything. He used to wait on Joe hand and foot. He just idolized Joe. He traveled with him everywhere. He was like Joe's valet. Even took Joe's clothes to the tailor, had his shoes shined, everything. Joe didn't have to worry about a thing as long as Solotaire was around.

"Anyway, when I get up in the room they're already in their beds and Joe says, 'Sleep over in that bed there,' and I'm set for the night.

The next morning at breakfast Solotaire says to me, 'Can I fix you a sandwich, Ernie?'

"A sandwich for breakfast? I say to myself. Well, what the hell, I'm a guest. So I say, O.K.

"Solotaire goes to work and starts making sandwiches. The next thing I know he hands me this big thing made of cream cheese and lox on a bagel. That's how I got introduced to bagels and lox. Solotaire was a Jewish fellow, grew up in New York. I guess he was a frustrated ballplayer or just liked to be around Joe. In his book Joe could do nothing wrong.

"The next day after I took the shots for my Yankee feature, I had to twin up the assignment and go to Miami to take pictures for a title fight. Well, the *Times* forgot to make reservations again. I'm like a traveling gypsy.

"So Joe says to Solotaire, 'Get on the phone and see what you can do for Ernie.'

"Solotaire picks up the phone and makes a call. In five minutes I've got a reservation in Miami. He was fabulous. Whenever I was down there at training camp or anyplace else with them, Joe and Solotaire always treated everybody like they were important. Even a photographer like me. You wanted something to eat, you took it if it was there, and if it wasn't, they ordered it for you."

Toots Shor was another of DiMaggio's close friends during his playing days in New York. DiMaggio ate his meals at Shor's restaurant two or three times a week. It was one of the few places where he felt completely at ease and relaxed. It was where he made the friendship, too, of some of the New York sportswriters and columnists who took a liking to him, studied his personality, and became instrumental in writing about the DiMaggio mystique in their columns. They were chiefly responsible for associating him with the aura of "class" as a personal characteristic. Shor, a huge, cigar-smoking bon vivant with a low tolerance for dilettantes and intruders, had started his saloon-keeping days as a bouncer. He saw to it that DiMaggio ate his meals free from distractions from the public.

Shor and Solotaire were garrulous, outgoing extroverts. Their businesses demanded that kind of personality. DiMaggio was the antithesis of his pals. The dichotomy of personality often puzzled the Broadway Bugles, the columnists who wrote about the Great White Way.

Shor put them at ease. "He's like anybody else," he said in discussing DiMaggio's friendship with him. "He has to talk things over with someone, and who is a better guy to talk things over with than a good saloon-keeper?"

There was considerable ground for these friendships. None of his cronies was well-read, yet their own celebrity had exposed them to a kind of popular finishing school. None had finished high school, but that did not seem to bother, sadden, or embitter them. In his own way each had talents he believed were marketable and on which he could turn a profit. They had been singularly attracted to New York fully aware of its mystique. They knew the city could transform and catapult personalities with all types of talent to the top rung of stardom. New York was where you could make a killing, no matter what your scheme—con man, professor, bartender, ticket broker, or professional athlete.

Shor was born and grew up in the tough section of south Philadelphia, a neighborhood thick with Irish and Italians, where a Jewish boy had to learn the tricks of survival as an underdog. Bartending, first through the speakeasy days of Prohibition and dodging the law, brought him to New York. His friendships with entrepreneurs of all shadings got him eventually into the legitimate restaurant business. In the 1940s and 1950s his restaurant at 51 West 51st Street in Manhattan, with its famous circular bar, was the mecca for anyone who had already attained status or anyone who sought to achieve it. His doors were rarely closed to anyone. It was America's most well-known name-dropping saloon, a chic atmosphere into which sauntered the famous and the near-famous. And the more famous the sainted or notorious names that were dropped, the merrier it made the patrons and Shor.

When DiMaggio first hit the sidewalks of New York and was being compared with Babe Ruth, it was only natural that he should take a place among the city's colony of celebrities. It was natural, too, that there would be a coterie of followers eager to rub shoulders with the talent they wished they possessed.

In this quid-pro-quo manner DiMaggio, Shor, and Solotaire struck up their friendship. They were on common intellectual ground and each had something to take and offer from knowing the other.

Shor, talkative and aggressive, capable of charming anyone on first meeting and sustaining it, was instrumental in bringing the shy and reticent DiMaggio out of his shell. He was also DiMaggio's staunchest defender. The aura of "class" that came to be associated with DiMaggio in later years as a player and then as a retired "gentleman sportsman" grew in part from his loyalty to Shor and his association with writers and other professional figures who were regulars at Shor's.

In the vernacular of the pub-hopping and celebrity set, the word "class" had a special connotation, akin to a kind of aristocratic behavior. To Hemingway, who had also been a patron at Shor's, it was called "grace under pressure."

Shor's contention was that the woods were filled with champions, but champions with class were like redwoods. To remain in Shor's good graces took extraordinary loyalty, and DiMaggio had to work hard to maintain it.

When Larry MacPhail was the president of the Yankees, he and Shor had several disagreements. What had once been a booming friendship, cooled rapidly into an icy relationship. MacPhail, a man who sought reprisal, indicated to his players that he would prefer it if they did not patronize Shor's restaurant, where several Yankees, besides DiMaggio, also occasionally ate dinner.

One night, after a Yankee game, MacPhail asked DiMaggio to have dinner with him.

"Thank you, but I can't make it tonight," DiMaggio said. "I'm having dinner with Toots."

This show of loyalty to Shor especially in the face of losing favor with MacPhail, became known to all the inner circle and put DiMaggio on the highest pedestal with them. Other Yankee players continued to eat dinner at Shor's knowing that MacPhail disapproved. Among the regulars at Shor's, DiMaggio's "leadership" in this instance became Exhibit A in their museum of illustrations of class—loyalty displayed under pressure.

It went even further. A sportswriter once encountered DiMaggio

running down 52nd Street as if he were chasing a fly ball at the
Stadium. The writer stopped him and asked what was happening.

"I had to eat lunch with the Yankees at '21' and I want to get over
and tell Toots before somebody gives him a bad report," DiMaggio
said, breaking again full-tilt into a sprint.

DiMaggio often visited Shor and his family at the restaurateur's
home in Deal, New Jersey, where he used to entertain friends with his
wife and three young daughters, who liked to call DiMaggio "Uncle
Joe." During the 1949 season when the Yankees were on the road, Shor
and DiMaggio exchanged phone calls nightly, with Shor eager to learn
how the slugger's heel spur was coming along. When DiMaggio's
aching bone spurs forced him into virtual seclusion that year, Shor
visited him often and arranged to have his meals brought to him by a
delivery man who took a cab every day from the restaurant to DiMaggio's hotel—and Shor never charged Joe for the meals. It was, of
course, a reciprocal friendship. DiMaggio remembered Shor on holi-
days and birthdays, sending him gifts, among them an alligator-skin
traveling bag, and a favorite of Shor's—a gold watch chain on which
was inscribed "To My Guy Toots—Joe DiMaggio."

Shor was eloquent at bombast. His description of DiMaggio as
"among the 10 most important living men" was surely that, but his
sincere affection for the player became public knowledge at the end of
the 1949 season when DiMaggio was honored with a "Joe DiMaggio
Day" at the Stadium for his comeback after missing the first 65 games
with his bone spurs.

Shor sent DiMaggio this message:

> You have given me more thrills than all the rest of the champions put
> together. You always won the Big Ones and never knew how to choke up.
> You are the biggest guy I know and the biggest thing about you is your
> heart. You gave us baseball fans the greatest moments we have ever had
> but something more than that, Joe, you gave me your friendship."

Toots Shor died in the winter of 1977.

Even before the Broadway Bugles came around to extolling DiMaggio's virtues, he received a far better press than any other top player in
other major league cities. For example, in Boston, Ted Williams played
under the heavy-handed criticism of a hostile press throughout his
career despite hitting exploits that even DiMaggio envied. Hank

Greenberg, a native New Yorker, got good press in Detroit, but it was minuscule compared to what he might have received had he had his great home-run-hitting seasons playing for New York.

Put in simplistic terms, DiMaggio seemed quite an ordinary person and he won over critics by rarely stepping out of character.

"Joe hasn't changed very much from the fellow I first met," Sisto said in recollection. "He's the same wherever he goes. No matter where I've been with Joe he's always been dressed like a prince. He's always neat and trim. He prides himself on that. He's got that real class, people can always pick him out. Sometimes I've had to spare him embarrassment, though. One night we left a hotel in Manhattan and we were walking up Broadway, heading someplace, I don't remember where.

"This big black guy is coming up the street with a woman. I recognize him right away.

"'Joe, Joe DiMaggio, how the heck are you?' he says and shoots out his hand to shake with Joe.

"Joe puts out his hand to shake, but I can tell Joe didn't recognize him.

"So right away I say, 'Joe Black, how are you?' and Joe says 'How are you Joe?' and they get talking. He had gotten so fat that Joe didn't recognize him.

"Later Joe said to me, 'Ernie, I'm glad you recognized him because I sure as hell didn't.'"

One of DiMaggio's Broadway columnist friends said: "Joe isn't backward, forward, or sideways. I've seen him develop where he can stand off 10 or 12 sportswriters, sign a couple hundred autographs, and get out with a big smile. There is tremendous pressure on him all the time and it's got so he has to duck into a movie on the sly if he wants to go at all. He's a good column name, but how often do you see his name in the gossip columns?

"It's just that he doesn't do anything. He doesn't give them the material to work on. Now, he's the sort of guy who's a dame guy and he isn't a dame guy, if you know what I mean. They go after him, but he just takes it in his stride like he does everything else. A lot of people think he is shy, but he isn't. He can keep a dame faded with small talk. He's no dud."

DiMaggio had learned, of course, how to make top dollar when it came to salary, but somehow he had not acquired the killer instinct for making money from endeavors outside of baseball. He had, of course, many things going for him, but even his lawyer during his playing days, Julian Rosenthal, estimated that if he had been more aggressive as an entrepreneur he could have doubled his take.

"Let's face it," Rosenthal said, "Joe just isn't very commercial."

He did dabble enough, however, to get a $50,000-a-year retainer from the Columbia Broadcasting Company to do a radio show in which he answered questions about sports. He produced an album of children's records worth about $25,000 in royalties, and endorsed cigarettes, T-shirts, sport shirts and sweaters, toilet articles, baseballs, bats, and gloves.

DiMaggio never gave the appearance of flashing or squandering money. He was known to tip generously, whether to bat boy, clubhouse attendant, or head waiter. He bought his parents a home in North Beach his second year in the majors; he bought a fishing boat for his brother Mike. He enjoyed wearing tailor-made suits and was named to several best-dressed lists. He favored double-breasted suits, most of them in shades of blue, and made by a tailor in Newark, New Jersey, for $125 each. Even when he was a sergeant in the Army Air Force his uniforms were trimmed and fitted by a tailor.

"Joe was not flashy or showy with money," said Sisto, who is now retired and living in Long Island, New York, "but he's a good tipper. I know the equipment man at the Stadium, Herb Norman, used to handle his things during the oldtimers days and he said, 'This guy DiMaggio, you do a little favor for him and he hands you a $10 bill.' But Joe doesn't squander his money.

"He's a guy who is loyal to his friends. If you're his friend and never did him any harm, you'll be his friend for life and he'll be your friend. He never forgets his friends. If you were his friend and you did something he might consider a double-cross, he wouldn't have anything to do with you again. I mean it would have to be something important because a petty thing wouldn't annoy him. But I know, he's a guy that if you did him a good turn he'd never forget it."

16

The Final Exit,
a Matter
of Pride

OLD COLONEL RUPPERT had said it all in prophecy during DiMaggio's holdout in 1938. "President's go into eclipse, kings have their thrones moved from under them, business leaders go into retirement, great ballplayers pass on, but still everything moves in its accustomed stride."

In April 1951, General Douglas MacArthur, fresh from his dismissal by President Truman as Supreme Commander of Allied Powers because of his criticism of the conduct of the Korean War, addressed a special joint session of Congress and echoed virtually the same sentiments with words from a military ballad. "Old soldiers never die, they just fade away."

Like Ruth and Gehrig and countless other great players before him, the Yankee Clipper was entering what was to be his last season in baseball. He had been despondent over the two previous seasons because he had been betrayed by his physical tools. His fierce pride and sensitivity would inevitably keep him from taking the field to perform simply as a journeyman player.

"The great DiMaggio" was 36 years old and his long battle with injuries and fatigue had drained his body. The mere act of getting out of bed in the morning became painful. Throughout the final season his knees and arms quaked and he was no longer able to bring the bat around with the swift, powerful wrist action that had made him one of baseball's most feared batters.

He would still have outstanding games and inspire the Yankees, but his batting average would dip drastically and, in his own estimation, reach a point of embarrassment.

The Yankees and Weiss could see the denouement—DiMaggio's era was coming to an end. His legions of fans remained loyal and still made him a premier gate attraction but the fact that he had slowed up was inescapable. Only through the physical effort he put into the 1950 season was he able to produce the statistics that warranted the Yankees extending him another $100,000 contract for 1951. They were personal figures that any journeyman player would have envied—a .301 batting average, 32 home runs, 33 doubles, 10 triples, 122 runs batted in, and 114 runs scored. For the last two months, after a dismal slump, he maintained a .400 average.

"Joe DiMaggio will be offered the same contract he had last year," Weiss said on January 5. "We have had only one contact with DiMaggio so far. Dan Topping called him just before he went to Florida and wished Joe a Happy New Year."

DiMaggio did not look gift horses in the mouth. When he received the contract in the mail he promptly mailed it back—with his signature on it, of course.

On February 7, the Yankees went through the public-relations charade of treating him with quiet dignity. They arranged a coast-to-coast news conference via telephone hookup between DiMaggio and the New York sportswriters. DiMaggio, speaking from his ailing mother's home in San Francisco (she would pass away in June), told the writers, who were jammed into the Yankees' Fifth Avenue office suite:

"They wouldn't have given me that kind of contract if they hadn't been happy about it. So I'm happy, too. I'll play for the Yankees as long as Stengel wants me and as long as this body holds out."

Among the press corps the sentiment was obvious that DiMaggio was being rewarded for services already rendered. There was some hope he might come up with one more stellar season, but even the fans were aware that a bad right shoulder and an ailing left knee had left him a shadow of the once effortless performer.

Then at Phoenix, Arizona, on March 2 at the Yankees' Instructional School, DiMaggio dropped a bombshell. With his third $100,000 contract safely tucked away and signed, he said 1951 would be his last year. His comment took the Yankees—players and officials alike—by surprise. Curiously, club officials reacted with as much doubt as surprise as if they refused to accept the inevitable. DiMaggio soon learned that the timing of his comment was unwise. It hounded him throughout the season and he wished he had left it unsaid, at least until the appropriate time.

"I haven't heard anything about it," Stengel said, officially. "But if that's the way he feels, that's his prerogative. I can't hold a gun at his head and say, 'You've got to play ball!' Of course, I'd hate to see it happen. But that's a decision the player makes himself."

Weiss also indicated that he and the rest of the club officials had not been consulted by DiMaggio officially and were as much in the dark as anyone.

"DiMaggio has not discussed this angle with any official of the club," Weiss said. "We regret to hear anything like this and we hope he will have the sort of season which will cause him to change his mind."

Weiss's words seemed protective—as much for the Yankees as for DiMaggio. If he decided to retire at the end of 1951, the Yankees might regret it, but their business enterprise would not crumble because of it. Weiss could always see out of the tunnel and for him the end of one era might be a welcome note on which to start building a new one. Hadn't Weiss invited Mickey Mantle to the Yankees' Instructional School in Phoenix for a close look in February? Although Mantle had been a shortstop in the minor leagues, he had tremendous speed and power, and on top of that he was a switch-hitter. Scouts were already telling the Yankees that he "might be a great center fielder" and "the great DiMaggio," in all his baseball wisdom and diplomacy, had called the 19-year-old Mantle "the greatest rookie I've ever seen."

If DiMaggio had in fact made up his mind to quit, he did so with the knowledge that his drawing power was still at its zenith. In an exhibition game in Los Angeles against the Los Angeles Angels of the Pacific Coast League, the Yankees attracted 22,355 fans, the largest crowd they had ever drawn for an exhibition game away from Yankee Stadium. Big league baseball would not expand to the West Coast until 1958 when the Brooklyn Dodgers and New York Giants would leave their generations of fans in tandem "for thirty pieces of silver." The Los Angeles crowd had turned out to get a glimpse of DiMaggio, sensing he would not pass their way again as an active player.

DiMaggio sensed that if he was going to retire, he would need some ballast to make his way in the marketplace as a celebrity once he had shed his uniform. He had already written a book, *Lucky to Be a Yankee*; signed a movie contract to play himself in a Metro-Goldwyn-Mayer production, *The Angels and the Pirates;* and entered into negotiations with M-G-M on a possible screen biography—an effort that was aborted when the studio and the player could not agree on terms.

At the beginning of 1950, the 39 players on the club roster at the time were sent questionnaires by the Yankees' front office asking them to reply to the question, "Who is your baseball model, and which player do you admire most?"

More than half the players answered: "Joe DiMaggio." It wasn't surprising, but the explanations told a lot about how some of the players regarded him. "He does everything better than anybody else," wrote Tommy Henrich. "He puts his heart into every inning more than any other player I have ever seen," said Billy Johnson; "He is grace, strength, power, all of it effortless," said Jerry Coleman.

Now the reaction among coaches and teammates to DiMaggio's

premature retirement announcement ranged from hero-worship to doubt. Some described it with locker-room and gallows humor, others measured it in monetary terms.

Bill Dickey, the laconic Arkansan who was now a coach under Stengel and had been with Ruth and Gehrig when they drew down the curtain, was philosophical about it.

"It's always sad when a great ballplayer moves out of the picture," Dickey said. "It's sad not only for his own club but for baseball generally. You know it's got to happen, but somehow, it's hard to take when the time comes."

Eddie "Junk Man" Lopat, the Yankees' left-hander whose change-up pitches gave him his nickname, put it more bluntly. "I'll believe it when I see it," he said. Lopat's irreverence stemmed mostly from his disbelief that a player would, as a matter of pride, walk away from a $100,000 salary.

Johnny Mize, one of only six players who had ever hit 50 home runs in a season (a feat neither DiMaggio nor Gehrig accomplished), was prosaic in his reaction. Mize had been acquired by the Yankees from the New York Giants and had produced many outstanding seasons with the St. Louis Cardinals. He had taken on the role of an extremely valuable and effective reserve and pinch-hitter with the Yankees. Affectionately called The Big Cat by the players, he was linked to the Babe Ruth era by kinship. Ruth's second wife, Claire, was Mize's cousin. When Ruth died she gave him Babe's pocket watch, inscribed with the initials "B.R.," as a memento. Mize proudly displayed the keepsake often to the players.

"We all feel that way in the spring," Mize said in his southern Georgia twang. "As you get along in years this training gets to be a trial, with its aches and pains and the torture of stiff and creaky joints. Sometimes I feel the ballplayers should be paid for spring training only and let them play the season for love of the game."

Frank Crosetti, who had chauffeured DiMaggio 3,000 miles to his first training camp 15 years earlier and now was making a second career as a Yankees coach, saw DiMaggio as a catalyst in helping to raise pay standards for players.

"When his time comes the effect will be felt by every player," Crosetti said. "Like when Babe Ruth bowed out. The Babe kept those salaries up there and Joe has done the same thing, so that every player has benefited from his presence."

—

As the season progressed, DiMaggio rarely had a moment without the press harping on his retirement plans. He regretted the statement even more. It seemed as if everyone wanted him to retract it. It got so bad, he said he would make no further comments about it until the season ended when he would talk to Topping and Webb about his future. He was caught in his own web, pledged to his word and too proud to go back on it.

In July he was selected for the 13th time to the All-Star team, but for the second time in his career injury would keep him sidelined. The ailment, a torn muscle in the back of his left leg, was aggravated while he was taking batting practice before the July 10 encounter at Briggs Stadium in Detroit. It would also drop him from the Yankee lineup for 10 days.

"I tried it out today in batting practice," he said in the Detroit clubhouse, "but I couldn't swing naturally. I couldn't get around on the ball, and I gave it up because I was afraid of aggravating the injury some more."

He missed the Yankees' next road trip, and on July 23 the team headed home with eight victories and eight losses to show for it, the last three losses occurring at Boston. The injury kept DiMaggio out longer than expected. The Yankees, only 2½ games in front, with Boston, Cleveland, and Detroit in close pursuit, were scheduled for a doubleheader at the Stadium on July 29 against the Chicago White Sox.

Since his earliest days with the Yankees, the saying, "As DiMaggio goes, so go the Yankees" had become something of a rallying cry, a forewarning by the New York fans to the rest of the teams in the league. He seemed to inspire the team even when his play was not extraordinary. He had an uncanny way of getting even after some of the gravest errors. He delighted the crowd of 70,972 with two home runs and five runs batted in the opener, then in the nightcap he made two superb catches to preserve a 2–0 shutout and a sweep.

The next day 39,684 were in the park to mark Stengel's 61st birthday. There had been a small clubhouse celebration. Detroit was the opposition. In the eighth inning, with one out, Gerry Priddy and George Kell hit consecutive doubles to send the Tigers ahead, 3–2. Steve Souchock drove a long fly to deep center field and DiMaggio sauntered back, made the catch, and leisurely started to trot into the infield with the ball. The crowd gasped. DiMaggio thought he had put away the third out of the inning. Kell tagged up and headed for third on the catch.

Dick Bartell, the Tiger coach at third base, alertly waved Kell around third, sending him home. By the time DiMaggio realized there were only two out he had no chance of preventing Kell from scoring and putting the Tigers in front, 4–2.

It was the kind of blunder for which a rookie certainly could lose his starting assignment on almost any team. But it was also part of baseball. Stengel had marked his 61st year, and DiMaggio, at 36, was getting on, too.

The Yankees scored twice and tied the score, 4–4, and in the ninth DiMaggio got his chance to save face. Jerry Coleman doubled and Bobby Brown walked and DiMaggio went to bat with two out. He lined a single to left field, scoring Coleman with the winner.

Through the heat of August, the Yankees weathered the challenge by the other clubs and clung to the lead. In the National League, the boys of summer also went through the annual rites. The New York Giants trailed the pace-setting Brooklyn Dodgers by 13½ games on August 11. Even the most loyal of Giants fans had written off their chances for recovery.

At that juncture the Giants began one of baseball's most memorable comebacks. They reeled off 37 triumphs in 44 games—13 of those victories by one run—and caught the Dodgers on the last two days of the season. They sent the pennant race into a two-of-three game playoff. The Giants won the opener, then felt the weight of Dodger bats in a 10–0 drubbing that seemed to signal the end of their valiant return.

In the deciding game the Dodgers went into the ninth leading by two runs. Then came "the shot heard round the world"—Bobby Thomson's three-run, two-out home run off Ralph Branca that capped the Giants' magnificent climb from oblivion to a championship.

The Yankees didn't have to wait so long to clinch their title. They did it almost routinely, beating the Red Sox twice on September 28, with Allie Reynolds pitching his second no-hitter of the season in the opener. It was a memorable feat not only for Reynolds, but for the tension it created. Yogi Berra had dropped a third-out foul hit by Ted Williams in the ninth inning, giving the Splinter another chance and almost dooming Reynolds's superb effort. Moments later, in a classic déjà vu, Reynolds got Williams to pop foul again behind the plate and this time Berra clung to the ball like glue to preserve the no-hitter. The second-game victory clinched the pennant, with DiMaggio contributing his 14th home run.

Despite Reynolds's no-hitter and another championship, the atmosphere in the Yankee clubhouse was subdued and restrained. There was no hoopla or celebration that had accompanied the clinching of past titles.

Phil Rizzuto, the shortstop, summed it up: "Three straight pennants. It's becoming monotonous."

It was the Yankees' 18th pennant and the 10th time DiMaggio had been a champion. Only Babe Ruth before him had played on 10 championship teams in the history of baseball. And Ruth had played on only seven Yankee winners—his three other title teams were at Boston. DiMaggio was the only player to play all 10 with one team—the Yankees.

He sat quietly in front of his locker holding a ball. It was the ball his brother Dom had hit to Gene Woodling in left field for the last out of the game.

"Gene gave it to me," DiMaggio told a reporter. "And this one I'm going to keep. With this ball the Yankees clinched the pennant—my 10th pennant."

Stengel went directly to DiMaggio as he came into the clubhouse.

"I want to thank you for everything you did," he said to DiMaggio.

Then he walked away to talk to the press.

"I never wavered in my belief that the boys would win it," he said, "but we never would have won it without DiMaggio. With the possible exception of his brother Dom, Joe is the best outfielder in the league. He saved me from looking bad many times when I should have removed a pitcher, but a great catch by DiMaggio took us out of a hole. And don't forget his timely hits and his excellent base-running. No, sir, without DiMaggio we never would have won it."

They were generous words from a manager not given to overpraise. They seemed to be kind words, too, coming from an old trouper who realized perhaps that DiMaggio's season had not been quite of the caliber of those of the past. Perhaps Stengel was aware that indeed this would be DiMaggio's last hurrah.

DiMaggio completed the season with a .263 batting average, the lowest of his career and 62 points below his lifetime average. That alone seemed to have convinced him that it was time to retire.

The Yankees would meet the New York Giants in the World Series and it was one more irony for DiMaggio to ponder. The Giants had been his World Series opponents in his first year in the majors. Now he had come full circle, facing the same team in what would be his final World Series appearance.

Most teams who were in contention to win a pennant and go on to the World Series usually sent scouts to get reports on the contenders from the other league who might be possible opponents. The Dodgers, who had been complacent enough to think the Giants could not overtake them, gave this job to Andy High, who had been a journeyman third baseman for 13 seasons from 1922 to 1934 with five National League teams and had played with three pennant winners at St. Louis. High had broken into the major leagues at Brooklyn and had landed the scouting job in their organization after he retired. Known as Handy Andy, he compiled a .284 career batting average. Like DiMaggio, he came from a family of ballplayers—two of his brothers, Charlie and Hugh, had also played in the big leagues.

High scouted the Yankees before the regular season had ended and had filed a report with the Dodgers. Once the Dodgers had been eliminated, however, they turned over High's scouting report to the Giants and from there it leaked out to the press. It became one of baseball's most famous scouting reports—not so much for what it had to say about the Yankees as a whole, but for what it said about DiMaggio.

"He can't stop quickly and throw hard. . . . You can take the extra base on him. . . . He can't run and won't bunt. . . . His reflexes are very slow and he can't pull a good fastball at all," was the way High's report, in essence, characterized DiMaggio.

It was a scathing indictment, businesslike but cruel, of what DiMaggio could no longer do. It was embarrassing not only to DiMaggio but to his teammates and to the many sportswriters who had seen him in his prime and had documented his greatest accomplishments.

"Andy High couldn't carry DiMaggio's jock, even now," said one sportswriter in a moment of anger over the report.

DiMaggio was hurt by the report and it seemed at the time that it figured, more than any other factor, in his decision to retire. Later DiMaggio said it had not bothered him that much and had not been crucial in his decision.

"When I said in Phoenix at the start of spring training that it might be my last season," DiMaggio said later, "I had just about made up my mind to quit. My right knee had been giving me trouble for a couple of years and both shoulders were bothering me. My swing was hampered, and I couldn't get around on the ball. Where I was fooled, though, was that I really thought I could make my last year a good one. I had a bad one, instead. I guess the reflexes just weren't there any more."

DiMaggio never took High's report publicly to task and his words later seemed to reinforce, at least in part, what had been obvious to High as a professional scout.

High was greatly distressed that his report had reached public print, however. He told that to Tom Meany, who covered the Yankees, and said he had for a long time regarded DiMaggio as the best player he had seen, but that as a scout he had had a duty to perform. His report was indeed prophetic.

The Series started as a nightmare for DiMaggio. He went hitless in the first three games, 12 straight times at bat, and the Yankees trailed, two games to one.

DiMaggio's inability to get any hits seemed to spread to the rest of the team. A rainout gave Stengel a day to think about making some changes and adjustments in his batting order. DiMaggio welcomed the rest.

Stengel's batting order for the fourth game astounded the critics for its sheer inventiveness. Hank Bauer, who batted eighth, was moved to leadoff; Gene Woodling, who had been the leadoff man, was moved to sixth; Yogi Berra was shifted from fifth to third, and the rookie, Gil McDougald, was placed fifth behind DiMaggio.

"I am just trying to shift around a bit to get some hitting in there," Stengel said. "I am not going to change the cleanup, DiMaggio's in there and he's going to stay. Sure, Joe hasn't been hitting. But he'll get started, and when he does start, everything will be all right.

"I gotta string along with the Big Fellow," Stengel went on, "I gotta keep him batting in the cleanup because he's been the heart of this ball club for so long and because, well, because he's still DiMaggio."

DiMaggio, however, looked upon himself as a pathetic figure.

"I'm not looking for sympathy. I don't want sympathy. I don't deserve sympathy. I've been lousy," he told Louis Effrat of *The New York Times.*

DiMaggio knew that Lefty O'Doul, his old friend and mentor who had batted .398 in 1929 with the Philadelphia Phillies, was in New York to watch the Series and to select personnel to make a trip to the Far East to entertain American troops in Korea and Japan. DiMaggio sought out O'Doul for advice on how to break out of his hitting slump.

O'Doul told him he was taking his eye off the ball and swinging too hard.

"You've been pressing, lunging at bad balls, your body is ahead of your arms, so that you're pushing the ball," O'Doul told him.

DiMaggio changed his stance and he and the Yankees began to roll. In the fourth game, DiMaggio laced a single in the third inning off Sal Maglie and the fans, knowing his ordeal, cheered him. It was his first hit in the Series. Whether it was from sympathy that the fans had cheered him, DiMaggio was too proud to rest on that alone. His next time up in the fifth inning he again faced Maglie, who was known as "The Barber" because his tantalizing pitches often gave batters a "close shave." DiMaggio slammed one of Maglie's pitches and drove a 400-foot clout into the upper deck of the left-field stands for a two-run homer and a 4-1 Yankee lead. It spurred their victory and tied the Series at two games apiece.

When DiMaggio's hit went into the upper deck, Yogi Berra, who had been on base, went into a jubilant dance, his fists thrust high into the air as if summing up the many years of Yankees power and domination. One reporter wrote: "Berra did a grotesque dance of joy on the basepaths, clenched fists help triumphantly above his head as he circled the bases ahead of DiMaggio." But Berra's joy was also for DiMaggio, who had mustered enough strength to answer the critics.

DiMaggio had hit a curveball off Maglie for his homer. After the game he was pleased and expansive in describing how it felt.

"It was a great feeling," he said, "to see it going out to the seats. I was doing a lot of things differently at the plate. Lefty O'Doul told me that I was swinging high and taking my eye off the ball. I corrected that, but Lefty wasn't here to see it. He went back to the Coast today. In batting practice today, Lew Fonseca was correcting things I was doing while he watched me. He's taken hundreds of pictures of me and knows more about my style than I do myself, because he's used to seeing them run in slow motion."

Fonseca, who had been a pitcher and manager in the majors in the 1920s and 1930s, had made a new career as a motion picture photographer, taking the official films of the World Series for the major leagues.

"Another thing," DiMaggio said, "I changed bats and got down from my 35-ounce bat to a 34-ounce bat, a Babe Ruth model. But don't forget that I struck out twice today. I don't want to look good today and make O'Doul and Fonseca look bad tomorrow if I don't connect."

In the fifth game, DiMaggio got two singles, drew an intentional walk to set the stage for Gil McDougald's grand slam, and cracked a two-run double as the Giants took a 13–1 drubbing, the worst rout in a Series game in 15 years. The Giants' pitcher paid him the ultimate compliment in the sixth game, walking him twice intentionally with runners on base to get to McDougald. The strategy worked the first time, but in the sixth inning, after DiMaggio's second walk, and another to Johnny Mize, Hank Bauer hit a triple to send the Yankees ahead, 4–1. Then in his last time at bat, his 199th appearance at the plate in 51 World Series games, both records, DiMaggio belted another double. He was out trying to reach third on a bunt by the next batter. As DiMaggio jogged from the field, the crowd, sensing perhaps it would be the last time they would see his majestic, loping stride, rose to its feet and cheered for five minutes. The Giants chipped away for two runs in the ninth, but the Yankees won, 4–3, and took their 14th world championship in 30 years.

For DiMaggio the exhilaration he felt in once again being a champion was only temporary. After 13 seasons, 10 pennants, and nine World Series titles, the hardest part would be to make the final exit.

The scenario that engulfed DiMaggio's final decision to retire took almost two months to unfold. After the final Series game, he dragged himself into the clubhouse, peeled off his shirt and said, "I've played my last game."

Stengel walked directly to DiMaggio, as he had done after the Yankees had clinched the pennant. He gave the player a handshake and a warm slap on the back, uncharacteristic shows of affection from the manager.

"Without you, we couldn't have done it," Stengel said to DiMaggio.

Some of DiMaggio's teammates congratulated him on the double he had hit in the eighth inning. It was to be his last major league hit.

"I'm glad I got it," he said. "It will give them [the fans] something to remember me by."

Now his teammates approached him with uneasiness, sensing that he had truly decided to quit, although since his first remark early in the spring he had refrained from any comment about it. It was an unusual scene, filled with unexpressed sentiment. As DiMaggio stood in front of his locker, smoking a cigarette, the players came to him, openly asking him to autograph bats, balls, gloves, and photographs—like children seeking out their hero. Several made requests for and received some of DiMaggio's pet bats and souvenirs.

It had taken DiMaggio a long time to shake off the reputation of being a loner. Although Yankee fans had virtually elevated him to sainthood, there were still critics who perpetuated the idea that he was the Greta Garbo of the sports world.

Late in the season, three of DiMaggio's friends from Newark had traveled to Philadelphia to watch him play. They were to return to New York on the same train on which the Yankees were booked. DiMaggio had promised them he would eat dinner with them in the dining car. He had asked them, however, to wait until all the Yankees had been served and had eaten so none of the players would have to wait for a seat.

DiMaggio was seated alone at a table for four, waiting for his friends, when he was spotted by a New York sportswriter. The next day, a story appeared in print that DiMaggio was avoiding and slighting his teammates. The story angered him and he had no chance for a rebuttal.

Later he explained what had happened.

"This writer saw me sitting alone in the dining car at a table for four and decided, without asking, that I was shunning the other players on the club," he said. "My friends never showed up. I found out later that they had been told it was a special dining car, not open to the public."

For him the outpouring of good wishes by his teammates after the last Series game, had taken some of the sting out of the story.

On October 12, DiMaggio left for home before joining O'Doul's all-stars for their trip to the Far East. On the same day, Bill Essick, the Yankee scout who had urged the Yankees to buy DiMaggio from the San Francisco Seals despite the player's knee injury, died in his sleep after a long illness at the age of 69 in Los Angeles. Besides DiMaggio, Essick had sent Tony Lazzeri, Lefty Gomez, and Joe Gordon to the Yankees.

Before his departure for the West Coast, however, DiMaggio indicated he had not changed his mind about retiring.

"I have made up my mind to retire and that is my present intention," he said. "I have given it considerable thought."

Still, the Yankees were hoping he might have a change of heart. They tried to persuade him to reconsider. That morning before he left for home, he was asked to visit Dan Topping in his office for a brief farewell chat. He spent two hours with Topping, going over the reasons why he thought he should retire. He cited the effects of night baseball, the toll his numerous injuries had taken on him physically, and not least, the fact that his pride was involved. Topping told him he would be welcome to play another season at his current $100,000-a-year salary. There was never any question that the Yankee management still considered him the biggest drawing card in baseball, and therefore still a sound investment.

Arthur "Red" Patterson, the Yankees' public-relations official, in reconstructing the meeting for The Associated Press, said that DiMaggio "came into the office with intentions of retiring but decided to give the subject a little more time at the request of Dan Topping."

"Joe," Topping said, "I'm not fully convinced that you have made up your mind. You might feel differently a month from now. Why don't you go on your trip to Japan and give this matter a little more thought? When you get back to the States in about a month from now, I'll be waiting here for you. Then we'll talk it over some more."

DiMaggio agreed in deference to Topping, but those close to him were convinced that he had played his last game.

"That was one of the great things about Joe," Ernie Sisto has said. "He didn't want to be remembered as a has-been. He always said to me that he quit for that reason. 'Might as well leave while I look fairly decent,' he'd say."

Solotaire, his close friend, put it candidly. "DiMaggio is just plain pooped out," he said. "Age simply has caught up with him. In other years he would visit nightclubs or go to the movies in the evening. Joe rarely left his hotel suite this year. He'd be so tired after a ball game, he'd go back to his hotel, order his dinner, and sit home watching television night after night until it was time to go to bed."

DiMaggio regarded the Yankees' willingness to pay him $100,000 to return as an honor. He had already earned more than $1 million in salary, World Series shares, and other off-the-field activities. There were reports that he might take a job as a manager; the general manager of the Portland Beavers of the Pacific Coast League offered DiMaggio the job of manager; and there were rumors that he might even take over the Yankees. DiMaggio quickly brushed them all aside. The strongest report, and a credible one, suggested that if DiMaggio did retire, the Yankees had him lined up as a radio and television commentator with the club. In this connection there were hints that DiMaggio and Topping had secretly talked about it before he left for the Orient.

So for three weeks following the World Series, the speculation over DiMaggio's retirement stayed on the nation's sports pages.

"The day DiMaggio quits," said Stengel, "part of the Yankees will be gone, too. In a sense, Joe was the Yankees. Just as Babe Ruth was before him. The Yankees can never repay him for what he has done for them."

Frank Lane, who had been a baseball executive in several cities, and in 1951 was the general manager of the Chicago White Sox, estimated that DiMaggio's retirement would cost each team in the American League, other than the Yankees who stood to lose a great deal more, about $25,000 a game. The Yankees visited Chicago and the other teams in the league 11 times a year.

"I figure he personally draws about 5,000 fans to our park every time the Yankees come to Chicago," Lane said.

DiMaggio fascinated not only the fans, but both veteran and young players. Gil McDougald, the rookie third baseman who had been outstanding in the Series, was in awe of DiMaggio.

"You know, I wish I could tell DiMaggio just how I feel about playing on the same team with him," McDougald said. "Just knowing that he may be watching me makes me try all the harder to do good. I still find it hard to believe that I am on the same team with him."

Other Yankees had similar reactions. "I'd hate to turn around and not see the Big Guy behind me," said Phil Rizzuto. Jerry Coleman, the second baseman, said, "All my life DiMaggio and the Yankees have been one and the same. The Yankees won't be the same without him." Gene Woodling, who like the other Yankees had reaped a share of World Series money for three straight seasons, summed it up this way: "Please, Joe, come back next year. I still need more money to buy shoes for my three kids."

DiMaggio would sit on his plans during his trip to Korea and Japan. On October 15, with his brother Dom of the Red Sox, Eddie Lopat and Billy Martin, his Yankee teammates, and 15 other players, Joe prepared to leave on a two-month tour. Mechanical trouble delayed the plane's takeoff from Los Angeles for two hours. After the departure, the plane developed more mechanical problems in the air and was forced to return to the mainland for repairs, causing another two-hour delay.

Finally, the troupe made its first stop in Honolulu. They were scheduled to play a pickup team of servicemen and semipro stars and a crowd of 15,000 waited two hours for them to arrive. When they took the field, DiMaggio, in his only trip to the plate in the game, struck out on three pitches thrown by Tuck Correa, a veteran Hawaii semipro. The O'Doul all-stars lost, 8–6.

The next day in Tokyo, the baseball-loving Japanese welcomed the American players as if they were heroes coming home from war. A crowd, estimated by the police at 1 million, jammed the downtown Ginza, Tokyo's counterpart of Broadway.

"Banzai DiMaggio! Banzai DiMaggio!" they shouted as magnesium flares lighted the sky and tons of paper scraps floated down from office building windows. The crush of the crowd on the players' motorcade and the police escort created such a traffic jam that for safety reasons the players were taken directly to their hotel. They had been scheduled for bows and speeches at the Yomiuri Shimbun building that housed Japan's leading newspaper only three blocks away.

The tour took the players to many major towns in Japan and Korea where crowds of 40,000 and 50,000 turned out for the games. DiMaggio was the No. 1 attraction and he responded with several home runs and standout fielding plays. Everywhere DiMaggio was deluged for autographs and interviews. The Japanese and the American Armed Forces press pursued the question of his retirement.

In an interview on the Armed Forces Radio Network on October 25, DiMaggio said, "I haven't changed my mind about quitting."

Early in November, tired and weary from the tour, DiMaggio announced that he was leaving the tour and flying back to the United States, ostensibly to keep a business engagement that had "nothing to do with my contract."

Before he left he played one more game in Tokyo against a team of Japan's best all-stars. He hit a towering 400-foot home run and the crowd of 50,000 at Meiji Stadium gave him a standing ovation, shouting once again, "Banzai DiMaggio!" It was his last competitive game.

Two days later, DiMaggio slipped into Los Angeles unnoticed and without fanfare after a flight aboard a Pan American Pacific clipper. He went to a Hollywood hotel, and visited his son who was a student at the nearby Black Fox Military Academy, a private and expensive preparatory school. Reporters discovered his whereabouts and DiMaggio, perturbed once again, was hounded about his plans.

"I'll make my announcement when I get good and ready," he said. "I'll go to New York sometime in the future, but I don't know how soon I'll go. It's my decision to make and I'll make it when I get ready."

Del Webb, co-owner of the Yankees, sent his private plane to Los Angeles to bring DiMaggio to Phoenix, where Webb was concluding a business engagement. The two planned to fly to New York together for the formal announcement, DiMaggio insisting that he make it there.

"I said I'd announce it in New York," he said, "and it wouldn't be fair to the sportswriters there if I said anything now. That's where I work, so I'm making the announcement there."

Webb and DiMaggio had lunch at the airport cafe in Phoenix, then flew to Kansas City, where they spent the night. DiMaggio had made his decision known to Webb, but they had chosen to join Topping and the sportswriters in New York to make it formal.

On December 11 at 2 P.M. in the Yankees' Fifth Avenue suite in the Squibb Tower, while newsreel and television cameras clicked, light bulbs flashed and nearly 100 reporters and photographers fought for space, DiMaggio made his farewell.

"I told you fellows last spring I thought this would be my last year," he said, somberly. "I only wish I could have had a better year, but even if I had hit .350, this would have been the last year for me.

"You all know I have had more than my share of physical injuries and setbacks during my career. In recent years these have been much too frequent to laugh off. When baseball is no longer fun, it's no longer a game.

"And so, I've played my last game of ball. Since coming to New York I've made a lot of friends, and picked up a lot of advisers, but I would like to make one point clear—no one has influenced me in making this decision. It has been my problem and my decision to make. I feel that I have reached the stage where I can no longer produce for my ball club, my manager, my teammates, and my fans the sort of baseball their loyalty to me deserves.

"In closing, I would like to say that I feel I have been unusually privileged to play all my major league baseball for the New York Yankees. But it has been an even greater privilege to be able to play baseball at all. It has added much to my life. What I will remember most in days to come will be the great loyalty of the fans. They have been very good to me."

Casey Stengel, usually garrulous, was subdued, but his three sentences seemed to sum it up.

"What is there to say?" he said. "I just gave the Big Guy's glove away and it is going to the Hall of Fame, where Joe himself is certain to go. He was the greatest player I ever managed and right now I still say there isn't another center fielder in baseball his equal."

Arthur Daley, the Pulitzer Prize winning sports columnist of *The New York Times,* wrote the next day:

> So he turned his back on the $100,000 and abruptly walked away. Only a man with character and an overwhelming pride could take a step like that. The Yankee Clipper has always been a proud man. That's why he was such a great ballplayer. He never was satisfied with anything less than perfection.

In Japan, where the two most popular Americans were General Douglas MacArthur and Joe DiMaggio, millions of fans were saddened by DiMaggio's retirement. Morita Fukui, the commissioner of Japanese baseball, said: "It is going to be difficult for us to realize that Joe DiMaggio is no longer a ballplayer. I want to pay tribute to his decision to retire when he believes a player should quit when baseball ceases to be fun. That is the decision of a true sportsman."

He was called the Yankee Clipper, equated for his style and grace with the tall ships, their great masts and booming sails clipping off miles with speed and precision in a bygone era, carrying riches, passengers, and seekers after gold over the seas, to California, where by the accident of birth he first touched base.

17

A Friend
Remembers

*Y*EARS AFTER HE had retired as a player, Joe DiMaggio still occupied a pedestal in the esteem of generations of fans who had grown older with him, perhaps not as gracefully, but happily enough to have remembered to "tell their kids his name."

In 1979, several months before his 65th birthday, the New York Board of Trade held a luncheon in Joe's honor at the Waldorf Astoria. He was presented with a big apple of crystal.

"He is Mr. New York, and Mr. Bowery, and Mr. Coffee," one speaker said.

"I should be thanking New York," DiMaggio responded. "Everything I have I owe New York."

Over the last decade his newspaper ads and radio and television commercials for the Bowery Savings Bank and the Mr. Coffee coffeemaker firm have kept DiMaggio's name a household word—a daily reminder to many New Yorkers of his baseball playing days. It was as if he had never gone away.

Indeed, Joe DiMaggio has had the best of all worlds—election to the Hall of Fame, numerous public relations jobs that kept his income in the six-figure range, a short stint as a broadcaster and then as a batting instructor for the Yankees, an official berth as an executive with the Oakland A's, whom he helped build into champions, countless trips abroad and honors from civic groups, the Medal of Freedom, and designation as "the greatest living ballplayer" in a poll conducted in celebration of baseball's Centennial.

His courtship of and marriage to Marilyn Monroe, their subsequent divorce, and her death had brought him happiness and grief, and also admiration from a sympathetic public for his demonstration of grace under pressure at her funeral.

His appearances at Oldtimers' Games in New York still brought thunderous applause and cheers. New York and Joe DiMaggio seemed to be inseparable.

Ernie Sisto, now 75 years old and retired on Long Island, recalls their friendship of more than 45 years.

"I can still see DiMaggio out there in center field. I saw him play so many games, almost every game he played in New York. When he was out there in center field it was like a song, he had that graceful rhythm. A guy would hit a ball. He'd take a look at it and then he'd turn away and he'd run to a certain spot. Then he'd turn around and be ready. He knew where that ball was gonna go before the ball got there. He made it look so easy. It was uncanny, the naturalness. It seemed like he was made for the game. I don't know how to explain it, maybe it was the other way around, like the game was made for him.

"I can still see him running out to his position. He used to step on second base all the time when he went out to the field and when he came back into the dugout. But he had another little thing. It wasn't a superstition, but everytime he went out to center field and got ready to play his position he'd spread his legs far apart and then pull down on the visor of his cap, sort of getting himself all set. He did it every time. I still see that picture of him out there.

"When he comes to New York now on business or for a Yankee reunion or something he always stays at the Americana Hotel [now the Sheraton Centre] and he always stays in the same two-room suite in the southwest corner, rooms 4501 and 4502. He used to smoke two or three packs of cigarettes a day, even when he was playing. But he gave them up quite a few years ago. I guess he got a scare or something. Well, whenever I'm around him and I've got a lighted cigar he goes into a panic.

" 'Get that thing out of here,' he'll say. 'I don't even like the smell of it. Put it in the ashtray. Don't hold it. Get rid of it.' That's the way he is.

"I see Joe almost every time he's in New York. He calls me up to say, 'How you doing, Ernie?' He never forgets a friend. He used to have an apartment on Lexington Avenue years ago. I'd visit him up there. I remember one night I walked in and he's cooking a kettle of spaghetti, and for sauce he's using that stuff in the jar, what's the name, uh, Ronzoni.

"I said, 'Whatta you doing? You can go out and get it in a restaurant.'

"He says, 'I just had a yen for some spaghetti.'

"Joe watches his diet, but he enjoys good food. He's kind of a gourmet. He used to go to the old Colony restaurant a lot in the old days. Joe likes Italian food, and he's proud of his Italian ancestry. But I never heard him speak too much in Italian. A few words now and then for a laugh or something, but I don't think he knows enough Italian words to sustain a conversation. I mean hold a conversation in Italian, I know that. He probably understands it more than he can speak it.

"Joe and I talked a lot about Marilyn Monroe. I know the guy was really in love with her. I used to drive him out to Kennedy Airport [then Idlewild] a lot to catch a plane back to Frisco after he'd been in town. Of course, I had to go out that way anyway to go home.

"One day I called him and said, "Joe, I'm leaving soon. I can pick you up and take you out to the airport.'

"He said, 'Oh, Ernie, I got somebody taking me out already. I'll meet you out there.'

"So I drove out to Kennedy and I'm waiting in front of the entrance and a car pulls up and it's Marilyn Monroe driving Joe. She gets out and the porter gets Joe's bags and I'm standing there, but Joe doesn't see me. She got back in the car and drove away. This was after they were divorced. They were still friendly.

"So when she's gone Joe sees me and comes over and says, 'What the hell are you doing standing there? Why didn't you come over?'

"I said, 'I didn't want to butt in.'

"And Joe says, 'Aw, heck, I wanted to introduce you.'

"I finally met her on a photo assignment for the *Times*. She was opening a movie in New York. He wasn't with her anymore. That only lasted such a short time. I often mentioned to him that I thought he had done a noble thing when she died. He arranged everything for her funeral. He was really torn by that, I know. He was angry, too.

"He said, 'All those monkeys. All they wanted was to get publicity. They hated her anyway. They were really jealous of her. So I put my thumbs down.'

"He was talking about all the people who wanted to be invited to the funeral, just for show.

"Joe's boy is a nice kid. He stood by his father. He's in the real estate business on the Coast. He spent a year at Yale. And he played football instead of baseball. You know what he said when they asked him why he didn't go into baseball? He said, 'How could I ever live up to my father's reputation? I'd never be that good.' I took a lot of pictures of him in the Yankee dugout with Joe when he was a youngster.

"Joe never lost his temper on the field. The closest I ever saw him really angry at himself was when Al Gionfriddo robbed him of a home run in the World Series. I remember he was running toward third and he kicked the dirt. I don't know what made him like that. He seemed to have respect for everything on the field. He loved the game so much and even though he looked nonchalant on the field, as if he didn't care, he was really a competitor. Inside, this guy really wanted to murder the ball every time up. When he had a bad day a lot of times I heard him say, 'Geez, that was a bad game, Ernie.' But, except when he had the bone spurs, he never seemed to brood a long time. It was done, forget it.

"Since Joe left baseball, he had never taken a job for less than $100,000 a year, but he's had to travel a lot. He's rarely at home. He still lives out of a suitcase. He doesn't like it, but he does it. He's connected with a lot of companies and with some golf tour and he's got to get around for those goddamned golf tournaments. But I think he's lonely. It's a tough country to make it in. You get as famous as Joe DiMaggio got and it's got to cost you something.

"Joe always liked the gals. I used to kid him when he went out on a date. 'How'd you make out?' I'd say. 'Did you score?' I was already married when I first met him. I'm 10 years older than he is, but we went out together. Joe never did anything off color when I was with him. It wasn't that he was afraid I'd leak anything about him to the press. He wouldn't hide anything from me, I know that.

"One season he was in New York for a Mets Oldtimers' Day. I'm out there taking pictures of some of the hostesses, some really beautiful girls. Each oldtimer was escorted out to the field by one of them during the ceremonies. So I took a picture of Joe with one of these girls. He liked her looks a lot.

" 'Geez, she's nice,' he says.

"After the game and party I'm visiting him at the Americana and he looks a little bored and lonely.

"So I said, 'You want me to fix you up with that gal, have a date?' He started to hem and haw and I told him to take my advice and let me call the girl. I made the call and said, 'Listen, you want a date with Joe?' She says all right. So I tell her to take a cab to the Americana and Joe'll pick up the bill. She was a really gorgeous Irish girl. I left the hotel and figured I'd give him a couple of hours.

"I called him back later and said, 'How'd you do, Joe?'

"He says, 'Ah, for God's sake, Ernie, she's just a kid. I sent her home.'

"I don't think he has gotten over Marilyn to this day. You know he still sends flowers to her grave three times a week. But with those kids he wouldn't take a chance. He never knows what one of them might pull on him. He's got to watch his step. Since then I never saw him in town with a woman. Every time he comes in, I could show up at the hotel in the early morning or the evening and he's alone. I think he's a lonely man. Fame took something from him. Gave him something and took something away.

"I'll never forget one night I'm up there visiting and he's a little nervous.

" 'What's the matter, Joe?' I asked.

" 'My skin is itchy as hell,' he says. 'Chrissakes, don't tell me I'm coming down with something serious.'

"It was around 10 o'clock on a Sunday night. Earlier I had been at Gough's Restaurant and Bar, a little place across from the *Times* where a lot of newspapermen hang out. I'm having a couple of drinks with a black guy who works as a nurse at the *Times* infirmary. We're having some drinks and making jokes. Then I said I was leaving and going over to see Joe DiMaggio. Everybody knew I was friendly with Joe. When Joe tells me about his trouble I called the bar right away to see if the black guy, the nurse, was still there. Sure enough, I got him.

"'Joe thinks he might have something bad,' I told him, 'he's itching like hell.'

"'Stay right there,' the black guy said, 'I'll stop at a drug store and get something for him and come right over.'

"He came up with some kind of ointment and Joe was better in no time at all. But this guy felt so honored that he had been able to help Joe DiMaggio.

"A lot of people say DiMaggio is a loner. To me he's not a loner, but for some reason he acts like a loner. I know he is definitely a lonely guy. At least that's the impression I get. A lot of it stems from not being really close to baseball. And I think he also still misses Marilyn Monroe. He has often said how much he misses her and maybe he'll never get over her.

"He loved baseball so much that now that he's not in it he feels kind of lost. Maybe he wanted to be a manager or a coach or in the front office. But then with him maybe nothing could match the actual playing, being out there. I think the Yankees made a foolish move when they didn't create some position for him to keep him before the public. He was a Yankee at the start and a Yankee at the end. They never capitalized on him that way. He always felt kind of bad the Yankees had no place for him.

"After he retired at spring training one year, Lee MacPhail [son of Larry MacPhail] came over to me and said, 'How's Joe? You think he might want to take something with the club?'

"'I don't know,' I said. "I'll feel him out.'

"I guess McPhail [then general manager of the Yankees and now president of the American League] figured I had some influence and wanted to use me as a go-between with Joe. It made me feel odd. What the hell's the matter with these guys, I thought. They know him as well as I do, why don't they make him an offer directly? It was a business, they should act like businessmen.

"I know Joe was hurt. He never admitted it, but I know he was hurt. He never would admit it. I know it just from the way he reacted when I told him MacPhail wanted to know how he felt.

"'Ah, fuck them,' Joe said. If he said a word like that you can imagine how peeved he was about it. He wanted them to be business-like, I guess. He wanted them to come and ask him. He wasn't going to bring up the subject because that's the kind of guy he is. He never would impose himself on anyone. A little thing like asking the equipment manager for some baseballs for some kids or a friend would be tough for him."

Early in January of 1980, Joe DiMaggio became a member of the Board of Directors of the Baltimore Orioles.

Sources

This book primarily covers the time span of the 1930s, 1940s, and 1950s. Besides interviews, articles from newspapers of that period were valuable sources for research. The papers included *The New York Times, New York Herald Tribune, New York Daily Mirror, New York Daily News, New York Post, New York World-Telegram and Sun, New York Journal American, Sporting News, San Francisco Chronicle* and *Boston Globe.* General interest magazines included *Collier's, Life, The New Yorker, National Geographic* and *Time.* Other sources for material were the New York Public Library, the Baseball Hall of Fame, and the Rutherford (N.J.) Library.

The following books also proved helpful:

Baseball Encyclopedia, The. New York: Macmillan Publishing Company, Inc., 1969

Danzig, Allison, and Brandwein, Peter, editors. *The Greatest Sports Stories from The New York Times.* New York: A. S. Barnes, 1951.

Durocher, Leo, with Linn, Ed. *Nice Guys Finish Last.* New York: Simon and Schuster, 1975.

Girdner, Audrie. *The Great Betrayal.* New York: Macmillan Publishing Company, Inc., 1969.

Goldstein, Richard. *Spartan Seasons.* New York: Macmillan Publishing Company, Inc., 1980.

Graham, Frank. *The New York Yankees, 1900-1946.* New York: G. P. Putnam's and Sons, Inc., 1946.

Hemingway, Ernest. *The Old Man and the Sea.* New York: Scribner's and Sons, 1952.

Honig, Donald. *Baseball When the Grass Was Real.* New York: Coward, McCann and Geohegan, Inc., 1975.

MacLean, Norman. *Casey Stengel, A Biography.* New York: Drake Publishers, Inc., 1976.

Murray, Tom, editor. *Sports Magazine's All-Time All-Stars.* New York: Atheneum, 1977.

Shoemaker, Robert H. *The Best in Baseball.* New York: Thomas Y. Crowell Company, 1962.

Spink, Taylor, J. G. *Judge Landis and Twenty-Five Years of Baseball.* New York: Thomas Y. Crowell Company, 1947.

World Book Encyclopedia. Chicago: World Book Publishing Company, Inc., 1963.

Index

A

B

C

#

12120